The One Year Life Recovery Prayer Devotional

THE ONE YEAR® LIFE RECOVERY PRAYER DEVOTIONAL

Daily Encouragement from the Bible for Your Journey toward Wholeness and Healing

STEPHEN ARTERBURN, M.Ed.
NICK HARRISON
with Misty Arterburn

A Tyndale nonfiction imprint

Visit Tyndale Momentum online at tyndalemomentum.com.

Tyndale, Tyndale's quill logo, *Tyndale Momentum*, and the Tyndale Momentum logo are registered trademarks of Tyndale House Ministries. Tyndale Momentum is the nonfiction imprint of Tyndale House Publishers, Carol Stream, Illinois.

The One Year Life Recovery Prayer Devotional: Daily Encouragement from the Bible for Your Journey toward Wholeness and Healing

Designed by Ron C. Kaufmann

Published in association with the literary agency of WordServe Literary Group, www.wordserveliterary.com.

For information about special discounts for bulk purchases, please contact Tyndale House Publishers at csresponse@tyndale.com, or call 1-855-277-9400.

ISBN 978-1-4964-5712-7

Printed in the United States of America

27 26 25 24 23 22 21
7 6 5 4 3 2 1

For the many who fight the war against addiction

May the victory be yours

Introduction

ADDICTIONS OF ANY KIND are life destroying. You know this firsthand. That's why you're in recovery. You're trying to shed your dependencies and "recover" a normal life. An important aspect of addiction recovery—an aspect often overlooked—is the spiritual component. Recovery involves not only overcoming the physical and psychological compulsion of our addiction but also becoming strong spiritually.

Our hope is that this book of devotions will stimulate you to more dependency on God as you go through the recovery process. We want you to know that God is for you in your battle. He is able to strengthen you. He works with you to overcome the weaknesses of the flesh. He does this through his Word, through your prayers, and through the encouragement of others on the same journey.

Our expectation for you is that you'll not only recover from your addiction but that God has a post-addiction plan for you that will bring you fulfillment and joy. Others in history have walked your path. The man we refer to as Saint Augustine was surely sexually addicted. Augustine claimed that even at the young age of sixteen, "the frenzy gripped me and I surrendered myself entirely to lust." William Wilberforce, leader of the abolitionist movement in England, was a solid Christian man who was addicted to opium first prescribed as a relief for his ulcerative colitis. More recently, it's all too common to read of celebrities who have had to fight a serious addiction. Some, sadly, didn't recover. Whitney Houston,

Elvis Presley, Amy Winehouse, and Michael Jackson come to mind. We don't want that to happen to you.

As you go through this year, remember that the devotions in this book are designed to supplement, not replace, your other recovery protocols. If you're not presently in a reputable recovery program, we hope you'll search for one. Life Recovery, Celebrate Recovery, and Teen Challenge are three good options. You can find others on the internet or through recommendations from friends, but do check them out first and make sure they're scripturally based and have a track record of helping people shed their addictions.

We say that because this book, too, is written from a decidedly Christian perspective and is part of Tyndale House's Life Recovery resources, which include the New Living Translation of *The Life Recovery Bible*, the version most often used in the devotions on the following pages.

Many of the ideas, Bible references, and prayers will only make sense to a man or woman who has made a commitment to Christ.

We expect many readers are drawn to this book because they're already Christians and want to follow biblically based principles in their recovery from addiction. We know, too, that many other readers may not have yet entered into a relationship with God through Jesus Christ. If you haven't entered into a relationship with God but want to, you can do this now by simply acknowledging your need for God's intervention in your life and asking him, in faith, to forgive your sins and make you a new creation. That new creation identity is the basis for Christian recovery from addiction.

We read in the New Testament book of Romans, "If you openly declare that Jesus is Lord and believe in your heart that God raised him from the dead, you will be saved. For it is by believing in your heart that you are made right with God, and it is by openly declaring your faith that you are saved" (Romans 10:9-10). And in the gospel of John, we read Jesus' words to Nicodemus, "You must be born again" (John 3:7). A wonderful verse affirming the believer's new identity is found in

2 Corinthians 5:17, which tells us, "Anyone who belongs to Christ has become a new person. The old life is gone; a new life has begun!"

Recovery is all about that new person you become when you confess Christ as your Lord. So if you're serious about your recovery and would like to commit your life to Christ, you can do so by simply praying in your own words or by praying this suggested prayer:

> God, I have failed to live the life I should. I've sinned and am in need of forgiveness. I ask you to forgive me for my sins, come into my life, and create in me the person you've always meant me to be. Help me as I recover my life from addiction.

If you prayed that prayer with even mustard seed–sized faith, God has made you his child. For further reading on this new life or more in-depth reading to help overcome your old life, see a list of useful Life Recovery resources on page 399.

When one becomes a Christian through the new birth, there comes a fresh supply of power from the Holy Spirit who will indwell you as your teacher, counselor, and comforter. The Holy Spirit will help you see areas in your life where you need to turn away from destructive behaviors and walk out the new post-addiction life God has planned for you.

Whether you're a new Christian or a well-seasoned believer who has become addicted to a substance or compulsive behavior, we hope this book helps you in your recovery. Please know you are being prayed for as you go through the next twelve months with us.

A final word: Make no mistake, being a Christian doesn't make addiction recovery an easy fix. For most people, including Christians, recovery is a long-haul process. There are rarely quick fixes. You must enter into recovery planning to stay the course—no turning back. You must be wanting and willing. *Wanting* recovery and *willing* to go through the process of recovery no matter what, enduring the challenges.

We think of the process of recovery as tearing down a brick wall that has slowly built up over the course of your addiction, separating you from the person you're meant to be. In recovery, that brick wall must come down, brick by brick.

To help you take down the wall, *The One Year Life Recovery Prayer Devotional* provides daily readings to encourage you in your recovery. Each day's reading starts with a Bible verse and follows it with a brief exhortation, a short prayer, and to cap it off, a quote from a prominent Christian, past or present, to reinforce the theme of the day's devotion. In quoting these people, we hope you'll see that, down through the ages, successful men and women went through very hard times to be able to instruct us with their wisdom. Even from those who wrote centuries ago, you will find words oddly contemporary and relevant to your recovery.

Over the next year, our prayer is that the bricks in your wall will continue to fall as you pursue sobriety. *We know you can do this.* God has called you to it, and he will empower you to remove that brick wall and step over into the real self you're called to be.

Remember, your best life is your post-addiction life. Pursue it.

A Word about Addictions

SOMETIMES THE FIRST STEP toward overcoming an addiction is to learn something about it. There are two general categories of addictions. One category, chemical or substance addiction, results from someone ingesting alcohol or some other drug simply to feel different. Not everyone develops a chemical addiction to alcohol, but other highly addictive drugs can trap anyone who tries them.

Those who have begun to use alcohol to ease pain should watch for danger signs that indicate they are susceptible to addiction. People who develop serious alcohol issues often have the ability to "handle" their drinking (that is, they can drink a lot without it having much effect on them). Another danger sign is binge drinking: when a person consumes a lot of alcohol in an evening or a weekend but doesn't drink again for several weeks. They point to their long stretches without alcohol as proof that they don't have a dependency problem, but they do. Another danger sign is having others in the family tree who have been alcoholics. Heredity is a factor and indicates a much higher probability of becoming addicted to alcohol. Watch for these signs—they spell trouble.

Becoming addicted to a drug can start innocently. We may use drugs in order to fit in with friends, not knowing how powerfully addictive the drugs are. Sometimes, people get a legitimate prescription from a doctor. It may help for a while, but then its effects wear off, and soon more and more is needed. Some people may end up actually getting prescription medications on the street as well as through a doctor. Others try to self-medicate by using illegal drugs. It begins as a way to escape the pain, but the need for more can easily become a compulsion and then an addiction. The user feels trapped and gradually gets loaded down with shame and guilt.

The other general category of addiction, process addiction, involves using less obvious methods to try to handle emotional pain. These compulsive behaviors are related to a process instead of a substance like drugs or alcohol. These behaviors start out in small ways and are seemingly innocent. Some people may think they can control these behaviors, but when they try to stop, they realize the repetitive behavior controls them.

Gambling or compulsively spending money may be a way we try to deal with our problems. We may find that we are always short of money or are drawn to the excitement of gambling with its random rewards. Even video games may become our escape from a painful reality. Check it out. Decide to not play any video games, gamble online, or spend money for thirty days and see how uncomfortable it is. Each of these activities can become a process addiction.

Process addictions involving eating can be a big issue. Eating is one of the things we think we can always control, but there are three ways eating can be a problem. One problem, overeating, happens when people look at food as a source of comfort. When they are in emotional pain, they turn to food in order to feel good again. Another eating problem involves binge eating and then having to purge what was eaten. And then there is the very serious problem of people not eating enough. Because they think they are fat, some people control their eating habits and chronically lose weight, leading to life-threatening physical problems.

Using the internet can become a problem that leads to devastating addictions. Spending too much time searching the web, or even too much interaction on social media, can keep us from living in the real world. Or our internet use may involve pornography. Many think that viewing pornography is a problem limited to men, but it can be just as big a problem for women. Research says that the age group most commonly looking at pornography on the internet is young people—as young as eleven years old. Habitually viewing pornography can affect the brain in the same ways as a chemical addiction and can have devastating effects on our relationships.

Sometimes, people inflict pain on themselves to distract them from their emotional pain. They usually do this by cutting themselves. The reasons for this behavior are complex, but it is basically a way to feel something different—physical pain instead of emotional pain—and it is a way for them to feel alive. If they bleed a little, they know they are still here and that they are not invisible. This can become a very serious addiction.

These are some of the ways we may attempt to handle life's problems. We can get caught up in one of these chemical or process addictions and then get angry with ourselves because we can't stop. We can begin recovery by recognizing that it's not all our fault, but then we also need to begin to take responsibility for the choices we make. What you do in response to these problems will determine the course of your life, whether you know it or not. You are in control of your choices right now. Look to the resources in this devotional and to others who understand you and love you. You should not—you cannot—walk this path of recovery alone.

An Early History of Life Recovery

IN 1935, BILL W. AND DR. BOB, who were deeply involved with the Oxford Group movement, founded Alcoholics Anonymous (AA). They were seeking to live out the Oxford Group's Four Absolutes—absolute honesty, absolute purity, absolute unselfishness, and absolute love—as they helped others find the sobriety they were experiencing.

In those beginning days of the program, there were no Twelve Steps. Instead, they had six precepts relayed by Ebby T., who was Bill W.'s sponsor. Here are the six precepts:

- We admitted we were licked.
- We got honest with ourselves.
- We talked it over with another person.
- We made amends to those we had harmed.
- We tried to carry the message to others with no thought of reward.
- We prayed to whatever God we thought there was.

From these precepts, the Twelve Steps emerged. Dr. Bob, Bill W., and Dr. Samuel Shoemaker spent hours discussing as they studied portions of the Bible that aligned with their Oxford Group experiences and supported their own recovery journeys.

Three portions of Scripture were specifically identified as foundational in the development of the Twelve Steps: the Sermon on the Mount, which includes the Beatitudes (Matthew 5–7); the book of James, which focuses on several Twelve Step fundamentals; and "the love chapter" (1 Corinthians 13). All three of these portions of Scripture clearly established the Christian and biblical roots of AA and the Twelve Steps. Having come out of their study of the Bible, these early pioneers were careful to include nothing in the Steps that would counter any truth found in God's Word.

In the early days of AA, when conservative Christian values and truths were unapologetically used to help others in recovery, the success rate was quite amazing. The book *Dr. Bob and the Good Oldtimers* tells how Dr. Bob called every newcomer to the first AA group to "say a prayer to God admitting you were powerless over alcohol and your life was unmanageable." Nearly 93 percent of those surveyed in the Akron, Ohio, group never relapsed. For an addiction that had resulted in hopelessness and helplessness for centuries, this result was truly amazing.

We can only imagine what it was like to hear of alcoholics being "cured" (as the unknowing world called it) when anyone getting better from a real addiction to alcohol was considered the result of a divine miracle. We can compare what was happening there to what people would think today if 93 percent of people with stage IV incurable and inoperable brain cancer who went to Akron, Ohio, miraculously found healing there. Every media outlet would send someone to discover what was going on. Back then, 93 percent of alcoholics getting better caused such a stir that the wealthy John D. Rockefeller Jr. sent his son to find out what was going on to produce this miracle. When he reported back, he told his dad that they all had experienced a conversion experience with God.

In order to remove any barriers to inclusion based on religious views, AA did not use explicitly Christian language in their literature. They referred to God mostly as "God as we understood Him" or as the "Power greater than ourselves," allowing for a variety of religious perspectives. As time passed, most people forgot the strong connection between the Twelve Steps and the Bible, and recovery became a secular practice with many connections to medicine and psychology. In recent years, it has been difficult to reestablish the connection between Christian values and successful recovery programs that use the Twelve Steps. We are honored to be part of a movement that brings the Twelve Steps back to Scripture through the publication of *The Life Recovery Bible*, the creation of additional Life Recovery resources, the formation of The Life Recovery Institute, and the establishment of Life Recovery groups around the world.

At a meeting in 1991, Tyndale House Publishers partnered with Stephen Arterburn and David Stoop to create *The Life Recovery Bible*, which includes traditional study Bible features along with devotionals to give fellow strugglers a meaningful connection to God's Word. This Bible is designed for people involved in Twelve Step recovery programs who have longed for a tool that integrates the Twelve Steps with Scripture. Introducing them to the true Power greater than ourselves, the God of the Bible, *The Life Recovery Bible* provides a strong biblical foundation for recovery. And for people who know the Bible but are in need of recovery, it introduces them to the Twelve Steps in a Christ-centered recovery program.

Using *The Life Recovery Bible* along with this devotional, in the context of Twelve Step meetings and working the Steps, your life can be transformed. You can become one of many people who have allowed God to take over what they could not control and now believe what they once found so hard to accept.

The Twelve Steps of Life Recovery

1. We admitted that we were powerless over our problems—that our lives had become unmanageable.
2. We came to believe that a Power greater than ourselves could restore us to sanity.
3. We made a decision to turn our wills and our lives over to the care of God.
4. We made a searching and fearless moral inventory of ourselves.
5. We admitted to God, to ourselves, and to another human being the exact nature of our wrongs.
6. We were entirely ready to have God remove all these defects of character.
7. We humbly asked God to remove our shortcomings.
8. We made a list of all persons we had harmed and became willing to make amends to them all.
9. We made direct amends to such people wherever possible, except when to do so would injure them or others.
10. We continued to take personal inventory, and when we were wrong, promptly admitted it.
11. We sought through prayer and meditation to improve our conscious contact with God, praying only for knowledge of His will for us and the power to carry that out.
12. Having had a spiritual awakening as the result of these steps, we tried to carry this message to others and to practice these principles in all our affairs.

The Twelve Steps of Alcoholics Anonymous

1. We admitted we were powerless over alcohol—that our lives had become unmanageable.
2. Came to believe that a Power greater than ourselves could restore us to sanity.
3. Made a decision to turn our will and our lives over to the care of God *as we understood Him.*
4. Made a searching and fearless moral inventory of ourselves.
5. Admitted to God, to ourselves, and to another human being the exact nature of our wrongs.
6. Were entirely ready to have God remove all these defects of character.
7. Humbly asked Him to remove our shortcomings.
8. Made a list of all persons we had harmed, and became willing to make amends to them all.
9. Made direct amends to such people wherever possible, except when to do so would injure them or others.
10. Continued to take personal inventory and when we were wrong promptly admitted it.
11. Sought through prayer and meditation to improve our conscious contact with God *as we understood Him,* praying only for knowledge of His will for us and the power to carry that out.

12. Having had a spiritual awakening as the result of these steps, we tried to carry this message to alcoholics, and to practice these principles in all our affairs.

The Twelve Steps and Scripture

THE TWELVE STEPS HAVE long been of great help to people in recovery. Much of their power comes from the fact that they capture principles clearly revealed in the Bible. The following pages list the Twelve Steps and connect them to corresponding Scriptures that support them. This will help readers familiar with the Twelve Steps to discover the true source of their wisdom—the very Word of God.

STEP 1: We admitted that we were powerless over our problems—that our lives had become unmanageable.

> "I know that nothing good lives in me. . . . I want to do what is right, but I can't" (Romans 7:18; see also John 8:31-36; Romans 7:14-25).

STEP 2: We came to believe that a Power greater than ourselves could restore us to sanity.

> "God is working in you, giving you the desire and the power to do what pleases him" (Philippians 2:13; see also Romans 4:6-8; Ephesians 1:6-8; Colossians 1:21-22; Hebrews 11:1-10).

STEP 3: We made a decision to turn our wills and our lives over to the care of God.

"Dear brothers and sisters, I plead with you to give your bodies to God because of all he has done for you. Let them be a living and holy sacrifice—the kind he will find acceptable" (Romans 12:1; see also Matthew 11:28-30; Mark 10:14-16; James 4:7-10).

STEP 4: We made a searching and fearless moral inventory of ourselves.

"Let us test and examine our ways. Let us turn back to the LORD" (Lamentations 3:40; see also Matthew 7:1-5; 2 Corinthians 7:8-10).

STEP 5: We admitted to God, to ourselves, and to another human being the exact nature of our wrongs.

"Confess your sins to each other and pray for each other so that you may be healed" (James 5:16; see also Psalms 32:1-5; 51:1-3; 1 John 1:2-6).

STEP 6: We were entirely ready to have God remove all these defects of character.

"Humble yourselves before the Lord, and he will lift you up in honor" (James 4:10; see also Romans 6:5-11; Philippians 3:12-14).

STEP 7: We humbly asked God to remove our shortcomings.

"If we confess our sins to him, he is faithful and just to forgive us our sins and to cleanse us from all wickedness" (1 John 1:9; see also Luke 18:9-14; 1 John 5:13-15).

STEP 8: We made a list of all the persons we had harmed and became willing to make amends to them all.

"Do to others as you would like them to do to you" (Luke 6:31; see also Colossians 3:12-15; 1 John 3:10-20).

STEP 9: We made direct amends to such people wherever possible, except when to do so would injure them or others.

"If you are presenting a sacrifice at the altar . . . and . . . someone has something against you, leave your sacrifice there at the altar. Go and be reconciled to that person. Then come and offer your sacrifice to God" (Matthew 5:23-24; see also Luke 19:1-10; 1 Peter 2:21-25).

STEP 10: We continued to take personal inventory, and when we were wrong, promptly admitted it.

"If you think you are standing strong, be careful not to fall" (1 Corinthians 10:12; see also Romans 5:3-6; 2 Timothy 2:1-7; 1 John 1:8-10).

STEP 11: We sought through prayer and meditation to improve our conscious contact with God, praying only for knowledge of His will for us and the power to carry that out.

"Devote yourselves to prayer with an alert mind and a thankful heart" (Colossians 4:2; see also Isaiah 40:28-31; 1 Timothy 4:7-8).

STEP 12: Having had a spiritual awakening as the result of these steps, we tried to carry this message to others and to practice these principles in all our affairs.

"Dear brothers and sisters, if another believer is overcome by some sin, you who are godly should gently and humbly help that person back onto the right path. And be careful not to fall into the same temptation yourself" (Galatians 6:1; see also Isaiah 61:1-3; Titus 3:3-7; 1 Peter 4:1-5).

In God's Image

God created human beings in his own image.
In the image of God he created them;
male and female he created them.

GENESIS 1:27

TO BE CREATED IN GOD'S IMAGE is to be made to desire the things God desires, to love the way he loves. When we were in bondage to our addiction, we experienced the demeaning of that image. We became less like our Creator and more like our abusive slave master. Our recovery is, in part, a restoration of the image of God in us as we turn from looking into the face of addiction and, instead, look into the Father's eyes. That gaze alone brings us closer to healing. Closer to once again bearing the image of God.

† *Father, that I was created to be an image bearer of you amazes me. In my addiction, I've allowed that image to be marred. In my recovery, Lord, I pray you'll fully restore your image in me. Remove the scars of my addiction. Allow me to be a reflection of you and your attributes—not just for my sake but for the sake of those who see me, know me, and interact with me. Renew me this year; bring recovery to every part of my being. Make me whole again.*

> Within each of us exists the image of God, however disfigured and corrupted by sin it may presently be. God is able to recover this image through grace as we are conformed to Christ.
>
> ALISTER McGRATH (1953–)

You can find today's Scripture passage on page 6 of *The Life Recovery Bible.*

Freedom Is Not Wishful Thinking

Christ has truly set us free. Now make sure that you stay free,
and don't get tied up again in slavery to the law.

GALATIANS 5:1

EARLY ON IN OUR ADDICTION, our prayers may have been wishful thinking along the lines of "I sure wish God would get me out of this life I'm in." God can answer that prayer, but since all of the Christian life is based on faith, at some point we must turn that wishful thinking into confidence in God's ability to fully bring us out of slavery and into freedom. When he does, we must forever after always "stay free." We must never again submit ourselves to any yoke of slavery.

For the apostle Paul's Galatian audience, the temptation was to submit to the law from which they had been freed by trusting in Christ. For us, the temptation is to waver from recovery and find ourselves back in the throes of addiction. Thank God wishful thinking is a poor substitute for saving faith. When Christ sets us free, we're free forever. As Paul reminds us in Galatians 5, "Now make sure that you stay free."

✝ ***Father, my hope in you isn't wishful thinking. Deliverance from addiction is reality. Staying in addiction is slavery. Lord, be with me as I continue on in faith, building my trust in you day by day, watching you bring about every change I need. Help me to remember that you are for my freedom even more than I am.***

> Trust is faith that has become absolute, approved, and accomplished. When all is said and done, there is a sort of risk in faith and its exercise. But trust is firm belief; it is faith in full bloom. Trust is a conscious act, a fact of which we are aware.
>
> E. M. BOUNDS (1835–1913)

You can find today's Scripture passage on page 1504 of *The Life Recovery Bible.*

Christ Welcomes Us

Accept each other just as Christ has accepted you
so that God will be given glory.

ROMANS 15:7

COMING TO CHRIST FOR THE FIRST TIME . . . or returning to Christ after a season of addiction, we might wonder at his response. We know of the returning prodigal in Luke 15, but is that just a Bible story? Or is it true for us who have wandered in addiction?

Yes! It *is* for us! We soon find ourselves not only accepted by Christ but *welcomed* by him. He has longed for our return and receives us without hesitation, without condemnation, without projecting shame on us. Christ reminds us we are his and are deeply loved by him, no matter how long it's taken us to come home to him.

Today, think about Christ welcoming you. Consider his deep desire for friendship with you. In his generous welcoming, would you refuse to also welcome him into your life?

✝ ***Lord, I come to you one day at a time, basking in your words of welcome. Thank you for taking me as I am. Thank you for the promise of recovery and wholeness. Father, in you, I find a true home and a sure rest after wandering so long in the desert of addiction.***

When you stray from His presence, He longs for you to come back. He weeps that you are missing out on His love, protection, and provision. He throws His arms open, runs toward you, gathers you up, and welcomes you home.

CHARLES STANLEY (1932–)

You can find today's Scripture passage on page 1451 of *The Life Recovery Bible*.

God Doesn't Count Our Successes and Failures

I focus on this one thing: Forgetting the past and looking forward to what lies ahead, I press on to reach the end of the race and receive the heavenly prize for which God, through Christ Jesus, is calling us.

PHILIPPIANS 3:13-14

IT'S DURING THESE EARLY DAYS of the new year when we recall our previous vows of sobriety, which by this date have often been violated, resulting in a plunge of our self-worth. We own up to another failure and assume God is adding another F to our divine report card. But the truth is that our failures are simply the enemy's tools to keep us in his clutches.

As Christians, we know our success doesn't depend on us anyway. Our strength is in the Lord himself. So we're able to forget what lies behind and strain ahead in full forgiveness and confidence that we aren't failures. We reach for the prize that is ours: sobriety here on earth and a heavenly home in eternity.

✝ ***God, thank you that my past failures have brought me to where I am now—seeking full recovery by trusting in you alone. I press on toward the greater goals you have for me in this life and the joys that await me when this life is over. May the one thing I focus on be forgetting what lies behind as I press forward to what lies ahead. Bring it to pass, Lord.***

If you are a true believer in Jesus, be of this mind—always to be pressing forward to something higher and better. If God has given you one form of maturity, press onward to a much higher form. Seek continually to rise. The eagle's motto is, "Higher, Higher!" Let it be your motto, too.

CHARLES SPURGEON (1834–1892)

You can find today's Scripture passage on page 1524 of *The Life Recovery Bible*.

A Clean Heart

Create in me a clean heart, O God.
Renew a loyal spirit within me.
Do not banish me from your presence,
and don't take your Holy Spirit from me.
Restore to me the joy of your salvation,
and make me willing to obey you.

PSALM 51:10-12

WHEN TEMPTATION COMES, we know two responses: One is the response of the clean heart and renewed, right spirit God has placed in us. At that point, we realize we no longer need to accept the invitation to renew our addiction. The other response is when we don't sense the Holy Spirit's upholding power, and we become as dry gunpowder, needing only a spark to set us off. But, praise God, he never takes his Spirit from us. He is *always* there to uphold us. We need only to have a willing spirit.

✝ ***God, because of Christ's death on the cross, my heart is clean. You are renewing my spirit each day. Lord, my hope is in you during times of severe temptation. Remind me often of the joy of my salvation. Uphold me with a willing spirit.***

As long as the Spirit dwells in my heart, he deadens me to sin, so that if lawfully called through temptation I may reckon upon God carrying me through.
But when the Spirit leaves me, I am like dry gunpowder.

ROBERT MURRAY M'CHEYNE (1813–1843)

You can find today's Scripture passage on page 715 of *The Life Recovery Bible.*

A New Life Has Begun!

Anyone who belongs to Christ has become a new person.
The old life is gone; a new life has begun!
2 CORINTHIANS 5:17

AT THE MOMENT OF OUR conversion to Christ, many amazing things happen to us. Perhaps the most miraculous is that we become a "new person." It's as we grow to understand and live out our new life that we overcome our old life, which, according to God, has passed away. Here's the thing: *You can't fully embrace your new identity if you won't let go of your old identity.*

✝ ***Lord, I belong to you! Because of that, I'm a new person. My old life is gone—truly gone—and a new life has begun. This life was born of you. Now, heavenly Father, I pray you'll nourish this life. Bring it to maturity. Protect me, care for me, use me. May I quickly learn to live out of this new reality and discard all that belongs to the old life with its addictions and wrong appetites. Use my life to help others, Lord. This will be true happiness.***

> Oh, the unimaginable blessedness of those on whom this new creation has taken place. Oh, the unutterable, the endless misery of those on whom no change has passed, in whom old things still remain!
>
> **HORATIUS BONAR (1808–1889)**

You can find today's Scripture passage on page 1486 of *The Life Recovery Bible*.

The New Birth

> You have been born again, but not to a life that will quickly end. Your new life will last forever because it comes from the eternal, living word of God.
>
> 1 PETER 1:23

THERE IS NOTHING LIKE THE new birth to set us right. Having been born again by the Spirit of God, we leave behind all our garbage: our sin, our dependency on chemical or other addictive crutches, our compulsions, our lost years. All those fall behind us when we're born from above. Now we simply daily live out the truth of a reborn life that can never end, rooted in the living Word of God.

Being born again *is* the gospel. And it's our ticket to freedom.

† *Thank you, Lord, for the living and abiding Word, through which I gain my freedom. I praise you for the new birth that ushers me into a far better life than the natural one that is so easily attracted to addiction. May my new birth bring a welcome infusion of true life into my being. I pray that this life within me, born of your Holy Spirit, will continue to grow and bring forth good fruit—the fruit of long-term sobriety.*

> The gift of sonship to God becomes ours not through being born, but through being born again.
>
> J. I. PACKER (1926–2020)

You can find today's Scripture passage on page 1612 of *The Life Recovery Bible*.

New Mercies Every Morning

I still dare to hope
when I remember this:
The faithful love of the LORD never ends!
His mercies never cease.
Great is his faithfulness;
his mercies begin afresh each morning.

LAMENTATIONS 3:21-23

EACH NEW DAY IS A GIFT FROM GOD, chock-full of a fresh supply of grace and mercy—all we need for the next twenty-four hours. Today is like no other day you've ever seen. And tomorrow won't be like today. Every day is one of a kind. Don't miss out on today because of regret for yesterday or fear of tomorrow. You're alive, so live another day of glorious sobriety.

✝ *Father, thank you for your new mercies every morning. They're always welcome and always needed. I look forward to this day as I put yesterday behind me, and I will allow no worries about tomorrow to derail me from the gift of today. Thank you for your faithful love that never ends. Great is your faithfulness!*

God's part is to put forth power;
our part is to put forth faith.

ANDREW BONAR (1810–1892)

You can find today's Scripture passage on page 1008 of *The Life Recovery Bible.*

Expectation

My soul, wait silently for God alone,
For my expectation is from Him.
He only is my rock and my salvation;
He is my defense;
I shall not be moved.

PSALM 62:5-6, NKJV

OUR EXPECTATIONS OF GOD ARE always too low. *Way* too low. God isn't just interested in our sobriety; he wants to use each of us in a unique, individual way. But first, we must have that expectation of use. We must expect continued sobriety, restored relationships, and success wherever God calls us—whether in a job, a ministry, or simply as a support to our brothers and sisters in recovery. Let's *expect* to be part of God's answer to our nation's addiction epidemic.

Are you in?

✝ *Dear Lord, I know my expectations of you have been low. But you see me as a person limited only by my meager expectations. Father, increase my ability to expect great things from you. Open doors that direct me in how you want me to serve you as I live the fruitful life of sobriety.*

God has great things in store for His people,
they ought to have large expectations.

CHARLES SPURGEON (1834–1892)

You can find today's Scripture passage on page 722 of *The Life Recovery Bible.*

JANUARY 10

Dismantling Satan's Lies

[Satan] was a murderer from the beginning. He has always hated the truth, because there is no truth in him. . . . He is a liar and the father of lies.

JOHN 8:44

SATAN'S INTENTION IS TO INCLINE our hearts away from the gospel by entangling us in the evils of his kingdom, including our addiction. We can probably remember the first lie he told us about our chosen vice. "Just this once," "It'll help you relax," "You deserve this," "You won't get hooked," and so on. From there, the deception continued until we were living a life far from the person of truth we were designed to be.

In addiction, our inner ear has become accustomed to hearing the enemy's lies and acting according to them. Now we must retrain that inner ear to identify and refute the falsehood, and then to hear God's truth so as to replace what was untrue. Today, do not give the lie a second's thought. Refute it at once—and keep on refuting as long as it persists.

✝ *God, I've been a victim of the enemy's lies for too long. I now renounce every false step I've taken as a result of the unfulfilled promises of Satan. I will be on my guard to immediately halt the enemy when he whispers a new or repeated lie to me. Lord, help me fend off the one who has been a hater of truth since the beginning. I know that, in my battle, you are with me, and I must prevail against this lying foe.*

Satan promises the best, but pays with the worst; he promises honor and pays with disgrace; he promises pleasure and pays with pain; he promises profit and pays with loss; he promises life and pays with death. But God pays as He promises; all His payments are made in pure gold.

THOMAS BROOKS (1608–1680)

You can find today's Scripture passage on page 1355 of *The Life Recovery Bible*.

The Spirit of God

We have received God's Spirit (not the world's spirit),
so we can know the wonderful things God has freely given us.

1 CORINTHIANS 2:12

IT TAKES FAITH TO BELIEVE IN something we can't see. Like our recovery, for example. We must recover by faith—a concept many can't fathom. For them, seeing is believing. But for us, believing is seeing. The plain truth is that we have the Spirit of God within us and, thus, can understand the wonderful things God has freely given to us. Gloriously, our recovery under the watchful eye and caring hands of God is one of those important "wonderful things."

✝ *Father, by faith I can perceive the spiritual realities that change lives. But, Lord, help me see those realities more clearly as relevant to me. Bring into focus the very truths I now only partly understand. Make vivid to me the power you bring to change my life through your Spirit. Thank you that your Holy Spirit is my guide to truth and sobriety.*

> God wants to make the things of the Spirit more actual in your life than the things of sense are in the lower world of the material, and to quicken every inward sense until you shall know and see the invisible realities of the world to come with a vividness that the things of earth can never have.
>
> A. B. SIMPSON (1843–1919)

You can find today's Scripture passage on page 1458 of *The Life Recovery Bible.*

Power from God's Word

All Scripture is inspired by God and is useful to teach us what is true and to make us realize what is wrong in our lives. It corrects us when we are wrong and teaches us to do what is right.

2 TIMOTHY 3:16

THE WORD OF GOD—THE BIBLE—is our rich resource for deliverance from our addiction. In its pages, we find the strength of the Lord portrayed in the stories of many men and women of God, often in dire circumstances. Those who overcame did so by trusting in God and his Word. Prayer and the Word go hand in hand in securing our deliverance. By walking according to the Word, we are set on the pathway out of addiction.

Learn to *love* God's Word. Feast on it daily. Read it and meditate on it as God's special message just for you. Incorporate its truths into your life. You will be changed.

✝ ***Father, today I thank you for your Word. I thank you for the power within its pages as it reveals your plan to rescue all who come to you in faith. I praise you that in living out the Bible daily, I'm not only enabled to overcome, but I'm transformed, day by day, into Christlikeness.***

The longer you read the Bible, the more you will like it; it will grow sweeter and sweeter; and the more you get into the spirit of it, the more you will get into the spirit of Christ.

WILLIAM ROMAINE (1714–1795)

You can find today's Scripture passage on page 1564 of *The Life Recovery Bible.*

No Looking Back

When they were safely out of the city, one of the angels ordered, "Run for your lives! And don't look back or stop anywhere in the valley!"

GENESIS 19:17

SODOM WAS ABOUT TO BE DESTROYED. Two angels appeared and warned Lot of the coming destruction. Lot and his family left as the Lord rained sulfur and fire on the city. Lot's wife, however, looked back with longing—and she became a pillar of salt (see Genesis 19:26).

After taking even that first brave step toward recovery, our mindset must forever be *No looking back. Ever!* Sometimes, the early steps out of addiction are the easiest—so easy, in fact, we may mistakenly think we're now strong in our own resolve. That error can set us up for a tragic relapse. When we are determined to never look back, we can anticipate and prepare for unexpected temptations and resist them in the full power of the Holy Spirit (and, if necessary, aided by a trusted friend we can call on to pray for us and stand with us until we're past the heated hour of temptation).

No looking back. *Ever.* Renew this commitment daily. Even when you don't feel like it.

† ***Father, my life is focused on what lies before me, not what I left behind. I need no reminders of the sulfur of addiction. For me, there can be no looking back. Strengthen me, Lord, when the enemy implores me to look behind me at what I've lost. What he sees as the glitter of addiction, I know to be only an illusion that profits me nothing.***

May the Spirit give us grace to be ready—safe in the only ark of safety—the blessed Jesus. By faith let us flee into His wounded side. By faith let us nestle in His very heart. Then, amid flames of a burning world, we shall be high above the reach of harm.

HENRY LAW (1797–1884)

You can find today's Scripture passage on page 28 of *The Life Recovery Bible.*

Triggers

Call on me when you are in trouble,
and I will rescue you,
and you will give me glory.

PSALM 50:15

A TRIGGER CAN SET OFF ALMOST ANYONE dealing with compulsive or addictive behavior. For some, stress is a huge trigger. For others, it can be something as seemingly innocent as certain music that perhaps once accompanied addictive behavior. It can be visiting a locale that triggers memories and the accompanying desires. It can be hanging with certain people with whom we once shared our addiction.

Disarming the power of a trigger involves recasting the trigger to an alternate pattern of response. At the moment a trigger is pulled, we must not entertain the accompanying temptation but, instead, immediately reject the thought, just as if it were a bullet aimed at our heart. We must insist that the trigger for our addiction now become a trigger for sobriety.

Each of us may find different ways to do this. It can be calling a trusted friend for support, attending a recovery-oriented meeting, reading the story of others who have left addiction, or engaging in a sport or some other physical activity. You may even turn your triggers into a summons for prayer.

† *Father, you know my triggers. You know when the next trigger will occur. I pray you'll keep me alert and prompt me to turn that trigger into a response to stand firm in your strength and to keep focused on the joy to be found in sobriety. Always help me remember that the pain after relapse is never worth the cost. Keep my eyes on the prize of wholeness. Lord, I will not return to the instability of the triggered life.*

Satan, like a fisher, baits his hook according to the appetite of the fish.

THOMAS ADAMS (1583–1652)

You can find today's Scripture passage on page 714 of *The Life Recovery Bible.*

Logic and Addiction

Whoever trusts in his own mind is a fool,
but he who walks in wisdom will be delivered.

PROVERBS 28:26, ESV

WE DISCOVERED LONG AGO that addiction doesn't respond to human logic. We may well know objectively that addiction is our enemy, that it harms us and those we love, and that, if not abandoned, it won't end well for us. But all logic fails in the face of temptation.

Our route to recovery may give assent to the logic of recovery, but to be effective, we must possess a power inherent in our recovery protocol that's stronger than logic. That power is, for Christians, the truths of the gospel that, when lived out, bring freedom. Of course, to many people, the power of prayer, faith, and the indwelling Holy Spirit to overcome addiction is not logical. And yet it's the very prescription for our best recovery.

We must stop trying to *think* our way out of addiction and learn to *faith* our way out. This faith is not abstract, passive faith but biblical faith that moves mountains—and addiction *is* a mountain.

Let us ground ourselves in the truth of the Word that offers us freedom through a new identity and the power to walk out that identity. The power of the Holy Spirit in a man or woman is a power that overrides the logic that fails us.

† ***God, you know the many times I've tried to think my way out of addiction. Logically, I know all the reasons to stop, but those reasons fail me when I'm sorely tempted. Lord, help me grow in my new identity as I abandon my addiction identity. Bring me into a wider place by faith—a place of freedom, not slavery.***

Prayer is not logical, it is a mysterious moral working of the Holy Spirit.

OSWALD CHAMBERS (1874–1917)

You can find today's Scripture passage on page 817 of *The Life Recovery Bible*.

Cutting Loose

Do not be deceived: "Bad company ruins good morals."

1 CORINTHIANS 15:33, ESV

ONE FACTOR IN RELAPSE IS returning to the lifestyle that supported our addiction, including maintaining relationships that hinder our healing. Breaking away from those who are hostile to healing is crucial. We may be tempted to think that since we're on the road to healing, we can bring others with us. However, that only works when we're fully healthy and *able* to help others out of their addiction. But while still on the road ourselves, it's best to cut loose from the people who can spell R-E-L-A-P-S-E. Though it may be hard to let them go, it won't be as hard as trying to bounce back after a relapse.

✝ *Father, I know that relapse often happens in the company of fellow addicts. Though they have been friends and fellow travelers on a downward path, I pray you'll give me the wisdom and the strength to sever the ties that are harmful to me. I do pray for those who have yet to make the decision to leave their addiction, but I cannot bring them with me. Only you can awaken them to the way out of addiction. I pray you do so, Lord.*

We must have a spirit of power towards the enemy, a spirit of love towards men, and a spirit of self-control towards ourselves.

WATCHMAN NEE (1903–1972)

You can find today's Scripture passage on page 1475 of *The Life Recovery Bible.*

Your "Last" Time

I have discovered this principle of life—that when I want to do what is right, I inevitably do what is wrong. I love God's law with all my heart. But there is another power within me that is at war with my mind. This power makes me a slave to the sin that is still within me. Oh, what a miserable person I am! Who will free me from this life that is dominated by sin and death? Thank God! The answer is in Jesus Christ our Lord.

ROMANS 7:21-25

HOW MANY TIMES HAVE WE DECLARED BOLDLY, "That was my last time. No more," only to relapse within days? To be sure, there *can* be a last time. It happens the day we grasp just how complete our deliverance from our addiction is from God's point of view. The apostle Paul must have wrestled with "last time" promises in order for him to write of our experience so well in Romans 7. But then he saw a deliverer from "this life that is dominated by sin and death." That deliverer was—and *is*—Jesus Christ our Lord. Thanks be to God!

† *Father, thank you for freedom from addiction. Thank you that indeed there was a "last time" for me. Once decided upon, and with your empowering Holy Spirit, that day is marked forever as my day of freedom. It's the day I decided that your promise is stronger than my temptation to fall.*

The flesh inclines us more to believe a temptation than a promise.

THOMAS WATSON (1620–1686)

You can find today's Scripture passage on page 1441 of *The Life Recovery Bible.*

The Life within Us

I can do everything through Christ,
who gives me strength.
PHILIPPIANS 4:13

BECAUSE OF OUR COMMITMENT to Christ, we have the life within us that can meet our needs, no matter what those needs are. Our inner life is more than equal to our daily tasks. This overcoming life that enables us to do "everything through Christ" is given to us freely. Our problem is, too often, we allow the demands of the outer life to stifle the inner life. But in reality, our inner life, when strengthened, enables us to do every necessary thing. Even live victoriously over our addiction.

✝ *God, how great is the knowledge that you strengthen me through Christ to do "everything." I have the fullness of power necessary for all my needs. You pour into my being the very life of Christ who provides the essential resource for every expected and unexpected event, temptation, or circumstance that confronts me. Father, allow those empowering times to teach me to trust you even more deeply than before. Move me ahead, Lord, in "everything."*

> Whatever our need, we must turn for its supply to the fullness of God in Christ. As we keep open the avenue of our soul to our Lord, He will pour his strength into our nerveless and helpless nature. Nay, He will not merely give us His strength, but will be in us the power of God unto salvation. We need not simply the strength of Christ, but Christ who gives strength.
>
> **F. B. MEYER (1847–1929)**

You can find today's Scripture passage on page 1526 of *The Life Recovery Bible.*

Not by Might nor by Power . . .

"Not by might nor by power, but by My Spirit,"
Says the LORD of hosts.

ZECHARIAH 4:6, NKJV

WE'RE MISTAKEN IF WE THINK WE overcome addiction by our own might or power. Haven't we tried that before—perhaps many times—and failed miserably? What then? God's word to us is to *not* trust in ourselves but to accept deliverance by his unfailing Spirit. What we cannot do, he *can* do.

The difficulties that look so great to us—what are they to him? Nothing at all! He can open a way for us, where there seems to be none. He can take away the cause of our greatest anxiety. He can quench our thirst. He can end our cravings. He can satisfy us fully without addiction.

† *Lord, it seems to me that addiction itself is a "power." And the power it brings enslaves those who partake of it. For full deliverance, I need a power greater than addiction. Sheer willpower won't do, Lord. I need help by your Spirit. Even the quiet voice of your Holy Spirit will prevail where my might and power fail.*

The mightiest of all the forces that are at work in this world is that "still small voice" of the Holy Spirit that whispers God's Word of truth and life into the listening heart.

JAMES SMITH (1802–1862)

You can find today's Scripture passage on page 1176 of *The Life Recovery Bible*.

Looking to Jesus

Looking to Jesus, the founder and perfecter of our faith, who for the joy that was set before him endured the cross, despising the shame, and is seated at the right hand of the throne of God.

HEBREWS 12:2, ESV

WE ERR WHEN WE FOCUS TOO MUCH ON our addiction and less on our remedy. With our eyes fixed on our troubles, we can't see clearly the healing of our wounds, including our addictions. The brick wall we've built up obscures our view of the man or woman we're meant to be. It's in tearing down the wall, brick by brick, that we can once again see our true selves in Christ. It's an amazing identity we're missing out on, so we mustn't delay our healing. The wall must come down. Look to Jesus and remove another brick.

✝ *God, sometimes it feels as if my addiction is the elephant in the room that is my life. So much that I do revolves around staying clean. My focus is set on my addiction, even as I'm overcoming it. Father, I pray instead that you'll help me look past addiction and focus intently on Christ, my remedy. Help me change my vision of the elephant in the room to an elephant-sized trophy of your power to overcome my addiction.*

Looking at the wound of sin will never save anyone.
What you must do is look at the remedy.

DWIGHT L. MOODY (1837–1899)

You can find today's Scripture passage on page 1592 of *The Life Recovery Bible*.

We Have an Enemy

Stay alert! Watch out for your great enemy, the devil. He prowls around like a roaring lion, looking for someone to devour. Stand firm against him, and be strong in your faith.

1 PETER 5:8-9

OUR ADDICTION WAS A "GIFT" TO US FROM our adversary, the devil. He knew our weaknesses and designed a way to entrap us by setting the snares that have led us into addiction and a devouring of our true selves. By soberly acknowledging our enemy, we must also acknowledge our strength in Christ. We are well on the road away from the lion's roar, but we must always remain watchful. He won't give up—and neither must we.

Stay alert! Stand firm, and be strong.

Father, it's a waste of time when I don't recognize my addiction as the enemy's attempt to "devour" me. I need to move past the usual rationalizations about my addiction and label it for what it is—and then fully engage in overcoming Satan's designs for me. Lord, remind me to always be sober-minded and watchful.

The first step on the way to victory is to recognize the enemy.

CORRIE TEN BOOM (1892–1983)

You can find today's Scripture passage on page 1617 of *The Life Recovery Bible*.

Be Thankful

Be thankful in all circumstances, for this is God's will
for you who belong to Christ Jesus.

1 THESSALONIANS 5:18

IF WE'RE AT A HIGH POINT IN OUR RECOVERY, we can rejoice and give thanks. But for us as believers, we should and can rejoice and give thanks in *all* circumstances. Even during our low points.

Rejoicing and expressing gratitude isn't a barometer of our state; it's an obedience to God that can change our state for the better. To get on an even keel and stay that way, we must learn the power of giving thanks . . . in *all* circumstances.

Thankfulness may include praising God, rejoicing, or blessing others in some tangible way. Gratitude doesn't require feeling grateful. In addiction, we may have become overly feelings oriented. But being thankful in all circumstances is something we *do*, feelings or no feelings.

Faith, rejoicing, and gratitude should *lead*, not follow, feelings.

† ***Lord, I give thanks to you for my every circumstance, knowing you're present with me in good times and not-so-good times. May my grateful attitude bring about a deeper satisfaction with your work in my life. May I fully experience the power that comes from a thankful heart.***

Yes, give thanks for "all things" for, as it has been well said
"Our disappointments are but His appointments."

A. W. PINK (1886–1952)

You can find today's Scripture passage on page 1542 of *The Life Recovery Bible.*

Biblical Self-Talk

Why are you cast down, O my soul,
and why are you in turmoil within me?
Hope in God; for I shall again praise him,
my salvation and my God.

PSALM 43:5, ESV

DAVID WAS A MASTER AT TALKING to himself, even reassuring his downcast soul to hope in God. Likewise, we can benefit by talking to our soul, urging ourselves to hope in God and to praise him, the author of our salvation.

Give your soul a good talking to today and every day. Point your soul to the Lord in all his goodness. When your soul is in step with the Lord, you're in the process of recovering.

Hope in God.

✝ *Father, my hope is in you. Only you can see me through the ups and downs of recovery. Help me as I speak encouragement to my soul. Help me as I remove the turmoil within me. Lord, I shall again praise you for my salvation. Bring reassurance to my soul. Renew my body. Allow peace to reign within me.*

Beloved, are you passing through storms, tempests, and trials?
Hope in God, whatever your trial may be.
Are you sick? He will make your bed, and sanctify your pain.
Are you poor? He will answer your prayers, and supply your need.
Are you sorrowful? He will comfort you, and give you joy for your sorrow.
Are you tempted? He will not suffer you to be tempted
above that you are able to bear.

JAMES SMITH (1802–1862)

You can find today's Scripture passage on page 709 of The Life Recovery Bible.

God in Creation

The heavens proclaim the glory of God.
The skies display his craftsmanship.
Day after day they continue to speak;
night after night they make him known.

PSALM 19:1-2

GOD'S GLORY IN CREATION IS DAZZLING. It brings health and healing to our deepest wounds. Nature isn't always readily accessible, but surely we can visit some part of God's creative world. Allow the beauty of the world outside of man's creations to renew your mind. Stop somewhere and drink in beautiful surroundings. Then consider the God who created it—and you as his greater creation. Worship him silently as you ponder his world and your unique place in it. Give thanks.

✝ *Father, renew my appreciation for your wonderful acts of creation. Open my eyes to see the wonders of nature through clear eyes, not the former vision-impaired lens of addiction. May the wonder of creation heal wounds and open my eyes to your glory. Lord, help me see myself as a part of your grander creation, created in your image.*

> The spiritual mind, fond of soaring through nature in quest of new proofs of God's existence and fresh emblems of His wisdom, power and goodness, exults in the thought that he treads his Father's domain. He *feels* that God, *his* God, is there.
>
> OCTAVIUS WINSLOW (1808–1878)

You can find today's Scripture passage on page 691 of *The Life Recovery Bible.*

Repentance

Prove by the way you live that you have repented
of your sins and turned to God.

MATTHEW 3:8

A KEY TO OUR RECOVERY IS deep-seated repentance. We have seen what our addiction has done to us and to those we love. But we may not be aware of our offense before God. We have wronged him as well as ourselves and our loved ones. To accomplish our recovery, we must repent for our past wrongs—a "turning away" from them—and bring forth the fruit of repentance, which is right living. Without repentance, there is no fruit. The wall remains high between us and our Lord.

† *God, you know I* do *repent of my sins—addictions and all. I repent of the lost time, wasted money, the deceitfulness, the broken relationships, and all else my addictions have cost me. Father, I know there is fruit to be born from repentance. I pray you'll help me not only by bringing healing to my own life but by restoring those things that can be restored. May the springs of repentance flow freely from my life.*

> Repentance is a grace, and must have its daily operation, as well as other graces. A true penitent must go on from faith to faith, from strength to strength; he must never stand still or turn back. True repentance is a continued spring, where the waters of godly sorrow are always flowing.
>
> THOMAS BROOKS (1608–1680)

You can find today's Scripture passage on page 1200 of *The Life Recovery Bible.*

Godly Decision-Making

Seek his will in all you do,
and he will show you which path to take.

PROVERBS 3:6

WE ENTER INTO RECOVERY BY making a decision. We look at our lives and see that we must change or we will likely die. So we *decide* that we will set aside our old life and enter into the new life of the Christian. A life that brings with it a new nature and a relationship with God that will sustain us through our recovery.

That one decision will change our destiny forever. By making this decision, we acknowledge God in all our present and future ways, trusting that he will direct our paths.

This decision, though, is just a beginning. We must make fresh decisions daily that impact our recovery and every other aspect of our lives. The secret is to make our decisions based on the Word of God. Any decision counter to the Word only sets our recovery back. Learning to make good daily decisions is a key component of our recovery.

Consider any decisions you must make today in light of God's Word. Your path will be made straight.

✝ ***God, I desire the happiness that comes from making and following through on wise decisions based on your Word. I pray for the influence of the Holy Spirit in helping me see the right choices I need to make from here on out. Help me, too, to make decisions about my former life of addiction that will reverse the damage done in my life and in the lives of those I've hurt. May I make healthy, life-affirming decisions, the fruits of which are happiness and contentment.***

As we trust God to give us wisdom for today's decisions, He will lead us a step at a time into what He wants us to be doing in the future.

THEODORE EPP (1907–1985)

You can find today's Scripture passage on page 789 of *The Life Recovery Bible*.

A Well-Boundaried Life

The boundary lines have fallen for me in pleasant places.

PSALM 16:6, NIV

JESUS SET THE BOUNDARIES REGARDING how we must come to our Father. It's through *him* and no other way. He is the boundary for the Christian life. Boundaries are useful to us in our recovery from addiction. Though they may vary from person to person, some of the boundaries are common to us all. By bitter experience, we have learned how foolish it is to set one foot out of the boundary keeping us from our addiction. Our boundaries are like guardrails on a mountain road, keeping us from a dangerous fall into the canyon below. Boundaries for our own behavior are as important as the boundaries we have in place with others who may have a negative effect on our recovery.

Define, respect, and stay well within your boundaries.

✝ ***God, my life in addiction was a life without boundaries. Even when there were boundaries, I constantly crossed those lines and suffered the painful results. Now, Lord, I pray for the wisdom and strength to walk within the designated boundaries you've drawn for me. And when there are boundaries you desire for me that I don't yet see, Lord, reveal them to me through your Word, other trusted friends, or through your Holy Spirit.***

> Boundaries define us. They define *what is me* and *what is not me*. A boundary shows me where I end and someone else begins, leading me to a sense of ownership. . . . *Boundaries help us keep the good in and the bad out*. Setting boundaries inevitably involves taking responsibility for your choices. You are the one who makes them. You are the one who must live with their consequences. And you are the one who may be keeping yourself from making the choices you could be happy with.
>
> HENRY CLOUD (1956–)

You can find today's Scripture passage on page 688 of *The Life Recovery Bible*.

Overcoming Discouragement

Why am I discouraged?
Why is my heart so sad?
I will put my hope in God!
I will praise him again—
my Savior and my God!

PSALM 43:5

TURMOIL HAPPENS. Adversity stalks us. But when bad things occur, our response isn't to be discouraged; it's to hope in God. It's time to praise him anew for his salvation. To laud him for being our God. Other people may fail us, unexpected news may sadden us, adverse circumstances may disappoint us, but God never fails. We must trust him and praise him. We must put our hope in him.

✝ ***Father, when I'm discouraged, remind me to hope in you. At such times, may I begin to simply praise you for your love, trusting your every move in my life. You are my God. You are my salvation. Turn my mourning into gladness. Trade my tears of sadness for tears of rejoicing. You never fail me, Lord. I find that especially true during trying times. I will praise you again, my God.***

> In the darkest of nights cling to the assurance that God loves you, that He always has advice for you, a path that you can tread and a solution to your problem—and you will experience that which you believe. God never disappoints anyone who places his trust in Him.
>
> **BASILEA SCHLINK (1904–2001)**

You can find today's Scripture passage on page 709 of *The Life Recovery Bible*.

Take Delight

Take delight in the LORD,
and he will give you your heart's desires.

PSALM 37:4

WHO AMONG US DOES NOT HAVE desires in life? Desires that, no doubt, God himself has placed in our hearts. To see those desires come to pass, we must learn the great secret of taking delight in the Lord. This means delighting in him *exclusively.* No other delights, including addiction, are allowed. The great thing is that delighting in the Lord is its own reward—and our avenue to a fulfillment of our heart's desires.

✝ *Lord, truth be told, I have often "delighted" in things other than you. Early on, my delight was in the afterglow of my addiction, not realizing where it was taking me. What was once my delight then became my horror. Father, I'm at the place now where I've abandoned forever the supposed delights of my addiction. Now, I delight exclusively in you. I find the knowledge of you extremely satisfying to my soul. My hunger is to know more of you, to know you better, to find even greater delight in you. That, Lord, is the desire of my heart.*

Our only business is to love and delight ourselves in God.

BROTHER LAWRENCE (1614–1691)

You can find today's Scripture passage on page 704 of *The Life Recovery Bible.*

The Blazing Fire of Addiction

Can a man scoop a flame into his lap
and not have his clothes catch on fire?
Can he walk on hot coals
and not blister his feet?

PROVERBS 6:27-28

ADDICTION IS A FIRE THAT BLAZES within relentlessly. It's not possible to escape serious burns if we do not put out the fire at first notice. Left unattended, the flames will consume us; the hot coals will bring painful blisters that cripple us.

Remember, fires begin as a spark. Beware of the sparks that precede acting out on your past addiction. Name them and avoid them.

✝ *Father, the fire of addiction nearly consumed me. The flames, left unattended, became a raging blaze. Had it not been for your intervention, I shudder to think where I'd be now. Thank you for the circumstances that have kept me safe during the fire. Thank you for the resources to extinguish the early sparks of fire. Thank you for shielding me now with your protection from future fires. I have learned to resist the first pulse of heat that seeks kindling in my soul. In you, I am now fireproof.*

Habit, if not resisted, soon becomes necessity.

SAINT AUGUSTINE OF HIPPO (354–430)

You can find today's Scripture passage on page 794 of *The Life Recovery Bible*.

Jesus' Unlikely Companions

Matthew invited Jesus and his disciples to his home as dinner guests, along with many tax collectors and other disreputable sinners. But when the Pharisees saw this, they asked his disciples, "Why does your teacher eat with such scum?"

MATTHEW 9:10-11

EVEN AT OUR WORST, we can know that Jesus would have no hesitation in dining with us, fellowshiping with us, *loving* us. We are a band of sinners whom Jesus specifically sought out for redemption, healing, and friendship. He is not ashamed to be seen with us, not now and not even in our past days of addiction. He was there then, and he is here now.

✝ *O God, you have not rejected me! In fact, you have called me to dine with you forever. You count me as a friend, as your child, your beloved. At my worst, you loved me. Even when I didn't show love toward you, your love still shone on me, protecting me, bringing me to this place of recovery. Such a thought transforms me, Lord. I am yours. Now and forever.*

Love shines forth in his reception of sinners. He refuses none who come to him for salvation, however unworthy they may be. Though their lives may have been most wicked, though their sins may be more in number than the stars of Heaven—the Lord Jesus is ready to receive them, and give them pardon and peace! There is no end to his compassion! There are no bounds to his pity! He is not ashamed to befriend those whom the world casts off as hopeless. There are none too bad, too filthy, and too much diseased with sin—to be admitted into his heavenly home! He is willing to be the friend of any sinner. He has kindness and mercy and healing medicine for all.

J. C. RYLE (1816–1900)

You can find today's Scripture passage on page 1209 of *The Life Recovery Bible*.

FEBRUARY 1

The Fiery Trial of Recovery

Dear friends, don't be surprised at the fiery trials you are going through, as if something strange were happening to you. Instead, be very glad—for these trials make you partners with Christ in his suffering, so that you will have the wonderful joy of seeing his glory when it is revealed to all the world.

1 PETER 4:12-13

IN RECOVERY, we experience a few easy days, some uncomfortable days, and quite a few hard days. We shouldn't be surprised when the latter arrive. It's often simply the unexpected hard days that throw us for a loop. But by expecting them, we can be prepared. We know that sometimes simply waiting out the temptation will eventually see it pass. At other times, we must actively resist the lure, refusing to take the bait.

Accept now that you will encounter difficult days, and prepare. And, of course, rejoice on the easy days. The remembrance of them will come in handy as we remind ourselves that hard days eventually give way to easier days—if we just stay the course.

† *Father, prepare me now for the times ahead that will be a struggle. Fortify me through faith; establish my roots in firm soil. Stretch my roots, enable me to be a strong resistance in the day of trouble.*

> Let us not be surprised when we have to face difficulties. When the wind blows hard on a tree, the roots stretch and grow the stronger. Let it be so with us. Let us not be weaklings, yielding to every wind that blows, but strong in spirit to resist.
>
> AMY CARMICHAEL (1867–1951)

You can find today's Scripture passage on page 1616 of *The Life Recovery Bible*.

The Treasure-Filled Field

The Kingdom of Heaven is like a treasure that a man discovered hidden in a field. In his excitement, he hid it again and sold everything he owned to get enough money to buy the field.

MATTHEW 13:44

UNLESS WE ACKNOWLEDGE THAT our addiction has cost us great amounts of money, time, and relationships, we may be unprepared to pay a price for our freedom. When we understand what freedom from addiction is and that it can be ours, we willingly do what's necessary to buy the treasure-filled field. It's the best investment we can make—and with lifelong benefits.

† *Father God, you have treasure awaiting me, not just in eternity but in this life also. I hear your invitation to do whatever's necessary to buy the field of freedom. I lay down my life, my habits, my addictions—all that is of me is now yours. Day by day, by faith, I uncover each and every treasure you have prepared for me. Nothing of my old life remains attractive to me as all is now invested in your Kingdom.*

To know God as the Master and Bestower of all good things, who invites us to request them of Him, and still not go to Him and ask of Him—this would be of as little profit as for a man to neglect a treasure, buried and hidden in the earth, after it had been pointed out to him.

JOHN CALVIN (1509–1564)

You can find today's Scripture passage on page 1218 of *The Life Recovery Bible.*

The Love of God

We love each other because he loved us first.

1 JOHN 4:19

IN OUR HUMAN RELATIONSHIPS, it's not unusual for us to love someone first and then have them return that love. But in our relationship with God, he is the initiator. His love is always upon us, even at our worst . . . perhaps *especially* at our worst. God's intense love is unlike human love. It continues to give in the face of our spiritual apathy and the dire straits we find ourselves in because of addiction. His love follows us through every trial and temptation, always persuading us to allow love to heal us. God's love is a great remover of the bricks that wall us off from our freedom. Let God's love find you . . . and keep you.

✝ ***Father, it's hard for me to grasp the fullness of your never-ending, faithful love toward me. Open my eyes, Lord, to the depths of this endless love that I will enjoy throughout eternity. Holy Spirit, in my weakness, may I find strength in the love of God.***

> When we pray for the Spirit's help . . . we will simply fall down at the Lord's feet in our weakness. There we will find the victory and power that comes from His love.
>
> ANDREW MURRAY (1828–1917)

You can find today's Scripture passage on page 1633 of *The Life Recovery Bible.*

Our Kind and Patient God

Don't you see how wonderfully kind, tolerant, and patient God is with you? Does this mean nothing to you? Can't you see that his kindness is intended to turn you from your sin?

ROMANS 2:4

THE KINDNESS OF GOD TOWARD US has a goal: causing us to turn away from addiction and securing our freedom. Have we looked back to recount God's kindness through our season of addiction? Have we seen his forbearance and his patience? Have we understood his presence during our addiction?

From time to time, we all need to reflect on how far we've come and how God has led us, even when we were unaware and unconcerned about his watching over us. Our reflection of God's patience toward us should reinforce our commitment to freedom. When we follow God's kindness, we will find ourselves in a place of repentance.

✝ ***Lord, you have been kind to me even when I was ignorant of your rich kindness and your commitment to secure my freedom. Father, please know that in glimpsing your kindness and your patience, I can do nothing other than repent for my lost years. Lead me forward now in living out this desired change of heart. Strengthen me when I'm weak, comfort me when I'm tempted, and rejoice with me when I celebrate my victories.***

Man is born with his face turned away from God. When he truly repents, he is turned right round toward God; he leaves his old life.

DWIGHT L. MOODY (1837–1899)

You can find today's Scripture passage on page 1432 of *The Life Recovery Bible.*

A Divinely Planned Destiny

The Lord will work out his plans for my life—
for your faithful love, O Lord, endures forever.
Don't abandon me, for you made me.

PSALM 138:8

PERHAPS THE WORST FRUIT OF our addiction has been the delay in fulfilling God's purpose for us. But God's steadfast love doesn't give up on seeing that divine purpose come to pass. He will never abandon us, because we were created for a divine destiny. His faithful love endures forever.

It's never too late to jump back on the path to our destiny. God has not and will not forsake us, the work of his hands. He *will* fulfill his purpose for me. For you. For all who trust in him.

✝ *Lord, to the extent that I've wandered away from your planned destiny for me, I sorrow for what I've missed. But, Father, I believe it's not too late to come back to the path you have set for me—a path leading to my ordained destiny here on earth. Lord, I know I was made for a larger end than the lonely life of addiction. Help me find that greater life you have for me. May nothing stop me from the restored future you have planned for me.*

We are made for larger ends than Earth can encompass.
Oh, let us be true to our exalted destiny.

CATHERINE BOOTH (1829–1890)

You can find today's Scripture passage on page 774 of *The Life Recovery Bible.*

Springs in the Desert

All my springs are in you.

PSALM 87:7, ESV

SPRINGS BRING REFRESHMENT. For too long, we tried to find springs in the desert places. The result was only dry sand, the arid climate of despair, and the joylessness of a life unfulfilled. But when we abandon those useless desert mirages and determine to find our springs in Christ alone, there arises an oasis in the middle of our personal desert. Whichever desert we find ourselves in, whatever our addiction, it doesn't delay God's intervention. When we seek his springs, we'll find an oasis of pure joy gushing up all around us.

✝ *God, daily I need joy. I need the joy that brings forth springs in the desert. I need the joy that never runs dry, the joy that's always available. I need the joy that knowing Jesus brings, the joy that overcomes the obstacles of temptation, loneliness, and barrenness of life. Lord, set the joy of Jesus Christ deep within me as a spring that never runs dry—and I will bathe in it day by day.*

> Joy is distinctly a Christian word and a Christian thing. It is the reverse of happiness. Happiness is the result of what happens of an agreeable sort. Joy has its springs deep down inside. And that spring never runs dry, no matter what happens. Only Jesus gives that joy. He had joy, singing its music within, even under the shadow of the cross.
>
> S. D. GORDON (1859–1936)

You can find today's Scripture passage on page 741 of *The Life Recovery Bible*.

Weakness as an Asset

"My grace is all you need. My power works best in weakness." So now I am glad to boast about my weaknesses, so that the power of Christ can work through me.

2 CORINTHIANS 12:9

IT'S A MISTAKE TO THINK THAT BEING weak means we are a disappointment to God or in some way inferior. Everyone has degrees of weaknesses. But the truth is that weakness in a person is an asset God can use. The power of Christ can rest on the weak in a way that it cannot rest on the strong. God's power is made perfect in our weakness. So much so that Paul boasted gladly of his weaknesses. We can do so too, confident that the power of Christ Paul experienced will also rest upon us.

✝ *God, grant me a life of permanent weakness, so that forever after, the power of Christ may work through me. Let me not despair of weakness, but may it become my boast. Lord, thank you for my many weaknesses, for in them I find I have many strengths.*

The strongest Christian is the one who feels his *weakness* most, and cries most frequently, "Hold me up, and I shall be safe."

J. C. RYLE (1816–1900)

You can find today's Scripture passage on page 1493 of *The Life Recovery Bible.*

The Blessing of Temptation

In your struggle against sin you have not yet resisted
to the point of shedding your blood.

HEBREWS 12:4, ESV

CAN ANYTHING GOOD COME OUT of temptations? Will there be a time this side of heaven when we're no longer tempted? Yes and no. No, there will always be temptations, and they are, of course, to be resisted. But as to any good to come from them, there is this: Resisting temptations makes us strong in the same way that lifting heavy weights at the gym makes us physically strong. When we've reached a plateau and want to become stronger, we add more weight for more muscle.

While we should never seek temptation, when it does come, we must quickly call on the inner strength God has given us to resist and overcome. When this becomes a habit, we begin to see our spiritual muscles made stronger. We can now bear temptations that once sent us over the edge.

The next time you're tempted, remember what you do at the gym when you're determined to increase your muscle mass.

† ***God, the only way I can envision good coming from being tempted is that, by continued resistance, I grow stronger with each confrontation with the tempter. Lord, though I pray that you will deliver me from temptation, I also pray you will deliver me in temptation so that my strength may increase.***

The higher the hill, the stronger the wind: so the loftier the life, the stronger the enemy's temptations.

JOHN WYCLIFFE (1328–1384)

You can find today's Scripture passage on page 1592 of *The Life Recovery Bible.*

FEBRUARY 9

God Gives the Victory

Thank God! He gives us victory over sin and death
through our Lord Jesus Christ.

1 CORINTHIANS 15:57

THE OPERATIVE WORD IN TODAY'S verse is *gives*. Victory over addiction is, like our salvation, a gift of God. And part of our lives in recovery is the ability to accept that gift of victory by faith and then continually enforce that victory in our lives, despite opposition. We have that power, though we often neglect it.

Give God thanks for this gift—and be quick to remind yourself that it *is* a gift from God to you. It's another evidence of his love for you.

✝ *Thanks be to God for my victory in Christ! Lord, my daily prayer is to meet forcefully my enemy of addiction and overcome through the gift of deliverance that you freely give. This gift is a treasure to me, and I do not take it for granted.*

> Any battle for victory, power, and deliverance—from ourselves and from sin—which is not based constantly upon the gazing and the beholding of the Lord Jesus, with the heart and life lifted up to Him, is doomed to failure.
>
> ALAN REDPATH (1907–1989)

You can find today's Scripture passage on page 1475 of *The Life Recovery Bible*.

Live Above!

Since you have been raised to new life with Christ,
set your sights on the realities of heaven,
where Christ sits in the place of honor at God's right hand.

COLOSSIANS 3:1

AS FIRM BELIEVERS IN CHRIST, we know we have been raised to new life with him. We now set our sights on heaven's realities as we discard the glitter of earth that once attracted us.

To seek heaven's realities, we must choose to turn our eyes away from where they're too easily drawn and cast them heavenward. How do we do this? One way is to have at the ready certain favorite Scriptures to lean on. One favorite is Isaiah 26:3: "You will keep in perfect peace all who trust in you, all whose thoughts are fixed on you!" Locate a few of your go-to Scriptures and commit them to memory. Draw upon them as necessary.

✝ *God, I've lived too long on the earthly plane with its so-called attractions. I now know that true happiness is found in seeking the things above. I know that I have been raised with Christ, and I can now set my sights on heavenly treasures. I choose, then, to live the risen life of victory.*

You say that you were dead with Christ, and that you have risen with Christ. Live, then, the risen life, and not the life of those who have never undergone this matchless process. Live above.

CHARLES SPURGEON (1834–1892)

You can find today's Scripture passage on page 1534 of *The Life Recovery Bible*.

Jars of Clay

We now have this light shining in our hearts, but we ourselves are like fragile clay jars containing this great treasure. This makes it clear that our great power is from God, not from ourselves.

2 CORINTHIANS 4:7

IT'S A MISTAKE TO THINK WE CAN overcome addiction by our own strength. That's a strategy doomed to failure as we know from our own experience. We are, after all, made of clay. The good news is that God is pleased to show off his great power in our jars of clay, for only then is it obvious that the strength to overcome belongs to him, not us—and that it is available to us at all times.

† *Father, thank you for the great treasure I have in this fallen human vessel of clay. It's a miracle that you would invest treasure within me—but you surely have. As I consider this treasure, I know that it serves to affirm the great power that belongs to you and not to me. Therefore, all the glory, all the praise goes to you. Break open this jar of clay so that the treasure might be seen in me.*

> The Treasure is in the earthen vessel, but if the earthen vessel is not broken, who can see the Treasure within? What is the final objective of the Lord's working in our lives? It is to break this earthen vessel, to break our alabaster box, to crack open our shell. The Lord longs to find a way to bless the world through those who belong to Him.
>
> WATCHMAN NEE (1903–1972)

You can find today's Scripture passage on page 1484 of *The Life Recovery Bible*.

We Are God's Delight

He rescued me from my powerful enemies,
from those who hated me and were too strong for me.
They attacked me at a moment when I was in distress,
but the LORD supported me.
He led me to a place of safety;
he rescued me because he delights in me.

PSALM 18:17-19

WHEN WE'RE AT OUR WORST, most of those we love find it hard to "delight" in us. But God isn't like that. The proof of God's delight is in his rescue of us, his bringing us out from a narrow, confining place, to a broad, spacious place of safety. He saved us from our powerful enemy of addiction that was too strong for us. Through it all, he has been our support—and will continue to be as long as we live.

Take this to the bank: We are God's delight, and he will never give up on us.

✝ ***God, I praise you for the miracle that you delight in me. I thank you that you are mine forever, that you have rescued me from my strong enemy, that you are my support and have brought me out into a place of safety, away from the narrow confines of my addiction. You rescued me—all because you delight in me. In me!***

It is the consciousness of the threefold joy of the Lord, His joy in ransoming us, His joy in dwelling within us as our Savior and Power for fruitbearing, and His joy in possessing us, as His Bride and His delight; it is the consciousness of this joy which is our real strength. Our joy in Him may be a fluctuating thing: His joy in us knows no change.

HUDSON TAYLOR (1832–1905)

You can find today's Scripture passage on page 690 of *The Life Recovery Bible*.

Battling Giants

David replied to [Goliath], "You come to me with sword, spear, and javelin, but I come to you in the name of the LORD of Heaven's Armies—the God of the armies of Israel, whom you have defied. Today the LORD will conquer you, and I will kill you and cut off your head. And then I will give the dead bodies of your men to the birds and wild animals, and the whole world will know that there is a God in Israel! And everyone assembled here will know that the LORD rescues his people, but not with sword and spear. This is the LORD's battle, and he will give you to us!"

1 SAMUEL 17:45-47

ALL BATTLES WORTH FIGHTING ARE against giants bigger than we are. Our addiction (our Goliath) is a good example. Though the battle is to be waged, it's not to be waged merely with sword and spear but by coming against our giant foe in the name of the Lord and by the power of his Spirit. Yes, the battle *is* the Lord's. But for us to face a Goliath, God must see a David in us. If we rely on him, he will deliver us from all our giants. To win the battle, we must engage in the battle—without fear.

† ***Father God, if there's one positive thing about addiction, it's an opportunity to show just how big a Goliath I can slay if I engage in the battle with faith and without fear. I pray that my addiction, though hell itself, would be an example of your power to perform a miracle. Give me the will, Lord, to enter the battle confident of your power to slay the Goliaths—all of them—in my life.***

The power of faith isn't based on who you are, it's based simply on who God is. Your faith is as big as the God you believe in. Like David facing the giant, sometimes God gives you a bigger-than-life problem so that He can show you His bigger-than-Goliath solution. Keep your eyes on Him, and keep the faith. He is faithful.

TONY EVANS (1949–)

You can find today's Scripture passage on page 368 of *The Life Recovery Bible*.

The Gift of Rest

He gives power to the weak
and strength to the powerless.

ISAIAH 40:29

IN OUR DAYS OF ADDICTION, we had no might. No strength. We were servants, not masters. But God offers us a trade: our weakness for his strength. When we make this trade, we find rest from the inner turmoil of our addiction. We have let go of our expectations that our own strength will carry us through. We depend on him alone. However, we do not become passive in our weakness. Our faith is an active faith, motivating us in ways our weakness could not. Our rest is a rest of confidence in God's strength in us.

† *Father, during the days of my addiction, what I often longed for was rest. Addiction does not produce rest—at all. You, Lord, give rest when you give your strength in trade for my weakness. Your strength plus faith equals quiet confidence and rest. Thank you for a true rest that refreshes and restores.*

> No soul can be really at rest until it has given up all dependence on everything else and has been forced to depend on the Lord alone. As long as our expectation is from other things, nothing but disappointment awaits us.
>
> HANNAH WHITALL SMITH (1832–1911)

You can find today's Scripture passage on page 892 of *The Life Recovery Bible*.

FEBRUARY 15

God Can Do What We Cannot

Is anything too hard for the LORD?

GENESIS 18:14

FOR US WHO GO THROUGH IT, deliverance from addiction is difficult. *Very* difficult. But is it hard to God? No, of course not. Nothing is too hard for God. In his plan for fallen humanity, God made the perfect way for us to be healed from our addictions. That way is to deliver the battle to the Lord, by faith accept his strength, and walk out his promises of freedom, even through the pain of withdrawal.

At times, we may wonder where God is as we agonize over what is likely to be a lengthy recovery. But God *is* there with us as we endure temptation, desperation, and even hopelessness on the human level. No matter what our present situation in recovery is, we must always, always, always know that nothing is too hard for the Lord—something millions who have walked this path before us can affirm by their post-addiction lives.

† *Lord, what is so hard for me is so easy for you. What I cannot do, you can do. When I can only fail, you can only succeed. When I say I'm weak, you declare me as strong. Father, so many men and women have walked away from addiction by relying on your strength because they could not free themselves. I affirm that I am included in that great cloud of witnesses who, by faith, have walked away from addiction . . . though hard for me . . . easy for you.*

See then, to whom we must look. Not to creatures, not to circumstances, not to ourselves; but to the Lord, for whom nothing is too hard. We cannot—*he* can.

JAMES SMITH (1802–1862)

You can find today's Scripture passage on page 26 of *The Life Recovery Bible.*

PTSD (Post Traumatic Stress Disorder)

O Lord my God, I cried to you for help,
and you restored my health.

PSALM 30:2

IF ADDICTION WEREN'T ENOUGH on our plate, some of us have the additional weight of PTSD, which, in fact, may either contribute to our addiction or be a result of it. No matter the cause of it, even PTSD isn't beyond God's ability to heal. Just as we can recover from addiction, so, too, can we recover from any traumatic event.

If we think we're free of PTSD, we might want to look closer because if we find a cause for our trauma, we can more easily recover from that as well as our addiction. Counseling is one good option. So is having someone with whom we can share our traumatic memories. The main thing is to never feel alone in our PTSD but to realize others suffer from this internal crisis and have made it through to the healing side, just as each of us will if we press on in Christ.

† *Dear Lord, you know my past. You know the events that have formed me for good and for bad. You know the tapes that loop in my mind, repeating the sorrow of trauma. Please heal the PTSD memories that haunt me. Bring your presence into each of those situations as I recall them. Remind me that you were there when the trauma occurred. Your desire, then and now, is that the pain pass me by. Help me here, Lord. It will surely enhance my recovery from addiction.*

> Few perversions of life, could be sadder than this *dwelling ever in the glooms and the shadows of past griefs*. It is the will of God that we should turn our eyes away from our sorrows, that we should let the dead past bury its dead—while we go on with reverent earnestness to the new *duties* and the new *joys* that await us.
>
> J. R. MILLER (1840–1912)

You can find today's Scripture passage on page 698 of *The Life Recovery Bible*.

Don't Compare

I'm not trying to win the approval of people, but of God.
If pleasing people were my goal, I would not be Christ's servant.

GALATIANS 1:10

IT'S ALWAYS A MISTAKE TO COMPARE our healing journey with others. We might look at colleagues who failed to overcome their addiction and become discouraged at their relapse. Or we might see someone who seemingly overcame with ease—perhaps was even miraculously delivered in an instant—and also become discouraged.

We must always remember that our journey is *our* journey, by God's design. While comparisons will often lead to a sense of discouragement, God's goal is always to encourage us. We must keep our eyes straight ahead at the unique path chosen for *us* by God.

✝ *Father, just as your love for me is uniquely mine, so, too, is your plan for my full recovery. When I'm tempted to look at others with envy or when I desire someone else's path to victory over addiction, I will refuse the comparison and take joy that you know best and that the healing path you have for me is just for me. Thank you for that designated path.*

You are good and all-powerful, caring for each one of us as though the only one in your care.

SAINT AUGUSTINE OF HIPPO (354–430)

You can find today's Scripture passage on page 1498 of *The Life Recovery Bible*.

The Worth of the Addict

This is how God loved the world: He gave his one and only Son, so that everyone who believes in him will not perish but have eternal life.

JOHN 3:16

A LIFE OF ADDICTION IS A LIFE OF negative self-worth. As we're beaten down by our addiction, our self-worth plummets. That's all part of the enemy's plan to destroy us, sometimes even to the extent of taking our own life. However, God has a plan too. He reveals his plan in his estimation of our true worth. In God's eyes, we're worth the life of his beloved Son, and in his plan for us, he reveals our true value. We all have a part—an important part—in the unfolding of the future.

Just think of it! Our value is measured by Christ's sacrifice on the cross for you and me. When our self-worth has plummeted, a full grasp of our real worth in God's eyes causes our self-esteem to skyrocket. God demonstrated his love for us first in our creation—our first, physical birth. Then he once again demonstrates his love through the Cross of Christ as we undergo a second birth—a spiritual rebirth.

The healthiest thing we can ponder is our worth in God's eyes as demonstrated by his sacrificial love for us.

† ***Lord, help me to see myself as your special creation. Help me to estimate my worth as you estimate it. Father, increase my appreciation for your plan for my life. Open my eyes to the true value of every addicted life.***

Jesus Christ has set a high value and estimate upon the soul. He made it and He bought it; therefore He best knows the value of it. He sold Himself to buy the soul.

THOMAS WATSON (1620–1686)

You can find today's Scripture passage on page 1344 of *The Life Recovery Bible.*

FEBRUARY 19

The Armor of God

Be strong in the Lord and in his mighty power. Put on all of God's armor so that you will be able to stand firm against all strategies of the devil.

EPHESIANS 6:10-11

IN ANY BATTLE, PROTECTION IS NECESSARY. In our war against addiction, we have been given an armor to put on—and it's a complete armor, ready to prevail against any onslaught of the enemy. This armor is only effective in battle because of the God who gave it to us. It's his power that protects us through the divine armor. Never get out of bed in the morning without being fully armored up.

(For a full list of your armor, check out Ephesians 6:13-18.)

† *Father, how foolish it is for me to engage in resistance to addiction without putting on the armor you've supplied for the battle. Remind me of each protective piece that will guard me against the enemy's onslaught. As I put on the armor, may I always remember it's not the armor that saves me; it's the God of the armor.*

We must not confide in the armor of God, but in the God of this armor, because all our weapons are only mighty through God.

WILLIAM GURNALL (1617–1679)

You can find today's Scripture passage on page 1517 of *The Life Recovery Bible*.

No Longer a Slave

Jesus replied, "I tell you the truth,
everyone who sins is a slave of sin."
JOHN 8:34

AFTER THE EMANCIPATION PROCLAMATION was issued in 1863 and the Civil War ended in 1865, slaves in the United States were declared free. Men and women were free to pursue whatever kind of life they could pull together. It was a daunting task. So much so that many slaves stayed with what they knew and worked as sharecroppers for their former masters. Some didn't even realize they had been freed or understand what freedom really meant.

So, too, with recovery from addiction; we often don't realize the extent of our freedom. It might be fear-inducing to think of life without our crutch. But happiness doesn't live with slavery; happiness lives—even thrives—in freedom. At some point, you will likely be tempted to go back to what enslaved you because it is familiar and once brought you momentary comfort. A better alternative is to embrace freedom and ask God to open doors for you—and as he does, walk confidently through them. You are free. Now *live* free.

† ***God, when I forget my freedom from the slavery of addiction, remind me that I no longer have that yoke to contend with. I'm truly free. Never let me forget that I've been saved out of slavery, never to return to it. Give me wisdom in living out the freedom to which you've called me.***

> Remember that if you are a child of God, you will never be happy in sin. You are spoiled for the world, the flesh, and the devil. When you were regenerated there was put into you a vital principle, which can never be content to dwell in the dead world. You will have to come back, if indeed you belong to the family.
>
> **CHARLES SPURGEON (1834–1892)**

You can find today's Scripture passage on page 1355 of *The Life Recovery Bible.*

FEBRUARY 21

Is Anyone Thirsty?

Is anyone thirsty?
Come and drink—
even if you have no money!
Come, take your choice of wine or milk—
it's all free!

ISAIAH 55:1

"COME AND DRINK . . . it's all free!" says God to every person with an addiction and to all who are on the recovery road. It's an invitation few can refuse when we grasp the richness of the offer. We who know what thirst is are invited to go to him and have our thirst quenched without cost. We contrast this free offer with the highly expensive offer of our addiction. How then can we not say yes to God—and to our own healing?

✝ ***Father, thank you for the invitation to simply "come" to you and have my thirst finally satisfied. I look back with regret at how I've spent time and money on that which didn't take away my thirst. Lord, bring the healing my soul so desperately needs. Lord, to your invitation, I say yes.***

Come, and eat; make it still more your own, and enjoy it. The world comes short of our expectations; we promise ourselves, at least, water in it, and we are disappointed; but Christ outdoes our expectations. We come to him, and we find wine and milk. The gifts offered to us are such as no price can be set upon. The things offered are already paid for; for Christ purchased them at the full price of his own blood. . . . On what easy terms is happiness offered us!

MATTHEW HENRY (1662–1714)

You can find today's Scripture passage on page 909 of *The Life Recovery Bible*.

The Nearness of God

The LORD is close to the brokenhearted;
he rescues those whose spirits are crushed.

PSALM 34:18

DOES GOD SEEM FAR AWAY? If so, that's only a sensory perception. The reality, apart from our fleeting emotions, is that God is near to us in our brokenheartedness, and he saves us from our crushed spirit.

God has always been for the broken person, never the proud, seemingly perfect Pharisee. Take your wounds to him. Take your broken heart. Be uplifted by his love for you. He has brought you this far and will not abandon you. He walks with you on every step of the recovery road.

✝ ***Father, you know my pain. You know the condition of my heart. To you I bring all my wounds for you to heal. Bind up my heart. Be near to me. Speak to me with assurance that you walk with me on the journey. I pray for a life free from addiction pain, shame, guilt, and remorse.***

> Jesus is the binder up of a broken heart. All the skill, all the efficacy, all the tenderness and acute sympathy needed for the office, meet and center in Him in their highest degree. Here then you can bring your wounded heart. Bring it simply to Jesus. One touch of His hand will heal the wound. One whisper of His voice will hush the tempest. One drop of His blood will remove the guilt. Nothing but applying to Him in faith will do for your soul now. Your case is beyond the skill of all other physicians. Your wound is too deep for all other remedies. It is a question of life and death, heaven or hell. It is an emergency, a crisis, a turning point with you. Oh, how solemn, how eventful is this moment!
>
> OCTAVIUS WINSLOW (1808–1878)

You can find today's Scripture passage on page 702 of *The Life Recovery Bible*.

FEBRUARY 23

Courage

This is my command—be strong and courageous! Do not be afraid or discouraged. For the LORD your God is with you wherever you go.

JOSHUA 1:9

THE BATTLE FOR FREEDOM FROM addiction takes courage. We can have the necessary courage if we heed God's Word and determine never to be frightened or discouraged, knowing full well that God is with us wherever we go. God actually *commands* us to be strong and courageous; it's not a suggestion or a hint. And when God gives a command, he always supplies the strength to obey. Joshua found that out as he believed God's promise about the land God was giving his people—a rich, lush land. They only had to believe and move forward. Courage brought the victory for Joshua, and it will bring the same victory to each of us in our battle for the rich, lush land of freedom from addiction.

✝ *Father, in you I find courage to endure all things. I obey your command to be strong and courageous, not frightened or discouraged, for you are with me wherever I go. Lord, as I take each step forward through an act of courage, I pray you will set my feet on the path designed especially for me.*

When God speaks, oftentimes His voice will call for an act of courage on our part.

CHARLES STANLEY (1932–)

You can find today's Scripture passage on page 267 of *The Life Recovery Bible.*

Why Me, Lord?

Trust in the LORD with all your heart;
do not depend on your own understanding.

PROVERBS 3:5

IF YOU'VE EVER ASKED, "Why did this happen to me? How did I allow this to happen?" you're not alone. We all look back and try to figure out when, where, and why our lives took such a dangerous and destructive detour. But at some point, we have to let all that go. Do the answers to those and other such questions really matter once we're on the road to recovery? How much more productive to trust in the Lord with all our heart and not depend on our own understanding. Isn't it enough that God knows the wherefores of our past? Concentrate then on the future. Look ahead, not back.

† *Father, it's a mystery to me when I think about my past and how my addiction became such a pivotal part of my life. To be honest, I know it's best to let it go. Knowing the wrong choices I made doesn't change those choices. How much better to let you redeem my past by bringing me into a positive future as I embrace a sober present. Now when I ask, "Why me?" it will be referring to why you have offered me such a wonderful deliverance.*

Being in Christ, it is safe to forget the past; it is possible to be sure of the future; it is possible to be diligent in the present.

ALEXANDER MACLAREN (1826–1910)

You can find today's Scripture passage on page 789 of *The Life Recovery Bible*.

Extended Darkness

Jesus . . . said, "I am the light of the world. If you follow me, you won't have to walk in darkness, because you will have the light that leads to life."

JOHN 8:12

WHEN ADDICTION CAME INTO OUR LIVES, the lights began to dim . . . and with each episode of acting out, the lights became dimmer, until finally there was only darkness. In darkness, we can't find our way forward. We're stuck where we are, with no light on our path.

But then Christ comes in and the path slowly or, in some remarkable cases, rapidly gets bright with light once again. The key is to follow Christ as he lights the path ahead of us. The longer we walk with him, the brighter the road.

✝ *God, you are my light in this dark world. You illuminate my path, allowing me to see obstacles in the road. With your light, I move confidently forward, the darkness receding behind me. I will follow you, Lord, into the brighter light ahead.*

It is only God Himself who can make it lightsome when the soul is in a dark, disconsolate condition. When the *sun* sets, none can make it rise but God. Just so, when it is *sunset in the soul* and the *dew of tears* drops—none can make *daylight in that soul* but God Himself.

THOMAS WATSON (1620–1686)

You can find today's Scripture passages on page 1354 of *The Life Recovery Bible.*

One Touch

They had come to hear him and to be healed of their diseases; and those troubled by evil spirits were healed. Everyone tried to touch him, because healing power went out from him, and he healed everyone.

LUKE 6:18-19

HOW MUCH OF CHRIST DO WE NEED to be healed? For those who crowded around Jesus, it took one touch. The woman who touched only the hem of his garment was immediately healed. Why, then, do we think that we must beg and continue to shed tears for our healing when all we must do is reach out and touch him? A lifetime of struggling can be put to rest with a single touch of Christ.

† ***Father, sometimes I think too much about the hardness of recovery, forgetting that one touch from you can bring about an enormous leap forward in recovery. Lord, you see my needs. I trust you and your timetable for recovery, but I also ask for an occasional leap forward as I, too, lean forward to touch the hem of your garment. Speed, then, Lord, your healing power.***

One touch of Christ is worth a lifetime of struggling.

A. B. SIMPSON (1843–1919)

You can find today's Scripture passage on page 1298 of *The Life Recovery Bible*.

FEBRUARY 27

Endurance

Patient endurance is what you need now, so that you will continue to do God's will. Then you will receive all that he has promised.

HEBREWS 10:36

RECOVERY REQUIRES SURRENDERING ALL. It requires total commitment (no matter what!), and it requires endurance. Once on the road to health, we can't turn back. Yes, the road can be bumpy and the desert dry. But this road is the will of God for us, and the farther we go on this road, the more we notice the scenery changes. Green sprouts up where there was only brown. The dry air gives way to welcome rain. At the end of the road, we find God's promise for us—a life restored—and we look back and see that endurance paid off in a big way. It was worth every bumpy mile.

✝ *Father, when the going gets rough, please remind me of the vital importance of endurance. Remind me that the reward for endurance is the fulfillment of the promise. May there be no turning back on my part—nor even the temptation to give up. Keep me looking ahead to the promise, Lord. It will be worth the effort.*

I can plod. I can persevere in any definite pursuit. To this I owe everything.

WILLIAM CAREY (1761–1834)

You can find today's Scripture passage on page 1590 of *The Life Recovery Bible*.

The Next Thing

Your word is a lamp to guide my feet
and a light for my path.
PSALM 119:105

HEADLIGHTS DON'T LIGHT THE HIGHWAY in its entirety. They light only the next few car-lengths. But as we move forward, with just the right amount of light we need to see a little bit ahead, we can make the whole trip home safely. Where each of us is now in our recovery is just that: where we are *now.* As we pray our way home, we'll find there's always a next thing to do. God's Word is our headlight keeping our path always well-lit. If we determine always to do the next thing we know to do, we'll make it all the way home.

† *Father, I need you always to reveal to me the next thing I need to do in my recovery, even if the next thing is simply to rest and heal. But when there's something I need to do—whether it's restitution, an apology, or moving to a location away from a tempting environment—please make that clear to me. I vow always to do the next thing in faith.*

Trust God and do the next thing.
OSWALD CHAMBERS (1874–1917)

You can find today's Scripture passage on page 767 of *The Life Recovery Bible.*

Be Content with Christ

Keep your life free from love of money, and be content with what you have, for he has said, "I will never leave you nor forsake you."

HEBREWS 13:5, NIV

ONCE ACTED UPON, addiction again takes its toll and then leaves us high and dry and with regret. But in Christ, we have a Lover of our soul who will never leave or forsake us. *Never.* For every time we feel alone, triggered, anxious, doubtful, or tempted, Christ is with us. He is not repelled and does not run away from us under any circumstance. Rely on him today in every encounter and every circumstance. Be content with Christ. He is enough.

✝ *Lord, my addiction was a craving for more. More of what, I can't really say. I was just always looking for something that I didn't think I had. Now, Father, I have Christ, and he is enough. Thank you for the unbreakable promise that you will never leave or forsake me. Yes, you are enough.*

God will meet you where you are in order to take you where He wants you to go.

TONY EVANS (1949–)

You can find today's Scripture passage on page 1594 of *The Life Recovery Bible*.

A "No Excuses" Life

Jesus replied with this story: "A man prepared a great feast
and sent out many invitations. When the banquet was ready,
he sent his servant to tell the guests, 'Come, the banquet is ready.'
But they all began making excuses. One said,
'I have just bought a field and must inspect it. Please excuse me.'"

LUKE 14:16-18

EARLY ON IN OUR ADDICTION, we may have made excuses for our behavior. Now that we know Christ, we no longer excuse our choices. We own them. When we make wrong choices, we acknowledge them, receive forgiveness, and move on without condemnation. Make it your practice to own your choices. Live a "no excuses" life.

† *Lord, it would be easy for me to dream up excuses for my choices. But whom would I be fooling? You know all the truth there is to know about me. Sometimes I wonder if my excuses aren't just an attempt to fool myself. As part of my recovery, I choose to live with no excuses for my choices. I am able to make wise decisions—or to default to making foolish decisions. You have bailed me out of many of the latter, but I pray now for the wisdom to make more of the former choices—wise and fruitful decisions.*

I attribute my success to this: I never gave or took any excuse.

FLORENCE NIGHTINGALE (1820–1910)

You can find today's Scripture passage on page 1317 of *The Life Recovery Bible*.

MARCH 3

Transformed into His Image

All of us who have had that veil removed can see and reflect the glory of the Lord. And the Lord—who is the Spirit—makes us more and more like him as we are changed into his glorious image.

2 CORINTHIANS 3:18

AS THE BRICKS COME DOWN, one by one, we continue the transformation process into the image of Christ. At our worst, when we were knee-deep in our addiction, we could not imagine a future where we would be transformed into the same image as Christ from one degree of glory to another. When we begin to see and experience transformation, we revel at the result and yearn for more. We lean into our transformation, expecting to be a more mature Christian a year from now. A prayer for transformation is one God is pleased to answer.

† *Father, the image of me in my addiction is a sad one. Thank you for not leaving me that way. Thank you for taking who I am, as I am, and over time molding me to more and more resemble your Son. I know it's a process that takes time, but then we do have eternity. Whatever it takes, Lord, to make me more like Jesus, I'm up for it.*

There are no ordinary people. You have never talked to a mere mortal.

C. S. LEWIS (1898–1963)

You can find today's Scripture passage on page 1484 of *The Life Recovery Bible.*

We Are His Masterpiece

We are God's masterpiece. He has created us anew in Christ Jesus, so we can do the good things he planned for us long ago.

EPHESIANS 2:10

IT SHOULD ASTONISH US AFRESH EVERY TIME we consider that God has created us to do good things that he planned for us long ago—before our recovery, before our addiction, before our birth. Our addiction created a wall that kept us from those good works, but as we remove the bricks during our recovery, we can get closer to doing the good things he planned for us. Let us hasten God's true work in us by living righteously, soberly, and boldly.

† ***Father, it amazes me that the works you have for me to do were planned before I was even conceived. It further amazes me that you would use me after the life I've been through so far. And yet you do choose to use me. Lord, move me ahead in the work you have for me. May it be a work with eternal effects.***

God has foreordained the works to which He has called you. He has been ahead of you preparing the place to which you are coming and manipulating all the resources of the universe in order that the work you do may be a part of His whole great and gracious work.

G. CAMPBELL MORGAN (1863–1945)

You can find today's Scripture passage on page 1511 of *The Life Recovery Bible.*

MARCH 5

When I Am Weak . . .

I take pleasure in my weaknesses, and in the insults,
hardships, persecutions, and troubles that I suffer for Christ.
For when I am weak, then I am strong.

2 CORINTHIANS 12:10

WHERE IS GOD'S STRENGTH FOUND? Oddly, it's found in our weakness. It seems that God sends our weakness to us as a blessing in disguise. Inside our weakness dwells the strength of God. And while our weakness can seem to be our downfall, from God's point of view, it's an open door for his strength to be unleashed. As Paul said in his letter to the Corinthians, let us take pleasure in our many weaknesses. They will give way for the power of God to be unleashed on our behalf.

✝ *Dear God, the truth is that, because I'm so aware of my weakness, I overlook the fact that, in my weakness, there dwells your strength—a strength I could never summon on my own. Daily I pray that you'll manifest this divine strength in my weakness. Remind me that to be weak in myself is to be fiercely strong in you.*

The acknowledgment of our weakness is the first step in repairing our loss.

THOMAS À KEMPIS (1380–1471)

You can find today's Scripture passage on page 1493 of *The Life Recovery Bible*.

A Divine Reckoning

The death that He died, He died to sin once for all; but the life that He lives, He lives to God. Likewise you also, reckon yourselves to be dead indeed to sin, but alive to God in Christ Jesus our Lord.

ROMANS 6:10-11, NKJV

DESPITE OUR FEELINGS TO THE CONTRARY, God reckons us as dead to sin (and addiction). We are, therefore, commanded to reckon as God reckons. What he says about our state is truer than what we assume to be true based on our faulty feelings. There is much "reckoning" that we can do as we discover more and more about how God reckons us. But for our recovery journey, reckoning ourselves as dead to sin and alive to God in Christ Jesus our Lord is the best place to start. For in so reckoning, we will find that reckoning will eventually silence the cries of our addiction.

✝ *Father, you are calling me to reckon myself dead to sin and all addiction. Though this wars against my fleshly senses, I know it is true. I am positionally dead to sin and alive to you through Christ. I pray to see this so clearly and certainly that what is true of me positionally quickly becomes true of me conditionally.*

We must reckon ourselves dead to sin and alive to God. This is true positionally, but it can be made true in our spiritual life only as we yield to the Holy Spirit's control.

THEODORE EPP (1907–1985)

You can find today's Scripture passage on page 1438 of *The Life Recovery Bible.*

MARCH 7

The Joy of the Christian

I will praise you with music on the harp,
because you are faithful to your promises, O my God.
I will sing praises to you with a lyre,
O Holy One of Israel.
I will shout for joy and sing your praises,
for you have ransomed me.

PSALM 71:22-23

THE SELF-ATTENDED LIFE LEADS TO TROUBLE, but the life surrendered to God leads to joy. We know that he can care for us far better than we can care for ourselves. It's not easy for us to grasp the sheer magnificence of being a person owned, cherished, and cared for by God, but that is our new reality.

We should shout for joy and sing the praises of the God who has ransomed us from our addictions.

✝ *Lord, I shout for joy as I thank you for ransoming me from my addiction and setting me free from the tentacles that had me bound. Joy is my song and ever increasingly so as I continue in recovery. This joy lights my way on the road ahead while fading the faulty footsteps of my past.*

> [Praise] cheers the day and brightens the night; it lightens toil and softens sorrow; and over earthly gladness it sheds a sanctifying radiance which makes it less liable to blind us with its glare.
>
> CHARLES SPURGEON (1834–1892)

You can find today's Scripture passage on page 728 of *The Life Recovery Bible*.

Surrender All

If any of you wants to be my follower, you must give up your own way, take up your cross daily, and follow me. If you try to hang on to your life, you will lose it. But if you give up your life for my sake, you will save it.

LUKE 9:23-24

GOD TAKES HIS GREATEST PLEASURE IN receiving what we surrender to him. Our part is to surrender, and his part is to receive. Yet we so often doubt that he will receive our burdens and worries, so our surrender is weakened by lack of faith. But if we can see with what great desire God takes our burdens as his, we will hold nothing back. Just so, friend, hold nothing back. Surrender all!

† *Heavenly Father, it takes a lot to bring a person to full surrender. I long ago reached that point of giving up. You know my desire to be rid of all the problems and addictions related to "self." Father, my surrender is complete. I hold nothing back. I bask in the pleasure you receive from me forsaking self and all the issues that spring from the evil root of my own desires.*

Whoever will labor to get rid of self, to deny himself according to the instructions of Christ, strikes at once at the root of every evil, and finds the germ of every good.

FRANÇOIS FÉNELON (1651–1715)

You can find today's Scripture passage on page 1306 of *The Life Recovery Bible*.

A Walking Faith

Someone may argue, "Some people have faith; others have good deeds." But I say, "How can you show me your faith if you don't have good deeds? I will show you my faith by my good deeds." You say you have faith, for you believe that there is one God. Good for you! Even the demons believe this, and they tremble in terror. How foolish! Can't you see that faith without good deeds is useless? Don't you remember that our ancestor Abraham was shown to be right with God by his actions when he offered his son Isaac on the altar? You see, his faith and his actions worked together. His actions made his faith complete.

JAMES 2:18-22

THOUGH THE LIFE OF RECOVERY IS ALWAYS by faith, that faith must be *walking* faith. It's not enough to *believe* in our recovery; we must show our faith by walking out that which we have received by faith. The walking out is not a "work" in the sense of doing something expecting payment. This walking out is a fruit of that victorious faith within us. Faith is completed by our walking out that which we believe. As we walk in faith, we will see victory upholding us every step of the way.

† ***Father, my faith is genuine. I evidence that by walking out the victory you've given me. I know that in myself, no such victory is to be found. But in Christ, I have all the victory for any battle I face. Be with me, Lord, in my daily walking out of my faith.***

> Faith and works should travel side by side, step answering to step, like the legs of men walking. First faith, and then works; and then faith again, and then works again—until you can scarcely distinguish which is one and which is the other.
>
> **WILLIAM BOOTH (1829–1912)**

You can find today's Scripture passage on page 1602 of *The Life Recovery Bible.*

Stabilizing

The godly may trip seven times, but they will get up again.
But one disaster is enough to overthrow the wicked.

PROVERBS 24:16

THOUGH RELAPSE NEED NOT OCCUR, if it does, our strategy must always be to stabilize *quickly*. This means a quick and meaningful repentance, a full acceptance of God's forgiveness, and—just as important—a refusal to accept continued condemnation for an act that has now been confessed and forgiven. The sting of guilt must be dealt with immediately. This is stabilizing—getting back on our feet and continuing on with our recovery. Relapse may momentarily *pause* our recovery, but we must not let it *end* our recovery.

✝ *Lord, in response to relapse, I've heard the refrain, "I've messed up; my father is going to kill me," versus the Christian response, "I've messed up; I'd better call my father." Lord, when I mess up—if I relapse—help me quickly stabilize by calling on you. May I quickly silence the enemy of his taunts and condemnations when I fall. Thank you that, though I fall seven times, I will always rise again, dust myself off, and get on with my recovery.*

> [Christ] foresees all the ambushes of Satan, searches into his intention, understands his strategies, and is as ready to speak to the Father for us, as He was to turn back and look Peter into a recovery at the crowing of the cock.
>
> STEPHEN CHARNOCK (1628–1680)

You can find today's Scripture passage on page 813 of *The Life Recovery Bible*.

Fulfilling Your Calling

Work hard to prove that you really are among those God has called and chosen. Do these things, and you will never fall away.

2 PETER 1:10

ONE OF THE WORST EFFECTS OF OUR ADDICTION is that it stalls the life God has for us. The longer we're in addiction, the longer our lives and usefulness to God are stalled. Tragically, if we never leave our addiction behind, we will die without having lived the productive life God meant for us.

The good news is that a delayed response to our calling is better than no response. As we embrace healing, we can more acutely hear our calling from God. Little by little, as our sadness and depression from addiction ebbs, our pleasure and joy from God increases. Finding our calling, then, is one of the most rewarding motivations to break free from our prison and enter into an abundant life.

✝ ***Lord, the realization that I'm called to something far better in this life than I've yet known amazes me. Though my past has stalled my calling, I believe you still have a good life for me to live and usefulness to others who are also stalling or ignoring their calling to an abundant life. Remind me, Father, as often as necessary, of what I would miss if I ever slipped back into my addiction. Thank you, God, for freeing me into the abundant life. Thank you for the ways you desire to use me.***

Next to faith this is the highest art: to be content with the calling in which God has placed you.

MARTIN LUTHER (1483–1546)

You can find today's Scripture passage on page 1623 of *The Life Recovery Bible.*

"I Promise . . ."

The LORD's promises are pure,
like silver refined in a furnace,
purified seven times over.

PSALM 12:6

MOST OF US—POSSIBLY ALL OF US—made a multitude of promises to quit our addiction. We promised our family, our friends, ourselves, and even God. And then within a short time, each promise was broken. This didn't happen just once. Nor just twice, but many times without fail.

We meant well, but meaning well doesn't give us the power to pull off the promises we make.

However, there is One who makes promises and keeps them without fail. Never once will God go back on a promise. Our response to the promises of God is to believe them and live them out. The promised power is there, but we must believe and step out, not accepting contrary feelings or doubts. A promise from God, empowered by faith, brings great results.

So much of recovery—in fact, so much of the Christian life itself—is simply discovering the promises of God in the Bible for any situation, believing them, and making them the cornerstone of our lives.

Be done with your fallible promises. Trust, instead, in the promises of God and walk them out daily. Hang upon his promises.

† *Father, as I read your Word, alert me by your Holy Spirit to the promises on each page. Help me discover the power that faith in each of your many promises brings. Forgive me for the many promises I made—and quickly broke. Lord, the only promises I can count on are* your *promises.*

To live upon Christ, and to hang upon a promise—is the way of ways to exalt Christ, and to glorify Christ.

THOMAS BROOKS (1608–1680)

You can find today's Scripture passage on page 687 of The Life Recovery Bible.

MARCH 13

Tell No Man

Jesus saith unto him, See thou tell no man; but go thy way, shew thyself to the priest, and offer the gift that Moses commanded, for a testimony unto them.

MATTHEW 8:4, KJV

OFTEN WHEN A PERSON HAS COME OUT of addiction, our tendency is to have them tell as many people as will listen. There may come a time for that, but we must first realize the very intimate and personal nature of the work God is doing in our recovery. What's happening to us is in some sense a private affair, and our testimony of healing can be premature. When we're quick to speak about our healing, we're also vulnerable to losing it temporarily.

"Tell no man" is simply a way of holding private for a while the special work God is doing in us. The work of healing must be private before it is public. There will be time later to share our victory widely. Till then, treasure the inner work God is doing.

† *Lord, thank you for the private, quiet, healing work you're doing in me. I pray that I will choose my words with wisdom when I share what's happening. Keep my tongue from speaking out rashly about a healing that's fresh. Keep me from speaking idle words.*

Idle words leak power.

WATCHMAN NEE (1903–1972)

You can find today's Scripture passage on page 1208 of *The Life Recovery Bible.*

Eternal Life Begins Now

Anyone who believes in God's Son has eternal life. Anyone who doesn't obey the Son will never experience eternal life but remains under God's angry judgment.

JOHN 3:36

SALVATION IS AN OFFER—A PROMISE OFFERED. When is a promise kept? It's kept when it's received by faith. So, though we're tempted to think eternal life is life that begins when we die, we must change our focus to see that when we have Christ in the here and now, our eternal life has already begun, only to be continued after we die. Taking possession, by faith, in eternal life now reminds us that we have the power within us that raised Christ from the dead. This is the same power needed to complete our recovery.

✝ ***Father, thank you for the unspeakable gift of eternal life. I praise you that I need not die physically to obtain the benefits of eternal life. Instead, I count on that power—the power that raised Christ from the dead—to so dwell in me that I experience eternal life daily. Lord, thank you that your judgment is no longer upon me—and never can be. Eternal life makes it so.***

Eternal life is not a peculiar feeling inside! It is not your ultimate destination, to which you will go when you are dead. If you are born again, eternal life is that quality of life that you possess right now.

MAJOR IAN THOMAS (1914–2007)

You can find today's Scripture passage on page 1345 of *The Life Recovery Bible*.

The Good News of the Gospel

I am not ashamed of this Good News about Christ.
It is the power of God at work, saving everyone who believes.
ROMANS 1:16

THE GOSPEL LITERALLY MEANS "GOOD NEWS." And for the recovering Christian, the gospel is very Good News indeed. For in the gospel, as God intends it to be understood and lived out, is the power of God for salvation—to be saved in eternity and to have that same power to live overcoming lives while here on earth. So strong is the gospel that the strength of our addiction pales in comparison. No matter what our addiction has been, it must bow to the Master of all.

† *Father God, what Good News is the gospel! Thank you that this Good News is meant for me. I know some see the gospel as just theology or part of a religious belief system. But no! The gospel is life itself. The living Christ who dwells in me, redeems me, makes me whole again is the power of God—and I am not ashamed!*

The Gospel that represents Jesus Christ, not as a system of truth to be received, into the mind, as I should receive a system of philosophy, or astronomy, but it represents Him as a real, living, mighty Savior, able to save me now.
CATHERINE BOOTH (1829–1890)

You can find today's Scripture passage on page 1431 of *The Life Recovery Bible.*

When God Is Silent

We know that God causes everything to work together for the good of those who love God and are called according to his purpose for them.

ROMANS 8:28

DISCOURAGEMENT MAY CREEP IN WHEN WE perceive God's silence as we battle on, often through temptations that are stronger than ever. "Where is God?" we ask. "Why is he silent now when I need him the most?"

Though God may seem silent at these times, the truth is that God is always working for our recovery, often behind the scenes. It's during these often-painful seasons we must trust him the most. And when we pray and God is seemingly silent, we may be tempted to doubt our recovery. But trust means believing that there is a reason for the silence. Perhaps a reason that will never be revealed in this lifetime but a reason nonetheless. The same is true for every yes or no God gives us regarding our lives. Never wrongly assume that God's silence is anything but God at work on your behalf behind heaven's curtain. Truly and fully trust his Word that *all* things work together for your good.

✝ ***Lord, your seeming silence during the tough days is hard to bear. It's on those days I need you the most. Yet I know that trusting you means trusting you in all situations—during times when you speak loudly and clearly and during the quiet times when I must take your active presence in my life by faith. Thank you for being there, even then, during the quiet days when my road is rocky.***

You say, "But He has not answered." He has, He is so near to you that His silence is the answer. His silence is big with terrific meaning that you cannot understand yet, but presently you will.

OSWALD CHAMBERS (1874–1917)

You can find today's Scripture passage on page 1442 of *The Life Recovery Bible*.

A Life of Prayer

Ask me and I will tell you remarkable secrets you
do not know about things to come.

JEREMIAH 33:3

A LIFE OF RECOVERY IS A LIFE BUILT ON THE sure foundation of prayer. Prayer is the beginning, middle, and end of recovery. The more we're committed to prayer, the more God is going to move visibly on our behalf. We must, therefore, learn to pray more effectively and allow God to increase our hunger for prayer. Prayer often requires boldness, and boldness often comes with practice. Never think that God is put off by bold prayer. On the contrary, he loves and rewards those who pray with confidence.

† *Father, forgive my often half-hearted, passive prayers. Instead, know that my heart is for you—only you—and that I desire a bolder, passionate prayer life. God, ignite my heart for deeper prayer! Enlist me as an intercessor for your people—especially those still caught up in the lies of addiction. Allow me a glimpse of your heart for the hurting. Inflame me for your people!*

> Flamed desires, impassioned, unwearied insistence delight heaven. God would have His children incorrigibly in earnest and persistently bold in their efforts. Heaven is too busy to listen to half-hearted prayers or to respond to pop-calls. Our whole being must be in our praying.
>
> E. M. BOUNDS (1835–1913)

You can find today's Scripture passage on page 976 of *The Life Recovery Bible*.

Tears

You number my wanderings;
Put my tears into Your bottle;
Are they not in Your book?

PSALM 56:8, NKJV

WHO AMONG US HAS NOT SHED TEARS over our addiction? And God has seen every one of those tears. Even as our pain may continue while in recovery mode, God treasures those tears, too, and puts them "into [his] bottle."

Our pain is important to God. He not only sees and saves our tears, but he also offers comfort in the person of his Holy Spirit. Never fear crying during your recovery. Know that God has seen your weeping, so rise up from your travailing and continue on with your recovery. Tears are a part of the healing process.

✝ *Father, my tears have been many—and you have seen every one of them. You have even saved them in your bottle. My tears of brokenness are, to you, a treasure. These tears have accompanied my many prayers—as you also know. Father, give heed to the bottle of my tears. Bring about the lasting change that turns my tears of pain into tears of joy. You are my treasure, Lord. Tears and all.*

You need not cry very loud; he is nearer to us than we think.

BROTHER LAWRENCE (1614–1691)

You can find today's Scripture passage on page 718 of *The Life Recovery Bible*.

Memories

[God said,] "I will forgive their wickedness,
and I will never again remember their sins."

HEBREWS 8:12

MEMORIES ARE WONDERFUL THINGS . . . except when they take us back to times we'd rather forget. One way to overcome the persistence of unwanted memories is to reframe them as reminders of how far God has brought us. In this way, the memory of past hard times of addiction can be turned into a trophy of God's power over addiction. Another option is to ask God to cleanse our memories of the past, so that we, like God himself, no longer remember the most harmful days of our past. If God remembers our sins no more, then we, too, should be able to forget the worst of our days.

† *God, you know about the times when my memory goes back to the days of my active addiction. Those painful memories can haunt me if I let them. Father, help me cleanse my mind. You have forgotten all my sins of addiction. Now, help me to do the same. Replace old memories of addiction with new memories of my sobriety. Fill my mind with images of peace and stability.*

Memories are the key not to the past, but to the future.

CORRIE TEN BOOM (1892–1983)

You can find today's Scripture passage on page 1586 of *The Life Recovery Bible*.

Guarding Your Heart

Guard your heart above all else,
for it determines the course of your life.

PROVERBS 4:23

WE MUST BE GUARDIANS OF OUR HEARTS. During our recovery, there will be attempts on our "hearts" to return to that which we previously craved. An unguarded heart will always fall prey to those cravings. So we must, with all vigilance, refuse to allow negative, destructive thoughts to enter our inmost being. We must fill our hearts with the words of Scripture. We must learn from other Christians ahead of us on the road to recovery. We must listen to messages from faithful men and women of God who teach biblical principles in our churches. The course of our lives is determined by the heart. Guard it above all else.

† *Lord, at times my heart is tugged back toward the world of addiction I left behind. I find myself caught between two worlds. Help me, Father, to instruct my heart to obey you, not to follow the downward path back into the dark world from which I escaped. Remind me always that I cannot live in two opposing worlds—and that I have now chosen the far better world—the one that leads to life, not death.*

A divided heart loses both worlds.

A. B. SIMPSON (1843–1919)

You can find today's Scripture passage on page 792 of *The Life Recovery Bible*.

Fellowship

Encourage each other and build each other up,
just as you are already doing.
1 THESSALONIANS 5:11

EVERY CHRISTIAN IN RECOVERY NEEDS encouragement, no matter how far along they've been on the journey. Sometimes we don't get the encouragement we need because we don't ask for it. Who in your life can you enlist as an encourager as you recover? Who in your life can you encourage in their journey?

Sometimes it takes only a brief email, a social media post, a phone call, a written note, or a face-to-face meeting to change a person's outlook from discouragement to encouragement. Train yourself to regularly offer encouragement and, if possible, build a team of several others who can encourage one another.

✝ *Father, you are my true and foremost encourager. And yet, from experience, I know it also helps to have another person to share my struggles with—someone who understands. Lord, I know many men and women share my situation. Bring across my path a fellow warrior or companion to uphold me in prayer, to encourage me to stay on the path to wholeness, and, most of all, to urge me in Christian maturity. Never let me overlook an opportunity to be all that to someone else who's tearing down their own brick wall of addiction.*

A helping word to one in trouble is often like a switch on a railroad track an inch between wreck and smooth, rolling prosperity.
HENRY WARD BEECHER (1813–1887)

You can find today's Scripture passage on page 1541 of *The Life Recovery Bible.*

The Christian Life Is Impossible but Not Hard

Don't be afraid, for I am with you.
Don't be discouraged, for I am your God.
I will strengthen you and help you.
I will hold you up with my victorious right hand.

ISAIAH 41:10

WHEN WE SEE HOW IMPOSSIBLE RECOVERY is without divine intervention, we wonder just how possible is it *with* divine intervention. God's reply is for us not to be dismayed at the seeming impossibility of freedom but to acknowledge his presence with us in the journey and depend on him to strengthen us, help us, and uphold us with his victorious right hand. Yes, healing is impossible on the one hand, but where possibility ends for us, it merely begins with God.

† *Father, all who have struggled with addiction know how formidable the battle to long-term sobriety is. In fact, many who have passed on and many who are still in the throes of their addiction attest to the impossibility of coming out of addiction alive. But God, with you, that which is impossible is more than possible. You are the magnet that pulls us toward wholeness as you uphold us with your right hand. Lord, when I seem dismayed, allow me to feel your strength; for you, O Lord, are my God and my Redeemer of the impossible situation.*

We never test the resources of God until we attempt the impossible.

F. B. MEYER (1847–1929)

You can find today's Scripture passage on page 892 of *The Life Recovery Bible*.

MARCH 23

Our Future Is Rooted in the Past

Have you forgotten that when we were joined with Christ Jesus in baptism, we joined him in his death? For we died and were buried with Christ by baptism. And just as Christ was raised from the dead by the glorious power of the Father, now we also may live new lives.

ROMANS 6:3-4

FOR A LONG TIME, many of us cried out to God to end our addiction. We surmised the answer to our prayer would be some future deliverance—whether in five minutes, five days, or five months. In short, we envisioned a deliverance happening in the future. But in reality, our prayers were answered in an event two thousand years ago.

When Christ died on the cross, we died with him—and so did all of our carnal, sinful appetites. As a result, everything we need in our recovery was provided through Christ's death by taking us into death along with him.

But that's not all. We were not just joined in his death; we were united with him in his resurrection. Thus baptism is the perfect picture of our death and resurrection with Christ.

Christ was raised by the "glorious power of the Father," and so were we. Today we are able to live new lives by the power of God—all because of that event so long ago. We no longer need to look toward a future deliverance. We have deliverance now. We live it out daily by faith.

✝ *Thank you, God, for including me in Christ's death and resurrection. Thank you, God, for a Christ-centered recovery that I can experience today and every day. May I live out my new resurrection future as I cast off the memories of my old, dead history.*

Our old history ends with the cross; our new history begins with the resurrection.

WATCHMAN NEE (1903–1972)

You can find today's Scripture passage on page 1438 of The Life Recovery Bible.

Restoring the Temple

Don't you realize that your body is the temple of the Holy Spirit, who lives in you and was given to you by God? You do not belong to yourself, for God bought you with a high price. So you must honor God with your body.

1 CORINTHIANS 6:19-20

IT'S A COMMON MISTAKE TO ASSUME GOD is interested in our souls but not so much in our bodies. And yet our body is the house of our soul and was created with care by God. As believers, our body has now become a temple of the Holy Spirit. How then should we treat our temples? With godly discipline. With care. With sacrifice. We must learn not to dishonor God by abusing our body. As we pursue healing from our addictions, let's also pursue health for our temples.

✝ *Lord, it seems every addiction takes a toll on the body. In many cases, the body is utterly destroyed, with death as the result. Father, as I live out my recovery, I pray for my body. Bring restoration to every organ negatively affected by my addiction. Cleanse not just my sins but also my earthly temple. Help me to be a good steward of this body you've given me. May I no longer bring destruction to my body, but may I work to bring restoration to my temple.*

Discipline, for the Christian, begins with the body. We have only one. It is this body that is the primary material given to us for sacrifice. We cannot give our hearts to God and keep our bodies for ourselves.

ELISABETH ELLIOT (1926–2015)

You can find today's Scripture passage on page 1463 of *The Life Recovery Bible*.

Following Jesus

[Jesus said,] "My sheep listen to my voice; I know them, and they follow me. I give them eternal life, and they will never perish. No one can snatch them away from me."

JOHN 10:27-28

AS BELIEVERS, we have all responded to the voice of the Good Shepherd calling us. But beyond the initial calling, the voice of the Shepherd continues to invite us to follow him. We can measure Christian maturity in part by our ability to hear our Master's voice and follow him. As we continue through healing, we'll find that the quieter the voice of our addiction, the more easily we hear the Shepherd's call.

✝ *Lord, thank you for the gentle call of the Shepherd that has led me to you. I do hear your voice, and I follow. I pray your voice will continue to bring me along the right path; even so that I might hear more acutely as I crane my ears and my heart toward heaven. Speak, Lord, for your servant listens. Lead, Jesus, for I will follow.*

A true shepherd leads the way. He does not merely point the way.

LEONARD RAVENHILL (1907–1994)

You can find today's Scripture passage on page 1358 of *The Life Recovery Bible.*

God's Presence

I can never escape from your Spirit!
I can never get away from your presence!
If I go up to heaven, you are there;
if I go down to the grave, you are there.

PSALM 139:7-8

IT'S A SOBERING FACT THAT GOD is always thinking about each of us. His eyes never leave us. Not for a second. He saw us at our worst during our addiction days, and he loved us through those hard times. His love, like his presence, is always with us, always wooing us, always bringing healing to us. Learning to live with an awareness of his constant presence speeds our healing immensely.

Remember that his presence is with us always. *Always!*

† *Lord, many were the nights I lived for my addiction—and you were there, despite my unawareness. I'm thankful that you never leave me, nor do your thoughts ever turn away from me. No matter which way I pivot, you are there—and there for me. Such a small taste of heaven, to know your presence at all times and in all situations.*

O slow of heart to believe and trust in the constant presence
and overruling agency of our almighty Savior!

ADONIRAM JUDSON (1788–1850)

You can find today's Scripture passage on page 775 of *The Life Recovery Bible.*

Spirit, Soul, and Body

May the God of peace make you holy in every way, and may your whole spirit and soul and body be kept blameless until our Lord Jesus Christ comes again. God will make this happen, for he who calls you is faithful.

1 THESSALONIANS 5:23-24

ADDICTIONS ARE DEADLY TO THE whole person: spirit, soul, and body. Our body weakens through addiction. Our soul becomes sick and unreliable. And our spirit deadens under the blade of addiction. The apostle Paul prayed confidently that God would make the Christians in Thessalonica every bit whole in all three of these vital areas. We, too, can pray for that wholeness with the same confidence, for "he who calls you is faithful."

† *God, I ask you to make me whole. Heal my broken spirit, renew my battered soul, mend my worn body. I pray for the blessings I don't deserve but that you pour out on your children because of your faithfulness.*

The spirit is the seat of our God-consciousness; the soul of our self-consciousness; the body of our world-consciousness. In the spirit God dwells, in the soul self, in the body sense.

ANDREW MURRAY (1828–1917)

You can find today's Scripture passage on page 1542 of *The Life Recovery Bible*.

Truth Heals

[Jesus said,] "You will know the truth,
and the truth will set you free."

JOHN 8:32

FOR SO LONG, we've been subject to lies about our addiction. Those lies and false promises have nearly destroyed us. To counter the lies of the enemy, we must apply the healing power of truth. Truth is stronger than lies. Truth heals where lies destroy. Truth is free, but lies are costly. Truth is found in Jesus who claimed to *be* the truth. Part of what we must do to heal is to seek truth and allow it to replace the myriad of lies we've believed during our addictive years.

✝ *Father, thank you for revealing truth to me. The lies of addiction have nearly destroyed me—yet you have brought me out and are still bringing me out of the web of lies that had me bound. Lord, more truth! Keep bringing me into the many Scriptural truths and promises that, when applied in my life, hasten my healing. I pray you will supernaturally bring bearers of truth that are confirmed by your Word into my life.*

An honest heart loves the Truth.

A. W. PINK (1886–1952)

You can find today's Scripture passage on page 1354 of *The Life Recovery Bible*.

The Secret of Victory

In Him dwells all the fullness of the Godhead bodily; and you are complete in Him, who is the head of all principality and power.

COLOSSIANS 2:9-10, NKJV

SELDOM DO WE FEEL COMPLETE. Instead, we often feel empty, half-human, and very much *in*complete. But if there is a secret to the over-coming life for a Christian who has an addiction, it is this: *Never see yourself as outside of Christ.* As a believer, you are *in* Christ. And in him, you are complete. Outside of him, you are still your old self, weakened and enslaved by addiction. By always seeing yourself in Christ, you break free from your old self with its many defeats.

✝ *Lord, yes, there is a secret to overcoming addiction and the various bad fruit of addiction (guilt, broken relationships, estrangement from you). That secret is to always see myself in Christ. In him, I am complete. I lack nothing. Thank you, Lord, for placing me "in Christ" as one of your children. When I'm tempted or discouraged, may I always recall this divine secret: I am complete in Christ and must never see myself outside of him.*

The secret to victory is never to look at ourselves apart from Christ.

WATCHMAN NEE (1903–1972)

You can find today's Scripture passage on page 1533 of *The Life Recovery Bible.*

I Will Tell What the Lord Has Done

I will not die; instead, I will live
to tell what the LORD has done.

PSALM 118:17

SO MANY OF OUR ADDICTED FRIENDS HAVE DIED . . . and prematurely so. We know what it's like to be on the road to the cemetery. Yet God has generously opened a detour from that dark grave and turned us onto the road of restoration. We who once were near death are becoming, day by day, more and more alive. And, yes, we *will* recount the deeds of the Lord who has saved us.

✝ ***Father, when I look back, I can recount the ways you've watched over me, even when I was at my worst. I will tell of your faithfulness in providing what I see now as narrow escapes. I will share about your grace toward me when I least deserved it. I'll boast about your mercy in spite of my many failures. You have saved me from the grave and set my feet on solid ground. Your detours have taken me off the road to destruction and placed me on the road to recovery.***

Let us seek to live to declare the works of God, and
to encourage others to serve him and trust in him.

MATTHEW HENRY (1662–1714)

You can find today's Scripture passage on page 763 of *The Life Recovery Bible*.

MARCH 31

The Forgetfulness of God

[The LORD said,] "I—yes, I alone—will blot out your sins for my own sake and will never think of them again."

ISAIAH 43:25

WHY DO WE CHOOSE TO REMEMBER WHAT God has chosen to forget? Too often our past sins are brought before us by our accusing conscience in concert with the enemy. But what does God say about our past? He asks, "*What* past?" It's one of the great secrets of Christianity that our God has forever blotted out our transgressions and, by an act of his will, chooses to remember our sins no more.

Tell me, why then are *we* remembering them? It's time to set the past well behind us and, by an act of our will, join God in forgetting our many sins. They now exist nowhere except in Satan's arsenal.

† *God, I'm thankful that you have utterly destroyed the memory of my sins, including my addiction. They exist nowhere in your world, nor in mine. They exist only as a weapon to discourage me and bring me down. Help me always to remember that my account with you is current. My sins are forever gone, along with guilt-stained memories of my addiction.*

Sins are so remitted, as if they had never been committed.

THOMAS ADAMS (1583–1652)

You can find today's Scripture passage on page 896 of *The Life Recovery Bible*.

God Is Mysterious at Times but Faithful at All Times

Great indeed, we confess, is the mystery of godliness.

1 TIMOTHY 3:16, ESV

GOD REVEALS MUCH ABOUT HIMSELF IN HIS WORD. But there remains a mystery that, on this side of eternity, we can't understand. For some of us, part of the mystery is why it is so difficult to put an end to our addiction. At times, it may seem our prayers are unanswered, our temptations too strong, our triggers too many . . . and yet we know God has called us out of our addiction to himself.

Faith requires us to move ahead with God's promises even when we don't understand the mystery of God's plan. Truth be told, the things we don't understand about God and his workings will one day be known by us. In the meantime, we can trust that the mysteries about God are part of a story with a glorious ending. Knowing what we do about God that isn't a mystery helps us let God be God, mystery and all.

✝ *Lord, sometimes you're a mystery to me. I don't understand your ways as well as I'd like. When I listen for your voice, I often hear only . . . silence. Father, in spite of this seeming absence on your part, I know that you are always present, always active, always listening, and always speaking. Give me ears to hear your voice when it's a whisper and the faith to trust you when I perceive only silence.*

When Christ delays to help His saints now, you think this is a great mystery, you cannot explain it; but Jesus sees the end from the beginning. Be still, and know that Christ is God.

ROBERT MURRAY M'CHEYNE (1813–1843)

You can find today's Scripture passage on page 1554 of *The Life Recovery Bible*.

Not Guilty!

Yes, what joy for those
whose record the LORD has cleared of guilt,
whose lives are lived in complete honesty!

PSALM 32:2

THINK OF IT—the blessedness we have in God clearing us of any guilt. With us fully and firmly in Christ, we can live in complete honesty. No masks! In seeking recovery, we have made ourselves transparent. We have nothing to hide, having confessed and forsaken our old way of life. Even though God sees us in Christ, the truth is we don't always see ourselves that way. And that's our problem. The Christian life is a life of narrowing the differences between how we see ourselves and how God sees us.

✝ *Father, I'm thankful that you have cleared me of all guilt. You do not store up my failures, my messes, my lapses, and my relapses. I can, therefore, be open with you, and you will find no deceit in me—only transparency as I confess all to you. Thank you for the blessedness of an empty sin account.*

> In Jesus Christ on the Cross there is refuge; there is safety; there is shelter; and all the power of sin upon our track cannot reach us when we have taken shelter under the Cross that atones for our sins.
>
> A. C. DIXON (1854–1925)

You can find today's Scripture passage on page 700 of *The Life Recovery Bible*.

The Flesh against the Spirit

The sinful nature wants to do evil, which is just the opposite of what the Spirit wants. And the Spirit gives us desires that are the opposite of what the sinful nature desires. These two forces are constantly fighting each other, so you are not free to carry out your good intentions.

GALATIANS 5:17

IT'S ODD TO THINK OF OUR TEMPTATIONS AND even our addictions as our instructors . . . but to be honest, the deeper we were into addiction and the life that went with it, the more we appreciate the freedom we have in deliverance.

We see the battle for what it is—the old nature versus the Spirit—and are thus able to relate to the gospel in a way many others cannot. We know what we're up against, and we know the weapons we must employ to stay clean.

Though we take no pride in our recovery, we are aware that having been forgiven much, we now love our Forgiver much.

✝ *God, for a long time now, I've hated my various temptations. I always will. But if there's anything to be said for being tempted, it's that my desires of the flesh catapult me into your presence. I willingly turn away from the old nature and commit to the desires of the Spirit. Lord, I've learned a lot from my temptations, but could we ease up on the lessons a bit for now?*

My temptations have been my masters in divinity.

MARTIN LUTHER (1483–1546)

You can find today's Scripture passage on page 1505 of *The Life Recovery Bible*.

APRIL 4

Establish the Work of My Hands

Let the beauty of the LORD our God be upon us,
And establish the work of our hands for us;
Yes, establish the work of our hands.

PSALM 90:17, NKJV

ADDICTION IS UGLY. At its worst, it makes us ugly too. But in Christ, we receive the beauty of the Lord as part of our deliverance. From our first moment of recovery on through the entire journey, we are being transformed. Further, God is establishing the work he has for us. Not only are we receiving the beauty of the Lord, but the work of our hands shall also thus be beautiful. Sobriety for the Christian always brings beauty to replace the ugliness.

† *God, what an awesome thing—that you share your beauty with your creation. Restore, O Lord, the beauty you see in me. Remove the telltale signs of my addiction, and where scars remain, may they now be turned into a testament of your power to bring new life into that which was dead. And, Lord, establish the work of my hands. Give me skill to bring more beauty out of the ashes of my past.*

> Humanity was made to be beautiful. God's ideal for man was spotless loveliness—man was made at first in God's image. But sin has left its trail everywhere. We see something of its debasement wherever we go. What ruins sin has wrought! . . . All Christ's work of grace is towards the restoration in human souls of the beauty of the Lord.
>
> J. R. MILLER (1840–1912)

You can find today's Scripture passage on page 744 of *The Life Recovery Bible.*

Hidden Pain

He heals the brokenhearted
and bandages their wounds.

PSALM 147:3

THE GREAT PHYSICIAN IS ALWAYS ON CALL. His ER is always open. His goal is always the same: to heal the brokenhearted, bandage our wounds, and even tend to our hidden pain. It's for certain that no one escapes the addicted life without wounds. It's just not possible. Therefore, recovery is many things, but among the most important is allowing God to bind our wounds and to heal our broken hearts. During recovery, God may even reveal the source of hidden pain we've been unaware of.

† *Father, as I recover from addiction, I pray you will take note of my pain and remember the times I've been brokenhearted, whatever the cause. Heal me, Lord. Calm my fears. Bind up my wounds. Tend to the hidden pains I'm not even aware of.*

How sweet the name of Jesus sounds in a believer's ear! It soothes his sorrows, heals his wounds, and drives away his fear.

JOHN NEWTON (1725–1807)

You can find today's Scripture passage on page 780 of *The Life Recovery Bible.*

APRIL 6

The Temple of God

Don't you realize that all of you together are the temple of God
and that the Spirit of God lives in you?

1 CORINTHIANS 3:16

ONE OF OUR GREATEST RESOURCES IN RECOVERY is the power of God living within us. God is not simply "out there"; he has chosen us to be the dwelling place of his Holy Spirit. The desecration of a temple is always a bad thing. How much more so the desecration of our bodies, wherein God's Spirit dwells? Consider in awe the fact that God abides in you. He has chosen to live within you. Marvel at this truth.

✝ *Father, I'm amazed that you have chosen people to be your temple—and more astonished that you have chosen to dwell in me. I pray you will use me as a channel to bring others to yourself. May I be faithful in my stewardship of this body you've given me. I deeply regret the damage my addiction has done to my body. May this temple be raised up once again to usefulness.*

> It ennobles a Christian immensely to know and to feel that
> he is a channel through which the life of Christ is to flow out.
>
> G. V. WIGRAM (1805–1879)

You can find today's Scripture passage on page 1459 of *The Life Recovery Bible.*

The Power of Giving

You should remember the words of the Lord Jesus:
"It is more blessed to give than to receive."
ACTS 20:35

IN OUR ADDICTION, we have been mostly takers. We would take whatever we needed to ensure our next high. It's hard for an addict to be a giver, to receive the blessing that comes with putting others and their needs first. But as we tear down the bricks in the wall, our hearts are changed.

Where we once had eyes to see what could be taken, we now begin to see with new eyes that compel us to help others by giving. It may be giving the Good News of freedom from addiction to others, or it may be simply giving time to someone who needs a good listener. It could be monetary giving. Whatever God puts in your hand to give, and whoever he puts in your path to help, act on that impulse. Every time you do, a brick falls from the wall.

✝ ***Lord, having been a taker for so long, I now need to learn to be a generous giver. Open my eyes, Father, to opportunities to give to others my time, my prayers, my friendship, my finances, and my story of freedom from addiction. Show me, Lord, how to give.***

How God loves to repay those who love to give!
GEORGE EVERARD (1828–1901)

You can find today's Scripture passage on page 1415 of *The Life Recovery Bible.*

Why Doesn't God Just Zap Me into Sobriety?

"LORD, help!" they cried in their trouble,
and he rescued them from their distress.

PSALM 107:6

WE HAVE ALL PROBABLY KNOWN ONE OR two people who were instantly set free from their addiction. Most likely, they couldn't tell us why God worked that way with them, nor why he hasn't worked that way with us. The only answer that makes sense is that God, in his sovereignty, knows best how to fashion a deliverance from addiction, and for some it is best fashioned in a moment's time. The wrong response when we witness this type of rescue in others is to covet their experience. The right response is to rejoice in their deliverance and accept God's timetable for our own recovery.

✝ *Lord, early in my recovery, I would have welcomed an instant deliverance, but as time has passed, I've come to respect your work in my life, including the speed with which you've chosen to work with me. God, please know that I trust in you and have abandoned watching the clock of recovery. You are the master timekeeper of my life.*

Set no time to the Lord the creator of time, for His time is always best.

SAMUEL RUTHERFORD (1600–1661)

You can find today's Scripture passage on page 756 of *The Life Recovery Bible*.

The Holy Spirit Teaches Us

You have received the Holy Spirit, and he lives within you, so you don't need anyone to teach you what is true. For the Spirit teaches you everything you need to know, and what he teaches is true—it is not a lie. So just as he has taught you, remain in fellowship with Christ.

1 JOHN 2:27

HOW WE LOVE TO HEAR GOOD TEACHING—and God has given us solid teachers in the body of Christ who can help us in our recovery. But one teacher stands out among all the rest: the Holy Spirit. God has sent each of us the Holy Spirit, who teaches us far more than our human teachers—and is always true to God's Word. Let the voice of the Holy Spirit instruct you in your recovery.

✝ ***Thank you, Lord, for the various men and women whose teachings have helped me. I pray you continue to send a parade of good, solid teachers my way through the remainder of my life. Father, I also pray I will become more adept at learning from the Holy Spirit speaking to me as he affirms the truth of your Word.***

If, through the teaching and testimony of the blessed Spirit, any portion of the word of truth is opened with divine light to our understanding, or laid with peculiar weight and power upon our heart, its solemn importance is at once seen and felt; it engages the whole of our attention, and we wonder how we could have been so blind to what is now so clear, or treated with neglect what is now so weighty.

J. C. PHILPOT (1802–1869)

You can find today's Scripture passage on page 1630 of *The Life Recovery Bible*.

APRIL 10

The Joy of the Lord

Don't be dejected and sad,
for the joy of the LORD is your strength!

NEHEMIAH 8:10

IT SEEMS ODD THAT WE SHOULD FIND strength in joy. But the joy of the Lord lifts the heaviest of burdens. It conquers grief and remorse. It's a great soother of pain. Joy allows no room for misplaced guilt. And the best thing about joy is that it is *ours*. God gives us joy readily. We have only to receive it by faith.

✝ ***God, I praise you for the strength-building aspect of joy. I thank you that joy isn't just a source of strength but*** **is** ***my strength. I praise you because joy is a gift from you to your people. And today, no matter what comes my way, I choose joy. I choose strength.***

> The joy of the Lord in the spirit springs also from an assurance that all the future, whatever it may be, is guaranteed by divine goodness, that being children of God, the love of God towards us is not of a mutable character, but abides and remains unchangeable. The believer feels an entire satisfaction in leaving himself in the hands of eternal and immutable love.
>
> CHARLES SPURGEON (1834–1892)

You can find today's Scripture passage on page 612 of *The Life Recovery Bible*.

Pray with Passion

I tell you, you can pray for anything, and
if you believe that you've received it, it will be yours.

MARK 11:24

PRAYER IS LIKE A LIFE PRESERVER TO A Christian in recovery. It keeps us afloat as the sea rages around us. As we pray, it helps us know we always have God's ear. He hears, he understands, and he responds with the right answer in the right time. But to be effective, prayer must be honest, and it must be offered in faith with the result that we will receive our answer in God's time.

Passion in prayer is also music to God's ears. In the Bible we often see desperation as a reason for God to move on behalf of the pray-er. We see a blind man, passionate to see. We see a demoniac begging to be set free. We read about a woman with an issue of blood for twelve years so desperate she knew if she could only touch the hem of Jesus' garment she would be healed—and she was right.

Pray often. Pray in faith. Pray with passion.

† *God, as part of my recovery, help me become a better pray-er. Teach me how to pray and how to have the kind of faith that brings about results. Remind me as I pray that honest prayers, offered with passion, are the ones you love to honor. Call me, Father, to a deeper place in prayer. Allow me to be an intercessor for the community of fellow men and women suffering from addiction.*

Those prayers God likes best, which come seething hot from the heart!

THOMAS WATSON (1620–1686)

You can find today's Scripture passage on page 1270 of *The Life Recovery Bible*.

APRIL 12

Waiting on the Lord

Wait patiently for the LORD.
Be brave and courageous.
Yes, wait patiently for the LORD.

PSALM 27:14

WAITING IS HARD FOR ANYONE, ADDICT OR NOT. We want what we want *now*. But a true test of our faith is in our ability to wait, to be strong, to take courage . . . to trust God that, in the fullness of time, our answer will come. Quick answers are seldom God's way. Sometimes the longer we must wait, the sweeter the answer will be when it comes.

† *Father, I have experienced many times of simply waiting in my life. Even in recovery, it seems that waiting—and becoming strong while doing so—is part of your prescription for wholeness. May I never become so anxious that I attempt to cut short the time of waiting you have measured for me. But may I also never lag behind when you want to lead me on to the next phase of my recovery.*

> Never was a faithful prayer lost. Some prayers have a longer voyage than others, but then they return with their richer lading at last, so that the praying soul is a gainer by waiting for an answer.
>
> WILLIAM GURNALL (1617–1679)

You can find today's Scripture passage on page 697 of *The Life Recovery Bible.*

Gratitude

Since we are receiving a Kingdom that is unshakable, let us be thankful and please God by worshiping him with holy fear and awe.

HEBREWS 12:28

GRATITUDE ON THE RECOVERY JOURNEY is crucial. Though we often feel shaken ourselves, we're receiving an unshakeable Kingdom. Our only response can be reverent and awe-filled worship for our great God. This moment, pause and express gratitude to the one who has brought us into his Kingdom. Gratitude has a profound effect on our memory. We recall with gratitude from where we have been called and look with thanksgiving to where we are called in the future.

† *Lord, I'm so grateful for my life—my recovered life. I thank you for keeping me alive, even with some narrow escapes. I worship you as my Creator, Redeemer, and Restorer. Thank you for offering me a Kingdom that cannot be shaken—a Kingdom I now call my true home. Praise you that the thoughts of my recovered future obliterate the painful memories of the past.*

Gratitude changes the pangs of memory into a tranquil joy.

DIETRICH BONHOEFFER (1906–1945)

You can find today's Scripture passage on page 1594 of *The Life Recovery Bible*.

Creativity

The LORD has filled Bezalel with the Spirit of God, giving him great wisdom, ability, and expertise in all kinds of crafts. He is a master craftsman, expert in working with gold, silver, and bronze.

EXODUS 35:31-32

ONE LOSS TO ADDICTION THAT'S OFTEN overlooked is the dulling of our creativity. God has gifted every believer with a measure of creativity that sometimes ends up as visual art, literature, music, woodworking, or many other worthy endeavors, including auto mechanics, construction, politics, or any endeavors where talent of any sort is required.

In recovery, we should expect to see the dullness lift and a fresh, though perhaps slow-appearing, return to normal in our creative endeavors.

As we recover, let's turn our focus back to the areas where God has gifted us, asking him to renew us with even greater creativity in our post-addiction life.

✝ *Father, in creating me, you put within me gifts of creativity, some of which I may not even be aware of yet. Lord, in my recovery, please reveal the ways you'd have me use my creativity. Restore my ability to truly be a creative person, made in your image. Remove any dullness that has set in due to my addiction. Allow my creative gifts to be useful to your purposes. May the fruit of my creativity be a blessing to many.*

A Christian, who realizes he has been made in the image of the Creator God and is therefore meant to be creative on a finite level, should certainly have more understanding of his responsibility to treat God's creation with sensitivity, and should develop his talents to do something to beautify his little spot on the earth's surface.

EDITH SCHAEFFER (1914–2013)

You can find today's Scripture passage on page 122 of *The Life Recovery Bible*.

Seeing Ourselves on the Other Side of Our Trial

God blesses those who patiently endure testing and temptation. Afterward they will receive the crown of life that God has promised to those who love him.

JAMES 1:12

REMAINING STEADFAST THROUGH THE TRIALS of recovery can be difficult—nigh on impossible it seems at times. But by faith, we can and must move forward through each trial, burden, and pain. We must see ourselves with the brick wall separating us from God's best life demolished forever. God has promised a crown of life to those who love him. Fix your eyes on God's reward, not on our Satan's desired end for your life.

† *Father, remaining steadfast isn't always easy. And yet, I can see myself on the other side of addiction, fully whole, fully free, fully joyful, and useful to you. I see steadfastness as a product of patience—and, Lord, you know how impatient I can be. Help me be content with the healing process and with myself. Keep my vision of my restored self in front of me always.*

Have patience with all things, but chiefly have patience with yourself. Do not lose courage in considering your own imperfections, but instantly set about remedying them; every day begin the task anew.

FRANCIS DE SALES (1567–1622)

You can find today's Scripture passage on page 1601 of *The Life Recovery Bible.*

Greater Is He

You belong to God, my dear children. You have already won a victory over those people, because the Spirit who lives in you is greater than the spirit who lives in the world.

1 JOHN 4:4

HOW DOES THE RECOVERING ADDICT OVERCOME? First by faith, of course. Faith in a God who hears and heals. We also overcome because Christ, who dwells in us through the power of the Holy Spirit, "is greater than the spirit who lives in the world," referring to our natural enemy, Satan.

When we rightly label our addiction as something from this present world and we realize that we are no longer connected to it, we can overcome all that would tie us to this world, including addiction.

We are not left worldless, of course. God has a world—a Kingdom of which we are now a part. Our citizenship in one world has been renounced as we learn to live in God's world.

✝ ***Father, I see my addiction as part of the system that is this world. Addiction has no place in your Kingdom, of which I'm now a citizen. The blessing for me is that, because you're in me and you're greater than the world, I'm enabled to overcome this present world with its addictions and evils.***

If you are a Christian, you are not a citizen of this world trying to get to heaven; you are a citizen of heaven making your way through this world.

VANCE HAVNER (1901–1986)

You can find today's Scripture passage on page 1632 of *The Life Recovery Bible*.

Untrustworthy Emotions

A fool gives full vent to his spirit, but a wise man quietly holds it back.

PROVERBS 29:11, ESV

MANY WHO SUFFER FROM ADDICTION FIND THAT mood swings and unexpected changes of emotion occur. With the promise of sobriety, we once again learn to hold back unworthy emotions and let go of our wild mood swings.

Like all aspects of recovery, this, too, is a growth process. Day by day, the changes come slowly. We are, after all, recovering that which has been lost. Recovery always takes time, whether it's after surgery, a broken relationship, job loss, or symptoms of addiction.

Go easy on yourself when the emotional pendulum swings wide. You will learn how to bring self-control into your emotional life.

✝ ***Lord, my emotions sometimes get the best of me. Anger, envy, sadness, and other negative emotions sneak up on me. I pray for the return of emotional stability. Help me let my emotions work as they should, under my control, and not vice versa. Thank you for my emotions. They serve important purposes in my life.***

We are only asking you to give to Christ that which you give to others, to transfer the old emotions, the blessed emotions, the exercise of which makes gladness in the life here below, to transfer them to Him, and to rest safe in the Lord.

ALEXANDER MACLAREN (1826–1910)

You can find today's Scripture passage on page 818 of *The Life Recovery Bible.*

Chosen to Be His Own People

We know, dear brothers and sisters, that God loves you and has chosen you to be his own people.

1 THESSALONIANS 1:4

THE DARKNESS OF OUR ADDICTION HAS BEEN replaced by God's wonderful light. In coming out of our darkness in response to God's call, we understand that we have been *chosen* by God. What we once were in the darkest days of our addiction no longer matters. What matters is that we are now part of a chosen race of people. We are God's own possession. And because of this, we proclaim his greatness. Praise God for his Kingdom of light and that he's chosen us to be part of his family!

✝ ***Lord, I cringe when I think of the darkness from which you saved me. Now, I dwell in your light, proclaiming your greatness, honored to be chosen by you. I'm content to be an instrument in your hands, knowing the care you give your chosen people. Guide me, Lord, as I live out the joys of one who is owned by God.***

Oh, happy they who have obeyed his summons and have made a complete surrender of themselves to him! He has already taken them for his own possession. . . . Once in darkness, now in marvelous light. Once not included among the people of God, now accounted as part of them. . . . Let us show forth his praise.

F. B. MEYER (1847–1929)

You can find today's Scripture passage on page 1538 of *The Life Recovery Bible*.

The Power of a New Nature

Throw off your old sinful nature and your former way of life, which is corrupted by lust and deception. Instead, let the Spirit renew your thoughts and attitudes. Put on your new nature, created to be like God—truly righteous and holy.

EPHESIANS 4:22-24

OUR OLD SELF WAS AN ADDICTED SELF. A slave to a merciless master. But everything that is from our past and from our old self no longer really matters. In recovery, we're putting off our former manner of (miserable!) life and are being renewed by God's Spirit. We have put on the new self, created after the likeness of God, truly righteous and holy. And—wonder of wonders—the new self cannot be subject to addiction.

✝ *Father, it was my old, corrupt nature that became addicted, but now I have a new nature—a new self that was created to be like you. Help me to live as the new creation that I am. I renounce the deceitful desires that belonged to my former life. Lord, I welcome my new nature.*

If God is adding to our spiritual stature, unfolding the new nature within us, it is a mistake to keep twitching at the petals with our coarse fingers. We must seek to let the Creative Hand alone.

HENRY DRUMMOND (1851–1897)

You can find today's Scripture passage on page 1514 of *The Life Recovery Bible*.

God Understands

How great is our Lord! His power is absolute!
His understanding is beyond comprehension!

PSALM 147:5

SOMETIMES IT MAY SEEM AS if God doesn't understand our plight. After all, what does God know about addiction? And yet, as he is our omniscient and omnipotent Creator, we have to assume that God knows *and understands* everything about us, even without having experienced addiction. That his understanding is beyond comprehension is what makes him God. When we aren't sure of his understanding, we must try to accept that God sees what we cannot see and, therefore, we can trust him more fully than ever.

† *Lord, you see all, know all, and understand all. You even see my post-addiction future, and each step I take forward toward that future is like another ribbon removed from the gift-wrapped package of your plan for me. Father, when I'm puzzled about a circumstance in my recovery, I will trust you and your understanding that is beyond my comprehension.*

> In perplexities,—when we cannot understand what is going on around us—cannot tell whither events are tending—cannot tell what to do, because we cannot see into or through the matter before us,—let us be calmed and steadied and made patient by the thought that what is hidden from us is not hidden from Him.
>
> FRANCES RIDLEY HAVERGAL (1836–1879)

You can find today's Scripture passage on page 780 of *The Life Recovery Bible*.

The Deceitfulness of Addiction

The human heart is the most deceitful of all things, and desperately wicked. Who really knows how bad it is?

JEREMIAH 17:9

MANY WHO ARE ADDICTED TRY TO REFORM themselves into sobriety. We, too, have likely tried to bring about a reformation on our own . . . only to be disappointed and relapse, which results in discouragement and shame. The truth is, for the Christian, it's no more possible to reform ourselves than to atone for our own sins. The latter could only be accomplished by Christ's death on the cross for our sins. The former, too, can only be accomplished by Christ's resurrection power at work in our lives. The human heart, apart from renewal in Christ, is desperately sick. We know this firsthand. Our only hope is not in our reformation but in our rebirth through Christ.

✝ *Lord, as I look back, I see how easily I was deceived in accepting my addiction. I believed and acted on certain lies that took my life in the wrong direction. Addiction, in its deception, cannot be satisfied. There is always the inward craving for more—a next joy ride, one that will end in a fatal crash. Father, I reject my addiction fully. I close my ears to its fresh promises and never-ending lies about the payoff of one more venture into addiction. Help me keep ever before me the sheer deceitfulness of any and all addictions.*

The deceitfulness of sin is seen in that it is modest in its first proposals but when it prevails it hardens men's hearts, and brings them to ruin.

JOHN OWEN (1616–1683)

You can find today's Scripture passage on page 956 of *The Life Recovery Bible*.

Destroying Strongholds

Though we walk in the flesh, we are not waging war according to the flesh. For the weapons of our warfare are not of the flesh but have divine power to destroy strongholds.

2 CORINTHIANS 10:3-5, ESV

TO HAVE AN ADDICTION IS TO HAVE A "STRONGHOLD." Recovery involves destroying the stronghold in which we're trapped. What may have started as just a thought or a whim evolved into a habit—and that's how addictions are acquired: usually slowly, inch by inch, until the addict is captive. Demolishing the stronghold requires spiritual warfare. That is, through prevailing, persistent, powerful prayer, we remove all traces of the stronghold. This spiritual warfare doesn't rely on the weapons of the flesh but on the divine power we have to destroy strongholds . . . to remove the enemy's power base.

✝ *Mighty God, I pray against this stronghold of addiction that's taken me captive. I pray for a breaking of the spiderweb that has me bound. Release me, Lord, through the power of Christ. Strengthen my resolve against the enemy's tactics to take me back under his power. Secure my freedom as I break away from every stronghold of the enemy. May I quickly see each brick removed, letting in the light of your presence. Lord, in your name, I am an overcomer, empowered by your Spirit to break the stronghold of addiction in my life.*

Spiritual strongholds begin with a thought. One thought becomes a consideration. A consideration develops into an attitude, which leads then to action. Action repeated becomes a habit, and a habit establishes a "power base for the enemy," that is, a stronghold.

ELISABETH ELLIOT (1926–2015)

You can find today's Scripture passage on page 1490 of *The Life Recovery Bible*.

God Sings over Us

For the LORD your God is living among you.
He is a mighty savior.
He will take delight in you with gladness.
With his love, he will calm all your fears.
He will rejoice over you with joyful songs.

ZEPHANIAH 3:17

WHAT A WONDERFUL REALITY TO KNOW THAT God rejoices over us with joyful songs. And why does he do this? He sings over us because he's excited about us. We are his people, his possession, and the objects of his greatest love. He loves to live among us. He delights in us with gladness, and he calms our fears.

Today, we can praise God for all we mean to him and all he means to us. Listen. Can you hear him singing a joyful song over you?

✝ *Father, when I'm in your presence, I'm on holy ground. I embrace the reality that you rejoice over me with a joyful song. And that you're not ashamed of me, nor disappointed. You are fully committed to me and will bring me through my recovery every step of the way. What a true and loving father you are!*

As the bridegroom rejoices over the bride—so shall your God rejoice over you.

JOHN MACDUFF (1818–1895)

You can find today's Scripture passage on page 1167 of *The Life Recovery Bible.*

Acting Out

Choose today whom you will serve. . . .
But as for me and my family, we will serve the LORD.

JOSHUA 24:15

WE ALL MUST CHOOSE WHOM WE WILL SERVE and from whom we will accept wages. If we claim to be God's child, we must act like a son or daughter of God. Our actions will answer the ownership question.

Acting out on our addiction is a denial of God's ownership. We're showing by our actions that either we don't believe in God's ownership of us or we don't care about his ownership.

On the contrary, when we acknowledge God's ownership—when we choose him as the one we will serve—we're empowered to be good stewards of what God has given us. The decision to never again act on our addiction must be irrevocable. That's a decision God honors.

✝ ***God, never again will I act out on my addiction. This decision is a choice that opens doors for me . . . doors of opportunity that are lost when I stray. Help me keep my eyes straight ahead on the path you have for me. Guard my eyes from being enticed to act out by closing those open doors.***

Here on earth, I am but a pilgrim—a transient lodger, for this world is not my rest.
I am seeking for and pressing towards, the magnificent city with eternal foundations—
a city designed and built by Almighty God!

THEODORE CUYLER (1822–1909)

You can find today's Scripture passage on page 296 of *The Life Recovery Bible*.

Poor and Needy

As for me, since I am poor and needy,
let the Lord keep me in his thoughts.
You are my helper and my savior.
O my God, do not delay.

PSALM 40:17

BLESSED ARE THE POOR AND NEEDY. When we experience a severe need we desperately want filled, we must realize that the need is simply serving as an arrow in our lives pointing us to God. If we seek him, he will be there—and so will the miracle we need. After all, God keeps us in his thoughts. He is our helper and savior. Consider today your present need. Can you trust God to provide the answer?

Yes, you can.

Because he will.

† *Father, by its very nature, addiction has brought me to a place of being poor and needy. But you keep me in your thoughts! You are my Helper and my Savior. Thank you for every miracle, large and small, that you bring my way to move my recovery forward.*

God is a powerful—an omnipotent helper; He has Heaven and earth at His command. It is nothing for Him to help. He can work deliverance by the weakest instruments; and often does, in order to confound the wisdom of the wise, and bring to nothing the understanding of the prudent.

JAMES SMITH (1802–1862)

You can find today's Scripture passage on page 707 of *The Life Recovery Bible*.

Overcoming Fear

I prayed to the LORD, and he answered me.
He freed me from all my fears.

PSALM 34:4

FOR MANY WHO ARE FIGHTING ADDICTION, fear has been a key component either leading to their addiction or resulting from their addiction. Thus, in recovery, overcoming fear of any nature must be a priority. Seeking the Lord and his power to deliver us from our fears is the way out. A fearful addict will have a tough time recovering. Building up our faith allows us to confront and banish our fears.

Are there specific fears you can list that keep you from moving ahead? Name them one by one and place them in God's hands. In prayer, commit them to him. Be done with your own meager efforts to overcome fear.

† *Father, if fear has been an issue with me, even an unknown fear, I pray against its influence in my life. I rise above every fear and cast it away. I turn my eyes away from my fears and direct them to you, the great Fear Banisher.*

> If the Lord be with us, we have no cause of fear. His eye is upon us, his arm over us, his ear open to our prayer—his grace sufficient, his promise unchangeable.
>
> JOHN NEWTON (1725–1807)

You can find today's Scripture passage on page 702 of *The Life Recovery Bible.*

God Knows All about You

O Lord, you have examined my heart
and know everything about me.
You know when I sit down or stand up.
You know my thoughts even when I'm far away.
You see me when I travel
and when I rest at home.
You know everything I do.

PSALM 139:1-3

FOR SOME OF US, it's sometimes unsettling to think that God knows everything about us. Those accusing thoughts, the times we were slow to forgive, the lustful thoughts. And yet because God knows all about us, we can rejoice in the uniqueness we each have. We were God-designed and made for great things, despite our wrong decisions and the crazy circumstances that derailed us for a while. God saw all of that. God has been with us all along. During our worst years, he saw what was happening, and he searched us out. Even today, we are constantly on his mind. He is acquainted with all our ways. Our past is not hidden from him (though he has forgiven and forgotten it), and our present is known by him. Best of all, our future as a recovered addict exceeds what we can imagine. Trust the one who knows us best.

✝ ***Father, my ability to know you fully is shadowed by the veil of my humanity. But from what you allow us to know of you, I'm grateful—and always desiring more. Lord, know that just as you know me fully, so, too, I count myself as fully yours. Yours in every way.***

> I am his by purchase and I am his by conquest; I am his by donation and I am his by election; I am his by covenant and I am his by marriage; I am wholly his; I am peculiarly his; I am universally his; I am eternally his.
>
> **THOMAS BROOKS (1608–1680)**

You can find today's Scripture passage on page 775 of *The Life Recovery Bible.*

We Have All We Need

This same God who takes care of me will supply all your needs from his glorious riches, which have been given to us in Christ Jesus.

PHILIPPIANS 4:19

FOR MANY, addiction came as a result of perceived need. Those needs may have varied from person to person, but the one commonality is that we tried to meet that legitimate need by illegitimate means. Illegitimate in the sense that they were not designed to meet our needs but only served as an artificial and short-term solution to our needs. In the case of every legitimate need, God wants to provide the true solution—and it's always according to his glorious riches in Christ Jesus. When we truly accept Christ as our "Need Meeter," we no longer seek the artificial solution.

✝ *Father, in times past, I had some serious needs. Some were real, and I now believe some were just perceived. In both cases, you had a solution—you would have had me fill my needs with your supply. Now I see more clearly that, in you, there are "glorious riches," which supply all my needs. Your cupboards are never bare.*

> The neediest of needy sinners find all supply in Him. He is salvation's overflowing well. He fills all vessels, so that they can hold no more. He is a treasure-house, in which gold never fails.
>
> HENRY LAW (1797–1884)

You can find today's Scripture passage on page 1526 of *The Life Recovery Bible.*

Made Right in God's Sight!

Since we have been made right in God's sight by the blood of Christ,
he will certainly save us from God's condemnation.

ROMANS 5:9

SATAN'S GOAL IN ADDICTION, prior to our destruction and death, is to entice us to act on our addiction and then to heap us with remorse and condemnation when we've submitted to his schemes. But when we are made right in God's sight because of the blood of Christ, condemnation can no longer bind us to Satan. His scheme fails due to God's wonderful way of taking away condemnation from all who trust in Christ. Condemnation is simply not compatible with being in Christ. When we realize this aspect of recovery, we will have made a great advance toward wholeness.

To be in Christ and yet allow condemnation—in any form and in any measure—into our lives is not just foolish and self-destructive; it's an affront to God.

No matter what your past has been—even yesterday's past—there is *no* condemnation for you.

✝ ***God, some of the worst aspects of addiction were the aftereffects of condemnation, shame, guilt, and remorse. But because of the blood of Christ, I no longer experience those things. Not only am I freed from addiction, but I'm also freed from the haunting condemnation that goes with it. Christ has borne all my guilt and shame in my place. Thank you, Father, for this unspeakable gift!***

> The freedom of the believer is just what it is declared to be—entire exemption from condemnation. From all which that word of significant and solemn import implies, he is, by his relation to Christ, delivered. Sin does not condemn him, the law does not condemn him, the curse does not condemn him, hell does not condemn him, God does not condemn him.
>
> OCTAVIUS WINSLOW (1808–1878)

You can find today's Scripture passage on page 1437 of *The Life Recovery Bible.*

Your Old Life

"Come now, let's settle this,"
says the LORD.
"Though your sins are like scarlet,
I will make them as white as snow."

ISAIAH 1:18

WE MUST BE CAREFUL IN THE WAY WE allow our fleshly lives to be shaped, for they will always default back to the most comfortable form of self-expression. We had no control over our childhoods, however, and if our flesh was bent in a certain destructive direction as children, we will have to overcome it as adults.

As Christians, we have God's power within us to change the contorted adult self that is the fruit of a dysfunctional childhood. Redeeming what was lost is God's specialty. Our past is truly *past.* It is dead as far as God is concerned. And yet, too often, we allow our past—even our distant past—to impact our present and our future. How foolish to allow something God reckons as dead to have any influence over us. Never let the past influence your present or your future. To do so is like carrying around a corpse on your back. What a useless burden!

† ***Father, a sure sign of healing is the ability to look confidently ahead, having put the past behind me. My former life is dead to you and dead to me. I now only look ahead to the joys of sobriety, and I wonder at how you will direct my future in my best interests, after all the time I spent working destruction on it. Praise you that you, not me or the enemy, have the last word on my future.***

> We ought not to live in the past. We ought to forget the things that are behind—and reach forward to the things that are ahead. "Forward, and not back," is the motto of Christian hope. The best days are not any days we have lived already—but days that are yet to come.
>
> J. R. MILLER (1840–1912)

You can find today's Scripture passage on page 850 of *The Life Recovery Bible.*

Miracle

You are the God of great wonders!
You demonstrate your awesome power among the nations.

PSALM 77:14

MAKE NO MISTAKE ABOUT IT: Recovery from addiction is a miracle. It might be a fast miracle or a slow miracle, but it's still a miracle, and God is still a miracle provider when a miracle is called for.

There are many needs that require a miracle. Physical healing, financial woes, relational problems, and, of course, addiction are just a few situations requiring a miracle. Often, when we're at a low point, we don't appreciate that being in need of a miracle is a good place to be. Needing a miracle means we're desperate. Nothing but God's intervention can help. That's when the God of great wonders steps in to demonstrate his awesome power.

Think now of your recovery as the needed miracle in your life. Claim it. Live it.

✝ *Lord, my life is a miracle. My recovery is a miracle too. Recovery is something I can't do on my own, but you have come through for me and are propelling me forward in restoration. I pray for every step ahead. Guide me, guard me, and keep me. Demonstrate your awesome power in me!*

I never have any difficulty believing in miracles, since I experienced the miracle of a change in my own heart.

SAINT AUGUSTINE OF HIPPO (354–430)

You can find today's Scripture passage on page 733 of *The Life Recovery Bible*.

Christ in Us

This is the secret: Christ lives in you.
This gives you assurance of sharing his glory.

COLOSSIANS 1:27

IN ACQUIRING AND THEN MAINTAINING our addiction, we didn't do very well in living a competent, happy life. The good news for the Christian is that Christ living in us can save us from ourselves. Perhaps that's why God has allowed us to fail so many times. Failure brings us resolutely to the end of ourselves. And that's exactly where we find the strength of Christ. What we *won't* find in ourselves or in this secular world, we will find only in Jesus—and that's enough to secure our victory.

✝ *Father, Christ in me is my hope. My full trust and faith are in him to continue my deliverance from addiction. Every day is full of opportunities for growth—or for relapse. Lord, you have seen me in my relapses, but you have remained faithful even then. What a blessing to know that when I have fallen, you have cared for me as you would a wandering sheep from the fold. What hope your loyalty to me brings.*

Whenever a Christian has fallen, and lies in defeat or failure—over him bends the heavenly Father in kindly pity, to raise him up and to help him to begin again.

J. R. MILLER (1840–1912)

You can find today's Scripture passage on page 1532 of *The Life Recovery Bible.*

Sanctified and Set Apart

You were washed, you were sanctified, you were justified in the name of the Lord Jesus Christ and by the Spirit of our God.

1 CORINTHIANS 6:11, ESV

TO BE SANCTIFIED IS TO BE SET APART. And, having been washed clean of our sins, fully justified in the name of Jesus, our Lord, we've been set apart for God's use. The Spirit of God has moved in us to bring about this miracle. The joy that's now before us is to embrace and enjoy our "set apartness." God now intends us to be useful to him—and we shall be if we continue to pursue him and his destiny for us.

✝ ***Lord, my salvation was by faith—and so, too, is my deliverance from addiction and my sanctification—my being set apart for your use. Build up this faith of mine, God. Increase my ability to walk this journey boldly, confidently, full of hope for my future. Keep me from expecting to be set apart by my own "religious" efforts to sanctify my old nature for my "apartness." My sanctification is in you.***

As from the cross flows all salvation, so from the cross flows all sanctification. What have not men done, to make themselves holy; and by this means render themselves, as they have thought, acceptable to God! What tortures of body, what fastings, scourgings, self-imposed penances to sanctify their sinful nature, and conform their rebellious flesh to the holiness demanded by the law! And with what success? They have landed either in self-righteousness or despair—though at opposite points of the compass.

J. C. PHILPOT (1802–1869)

You can find today's Scripture passage on page 1462 of *The Life Recovery Bible.*

Loss of Control

Prepare your minds for action and exercise self-control.

1 PETER 1:13

JUST AS LOSS OF CONTROL IS A HUGE ISSUE while addicted, so is regaining control a large part of recovery. Having lost control of our lives for a while, we may struggle in taking control of our lives again. We may be plagued with self-doubt (a possible trigger for relapse), indecision, the making of wrong decisions . . . and more. But as we continue on the recovery path, we learn the joys of taking control again. Our self-doubt diminishes, and our decisions become more certain and, more often, the right ones. Give yourself grace in taking control again. Never let one bad decision lead to relapse. God is teaching you something, even during your bad decisions. You will once again enjoy the self-imposed (and safe) boundaries that come with self-control.

† *Lord, in my addiction, all control was lost as I surrendered to my enemy. That enemy chose for me things no right thinking, self-controlled person would ever consider. Now, though, you have returned to me the ability to control my thoughts and actions. Continue to teach me how to rightly use this privilege. Show me the areas where I need to step up and put in place some controls that will aid my recovery. Remind me when I'm relinquishing self-control or using it inappropriately. Guide me toward a secure future with my ability for self-control.*

> I am a spiritual being. . . . After this body is dead, my spirit will soar. I refuse to let what will rot rule the eternal. I choose self-control. I will be drunk only by joy. I will be impassioned only by my faith. I will be influenced only by God. I will be taught only by Christ.
>
> MAX LUCADO (1955–)

You can find today's Scripture passage on page 1611 of *The Life Recovery Bible.*

Covenant

He always stands by his covenant—
the commitment he made to a thousand generations.

PSALM 105:8

WHEN WE THINK OF THE TWO SECTIONS OF the Bible—the Old Testament and the New Testament—we may forget that a synonym for *testament* is *covenant.* God has entered into a covenant with all who will come to him in faith. In the Old Testament, the old covenant was based on law—on our performance. The new covenant is based on the perfect performance of Christ in our place and the shedding of his blood to atone for our sins. And here's the thing: This covenant is backed by God's own integrity and righteousness. In short, it's a covenant that, once entered into, cannot be broken. Our recovery, our promise of deliverance from sin and addiction, is inherent in our covenant with God. He remembers his covenant with us *forever*. What a mighty God we serve!

✝ *Lord, in your covenant with me, I find my deliverance. Your covenant promises forgiveness of sins, new life that overcomes every evil, and your Holy Spirit as my guide. Though I may not be very good at covenant keeping, you never fail in seeing your covenant fulfilled in your children. God, I thank you that the new covenant of grace is what saves me from my destroyers.*

> The covenant of grace is so well ordered by the unsearchable wisdom of God, that you may find in it remedies to cure all your spiritual diseases, and cordials to comfort you under all your soul-faintings, and a spiritual armory to arm you against all sorts of sins, and all sorts of snares, and all sorts of temptations, and all sorts of oppositions, and all sorts of enemies, whether inward or outward, open or secret, subtle or silly.
>
> **THOMAS BROOKS (1608–1680)**

You can find today's Scripture passage on page 752 of *The Life Recovery Bible*.

Back to Reality

Just as you accepted Christ Jesus as your Lord, you must continue to follow him. Let your roots grow down into him, and let your lives be built on him. Then your faith will grow strong in the truth you were taught, and you will overflow with thankfulness.

COLOSSIANS 2:6-7

THE WORLD OF OUR ADDICTION WAS a false world. There was no reality to it. As we partook, we, in a sense, left the world of reality and entered into a world of fantasy. Recovery brings us back into reality, but it's a new reality. Where previously we may have wanted to escape reality and thus entered into addiction, we now have a reality in Christ that far exceeds the reality we once escaped and the false world of addiction.

Every day, we have the choice of which world we will live in.

Which reality are you going to live in today: the false reality with all its bumps, twists, and shifting sands or the reality that plants you firmly in Christ with all its gifts, blessings, and joys?

✝ ***God, you have brought me back from the world of fantasy to the real world—and in so doing, you've equipped me to deal with the realities of life without the crutch of addiction. Father, may my eyes always be clear so I can distinguish the real world and the possibilities therein for me—and may I remember that the world of addiction offers only a false future built on lies.***

Faith beholds invisible realities! It is the conviction of things not seen. It brings the great realities of the spiritual world within my reach: God, in His glory; Christ, in His beauty and love; sin, in its deformity; holiness, in its excellence; the solemn judgment to come; eternity, so blessed—or so sad. Faith gives me a firm persuasion of these unseen realities. It invests them with a transforming influence over my heart. I look out, with the eye of faith, and I find myself in their midst.

ALEXANDER SMELLIE (1857–1923)

You can find today's Scripture passage on page 1532 of *The Life Recovery Bible.*

Death to the Old Self

Don't lie to each other, for you have stripped off your old sinful nature and all its wicked deeds.

COLOSSIANS 3:9

PAUL KNEW THAT BECAUSE THE COLOSSIAN believers were now new creations in Christ, he could admonish them to change their lying behavior *because* they had put off the old self with its practices. Make no mistake about it, our addiction belongs entirely to the "old self." It is not and cannot be part of the new creation that is now ours. Just as Paul could tell the Colossians to stop lying by putting off the old self with its practices, so he would tell us to put off our addictions as one of the "wicked deeds" of our old selves. This we can do! This is our recovery: putting off the old and its practices and embracing the new self with its self-control, patience, joy, and all the other fruit of the Spirit (see Galatians 5:22-23).

✝ *God, when you save a person, that person is fully saved. You give a new self in place of the old self with all its addictions and deadly practices. Thank you that all things in my life are new. The newness of salvation affects all my life—nothing is left untouched. Therefore, by faith, I can put off all the practices that originated with my old self.*

> The true Christian is quite a new man, a new creature—all things are become new. Conversion is a deep work, a heart work. It makes a new man in a new world. It extends to the whole man—to the mind, to the members, to the motions of the whole life.
>
> JOSEPH ALLEINE (1634–1668)

You can find today's Scripture passage on page 1534 of *The Life Recovery Bible.*

Giving God the Glory

Whether you eat or drink, or whatever you do,
do it all for the glory of God.

1 CORINTHIANS 10:31

OUR SOBRIETY MAY BRING THE OCCASIONAL applause and acclaim of those who knew us at our worst. But we know the truth: Our healing up to this point has been the work of God for the glory of God. And so it will be as we continue our recovery. Make sure that you're clear on this: Your recovery is of God and for his glory. Be prepared to give God credit for your continued sobriety.

✝ *Father, at times when I see how far I've come, I may be tempted to think well of myself for having succeeded. But, Lord, we both know the truth. All I do as a Christian recovering from addiction is a reflection of your work within me. With every passing day of sobriety, you, Lord, are the one due the praise. May I never forget that.*

The glory of God is a silver thread which must run through all of our actions.

THOMAS WATSON (1620–1686)

You can find today's Scripture passage on page 1468 of *The Life Recovery Bible.*

Grace

From his abundance we have all received one
gracious blessing after another.

JOHN 1:16

WHO BUT SOMEONE WHO HAS KNOWN addiction desires one gracious blessing after another? God knows how we failed without grace—the unmerited favor of God. We were judged by others and by ourselves. But now, from his abundance of grace, we receive blessing after blessing.

We find grace only when we truly desire it. And we mostly desire it when the road is rugged and narrow. Many who remain in addiction have no understanding of grace, nor the depths of God's love and commitment to the addict, even at his or her lowest.

Do you desire grace today? Grace upon grace? Then it is surely yours.

✝ *Dear Lord, thank you for your grace. Without it, my case is hopeless. I deserve no favor from you—and yet you pour out favor upon me in the form of grace, grace, and more grace. May it ever be so. May your grace always be upon me.*

The road is rugged, and the sun is hot. How can we be but weary? Here is grace for the weariness—grace which lifts us up and invigorates us; grace which keeps us from fainting by the way; grace which supplies us with manna from heaven, and with water from the smitten rock. We receive of this grace, and are revived.

HORATIUS BONAR (1808–1889)

You can find today's Scripture passage on page 1341 of *The Life Recovery Bible*.

Are We There Yet?

Dear friends, I warn you as "temporary residents and foreigners" to keep away from worldly desires that wage war against your very souls.

1 PETER 2:11

AS KIDS ON THE LONG CAR RIDE TO Grandma's house, it was usual for us to ask, "Are we there yet?" It was a question we asked over and over . . . until we were indeed there.

Spiritually, the journey to the end of ourselves is somewhat like that seemingly endless car ride. Ours is a perilous, bumpy, jarring journey. And yet it's the journey we all must take to be free. As we look back, we wonder how we made it this far as we ask, "Are we there yet?" And be assured, we *will* arrive at our destination at the very moment the road of "self" comes to an end and we find ourselves fully recovered and at ease in the Father's house. Until then, we're only here as temporary residents and foreigners. Losing our lives includes keeping away from the desires that war against our souls, that pull us back from the life of freedom into slavery again. We will only arrive at Grandma's house by staying the course.

✝ *Father, sometimes the journey to full recovery seems so long. The road is bumpy, the air is dry, and there are so many twists and turns. The road map instructs me to lose my life here so that I will find it.. To be honest, I lost my life when I embraced my addiction. In losing my old life, I awake to find a new life—a life that brings sobriety and contentment. A life that has overcome the desires that wage war against my soul. Daily, Lord, I press on in victory, never stopping.*

Press forward. Do not stop, do not linger in your journey, but strive for the mark set before you.

GEORGE WHITEFIELD (1714–1770)

You can find today's Scripture passage on page 1613 of *The Life Recovery Bible.*

The Capacity for Great Joy

You love him even though you have never seen him. Though you do not see him now, you trust him; and you rejoice with a glorious, inexpressible joy.

1 PETER 1:8

HOW ODD IT SEEMS FOR US TO FIND inexpressible joy in someone we cannot see. How amazing to love an invisible Christ. But, of course, he's not invisible. His hands are shaping our lives. His mouth speaks words of comfort in our discomfort. His eyes never take leave of our every move. His ears hear our every prayer. This glorious joy is one of our major antidotes to the depression that often accompanies addiction—and sometimes accompanies recovery, too.

If we are believers in Christ, we have the capacity for this inexpressible joy. It's a joy that's our daily strength as we battle addiction.

† *Father, thank you for the capacity for great joy you've given me. This joy, coming from you, is a great tool in my recovery. It relieves me when I become depressed. It enlivens me when I become sluggish. It keeps me on the road to wholeness. Thank you for your divine joy!*

The believer in Jesus is essentially a happy man. The child of God is, from necessity, a joyful man. His sins are forgiven, his soul is justified, his person is adopted, his trials are blessings, his conflicts are victories, his death is immortality, his future is a heaven of inconceivable, unthought of, untold, and endless blessedness. With such a God, such a Savior, and such a hope, is he not, ought he not, to be a joyful man?

OCTAVIUS WINSLOW (1808–1878)

You can find today's Scripture passage on page 1611 of *The Life Recovery Bible*.

God Redeems Our Past

The LORD says, "I will give you back what you lost to the swarming locusts, the hopping locusts, the stripping locusts, and the cutting locusts."

JOEL 2:25

WHEN WE LOOK BACK AT OUR LOST YEARS in addiction, what do we see? For some, the view is too depressing to revisit. But if we look beyond what the swarming locust of addiction has devoured of our lives, we see a God of restoration who can reclaim and repurpose our past into a monument to his faithfulness. The enemy wants to keep us focused on past failures and wasted time. God, however, has dealt kindly with us in sweeping away our past, giving back what we lost—and more.

We will praise the name of the Lord our God who sees our past as raw material for his redeeming power.

✝ *God, of all your attributes we who have known addiction can appreciate, perhaps your ability to restore is most appreciated. My natural tendency is to think that restoration to all I had before my addiction—and even greater than that—is impossible. Too much time has passed. I've lost too much. But no, you do restore beyond what I deserve. I pray for continued restoration. I pray that, by faith, I can glimpse the restoring years ahead.*

It is God who says, "I will restore." Only the divine hand can do it. Christ is the restorer, for he has made atonement for us.

J. R. MILLER (1840–1912)

You can find today's Scripture passage on page 1117 of *The Life Recovery Bible*.

Less Becomes More

[John the Baptist said,] "He must become greater and greater, and I must become less and less."

JOHN 3:30

JOHN THE BAPTIST WAS A GREAT MAN. Jesus even lauded him by saying, "I tell you the truth, of all who have ever lived, none is greater than John the Baptist" (Matthew 11:11). John, of course, knew his role was that of a forerunner to Jesus and thus claimed, "He must become greater and greater, and I must become less and less" (John 3:30). We, too, must become less and less in ourselves and allow the presence of Christ in us to increase. Jesus' assessment of John the Baptist continued with these words: "Yet even the least person in the Kingdom of Heaven is greater than he is!" (Matthew 11:11).

If we're willing to become less, we shall experience greatness in the eyes of God. As *we* decrease, so does our addiction. As Christ increases, so does our freedom.

† *Father, my prayer is that my life from here on out would be one of becoming less and less so that Christ in me might become more and more. In myself, I have nothing to offer. But it's as I abide in Christ—and allow his increase in my life—that I find full freedom and joy. I shall find more.*

If our hearts are right with Him, there will be fullness of joy at the increase of Christ and the decrease of self.

JAMES SMITH (1802–1862)

You can find today's Scripture passage on page 1345 of *The Life Recovery Bible.*

Is Satan Afraid of You?

Humble yourselves before God. Resist the devil, and he will flee from you.

JAMES 4:7

JAMES OFFERS A TWO-STEP STRATEGY TO OVERCOME the enemy. First step: Submit to God. Second step: Resist the devil. Result: He will flee.

Where we often fail in this strategy is in not resisting the enemy soon enough. One of his weapons is to insert temptations into our thoughts. And if we receive the tempting thought, we're very likely to act on it. But if part of our recovery is developing the habit of *immediately* resisting tempting thoughts, those thoughts will vanish along with their instigator, the devil. Learning to resist our temptations is key to recovery. We must quickly and resolutely resist the enemy's temptations. And if they occur again five minutes later, we resist again. It won't take long for resisting the enemy to become a successful response to his tactics so he will flee.

If tempted today, submit to God and resist the enemy. Repeat as necessary.

† ***Father God, one of your great tools in building my strength is the ability to resist the enemy in all his strategies. You have called me to submit to you, resist the enemy, and watch him flee. This, Lord, I do daily—and early before he begins his whispers to capture my ear.***

> Our resistance must be thorough. The approaches of Satan to the soul are gradual: he asks us to yield but a little at first. Many promise themselves they will stop after they have conceded a trifle, but when a stone at the top of the hill starts rolling down, it is hard to stop. We see this principle forcibly illustrated in the case of [addicts]. Take heed unto thyself. Our resistance must be constant and continuous: not only against his first attack, but his whole siege. The Devil is very persevering, and we must be so too.
>
> **ARTHUR PINK (1886–1952)**

You can find today's Scripture passage on page 1605 of *The Life Recovery Bible*.

True Wisdom

The wisdom from above is first of all pure. It is also peace loving, gentle at all times, and willing to yield to others. It is full of mercy and the fruit of good deeds. It shows no favoritism and is always sincere.

JAMES 3:17

WISDOM IS THE RIGHT USE OF KNOWLEDGE. As we learn about addiction and consider our past bondage, we're wise if we fully implement what we learn about ourselves. Knowledge unused is a waste. As we learn, we must depend on God to give us "wisdom from above" and allow the good fruit to flourish in us.

† *Lord, one thing I lost in my addiction was wisdom. As I live out my freedom, I pray for the wisdom from above. Father, I want to enjoy the pure, peace-loving, gentle, yielding, merciful, fruitful, impartial, and sincere wisdom that comes from you. This wisdom is crucial, Father, to my recovery. You know how faulty my own wisdom is. Renew my mind, Lord. Give me wisdom from above that will allow me to use knowledge properly.*

The all-seeing eye of God beheld our deplorable state; infinite pity touched the heart of the Father of mercies; and infinite wisdom laid the plan of our recovery.

DAVID BRAINERD (1718–1747)

You can find today's Scripture passage on page 1605 of *The Life Recovery Bible*.

Superman or Clark Kent?

Be strong in the Lord and in his mighty power.

EPHESIANS 6:10

OUR ADDICTION HAS BEEN OUR KRYPTONITE. Slowly, over time, it has sapped away our strength, leaving us as weak as Clark Kent appeared to be. God's Word to us now, as we recover from our addiction, is to be strong in the Lord and the strength of his might. In short, we're not called to be strong in our own might but to depend on his strength. Day by day, his strength, his might, is more than enough. We ditch our Clark Kent suit and tie, take off the glasses, and don the cape that reflects who we really are: supermen and superwomen who survive by staying strong in the Lord and in his mighty power.

✝ *Father, you know full well how weak I am in my own strength. Time after time, I've tried to overcome by sheer willpower—only to fail once more. Lord, help me to stop the useless striving and count on your strength to overcome. I long to be strong in you and in the power of your might. I have full confidence that you are with me and in me to bring about this supernatural strength to overcome every obstacle to my recovery.*

> Do not strive in your own strength; cast yourself at the feet of the Lord Jesus, and wait upon Him in the sure confidence that He is with you, and works in you. . . . Strive in prayer; let faith fill your heart—so will you be strong in the Lord, and in the power of His might.
>
> ANDREW MURRAY (1828–1917)

You can find today's Scripture passage on page 1517 of *The Life Recovery Bible.*

The Promises of God

Because of his glory and excellence, he has given us great and precious promises. These are the promises that enable you to share his divine nature and escape the world's corruption caused by human desires.

2 PETER 1:4

HOW DO WE ESCAPE ADDICTION? Through the great and precious promises of God. A good exercise is to search the Bible for a promise relevant to our present need and meditate on it, believe it, and trust its power to benefit us. It's through the promises that we become partakers of God's divine nature—which, we know, is the means of implementing the promises and escaping the corruption in the world.

† *God, your promises are golden to me. It's by your promises that I partake of your nature. It's by your promises that I escape the corruption in the world because of my own human desires. Lord, today, show me a promise from your word that I can meditate on throughout the day.*

A person who wholly follows the Lord is one who believes that the promises of God are trustworthy, that He is with His people, and that they are well able to overcome.

WATCHMAN NEE (1903–1972)

You can find today's Scripture passage on page 1622 of *The Life Recovery Bible*.

The Power of Worship

Exalt the LORD our God!
Bow low before his feet, for he is holy!

PSALM 99:5

AS WE PROGRESS IN RECOVERY, worship becomes an important element in our healing. We worship God first for who he is. He is worthy of our worship. We can also worship God for what he does and for his healing power in our lives.

Go off by yourself today and begin to worship God in your own words, even if they come slowly at first. As you progress in worship, the words will come more easily.

Worship God aloud. Hearing your own lips worship him is an added benefit to an already rewarding practice.

† *Father, I love to enter into your presence through worship. Teach me, Lord, how to worship you more fully, more effectively. Surely as I watch you work through my recovery, I feel more and more compelled to worship. Daily, I find worship easier as I experience your work in my life.*

Worship is adoring contemplation of God.

R. A. TORREY (1856–1928)

You can find today's Scripture passage on page 748 of *The Life Recovery Bible.*

Life-Giving versus Life-Destroying

[Jesus said,] "The thief's purpose is to steal and kill and destroy. My purpose is to give them a rich and satisfying life."

JOHN 10:10

WE ARE AMONG THOSE ALMOST DESTROYED by addiction. We know some friends who didn't make it through the war to victory. We can see that the enemy did indeed invade their lives, stealing from them the years they could have had and destroying their personhood, leading them to the grave. There are always two competing voices at work: the voice of the thief trying to add us to his list of conquered souls and the voice of Christ who speaks to us of a promised abundant life. How hard is it to choose life over death?

✝ ***Lord, you know my choice. You know I crave the rich and satisfying life promised to all believers. You know the friends I've lost to the grave. I shall not follow them to that end, but I shall live and prevail in this life. I shall live a whole life, not the partial life the enemy tempts me with. Father, with your strength, I shall prevail!***

> If you have truly trusted the Lord Jesus Christ to be your Sin-bearer, then you have life abiding in you, despite what may look like obvious signs of death. Simply put, what you need is more growth—spiritual growth, not more life. Spiritual growth is the process by which we allow the indwelling Christ to increasingly express Himself in and through us, resulting in a greater capacity on our part to bring God greater glory and experience His greater good for ourselves. In short, spiritual growth is less of you and more of Christ being expressed in your life. If you are struggling to see His life in you then it's time to commit to growth.
>
> TONY EVANS (1949–)

You can find today's Scripture passage on page 1358 of *The Life Recovery Bible*.

Our Sufficiency

Not that we are sufficient in ourselves to claim anything as coming from us, but our sufficiency is from God.

2 CORINTHIANS 3:5, ESV

EARLY ON, we discovered our insufficiency in dealing with addiction. In retrospect, that was a happy day, though we couldn't see it then. Happy because, when we're no longer sufficient in ourselves, we're drawn to God's sufficiency. There we find our need met. There we find rest.

Day by day, God renews our awareness of insufficiency so that we must turn to him to find sufficiency. And it will always be there.

✝ ***Father, in you I find all I need. I find sufficiency in all things. Thank you for removing all the props in my life that tried to make me believe my own sufficiency was enough. Daily, I look for reminders of my own lack, which then sends me to drink of your sufficiency.***

We have no sufficient strength of our own. All our sufficiency is of God. We should stir up ourselves to resist temptations in a reliance upon God's all-sufficiency and the omnipotence of his might.

MATTHEW HENRY (1662–1714)

You can find today's Scripture passage on page 1483 of *The Life Recovery Bible*.

Our Security

[Jesus said,] "Those the Father has given me will come to me, and I will never reject them."

JOHN 6:37

WHAT SECURITY IT IS TO KNOW THAT WE'RE fully and forever his. We have gone to the one who will never reject us. His love for us—even in our past addiction—has never wavered. He's brought us this far and will be with us for the entire journey.

God's love for us declares his full acceptance of us. This is transforming. Therefore, we must let God's love and acceptance have its full effect in our lives.

✝ *Lord Jesus, thank you for the security I have in you. Thank you that in your eyes I'm rejection proof. Nothing can woo me away from you nor you from me. Though I have come to you by a decision I made, that decision was prompted by the fact that I've been given to you by the Father. So I come to you 24/7 to draw from you the power to live another sober day. Thank you for this strong, safe security.*

> Where does your security lie? Is God your refuge, your hiding place, your stronghold, your shepherd, your counselor, your friend, your redeemer, your saviour, your guide? If He is, you don't need to search any further for security.
>
> ELISABETH ELLIOT (1926–2015)

You can find today's Scripture passage on page 1350 of *The Life Recovery Bible*.

Temptation

Temptation comes from our own desires, which entice us and drag us away. These desires give birth to sinful actions. And when sin is allowed to grow, it gives birth to death.

JAMES 1:14-15

GOD DOES NOT TEMPT US. Our own addictive flesh entices us to whatever sins and addictions will work toward our destruction. The result is deception and spiritual sickness and, if not checked, often death. Addictions start small, like a crack in a dam. Eventually, the crack enlarges—it never gets smaller. The crack, however, must be mended because the sooner the fix, the easier the fix. It's the same with addiction. The sooner the impulse to indulge in our addiction is stopped cold, the easier the recovery.

God is our go-to when we are tempted. He repairs the breach in the dam. Only through him can we live a better life. But we must see our plight for what it is. We must no longer be deceived by our addiction. Its promises are lies. Let us be strong today and say no to lies and deception.

✝ ***Father, thank you for the power within me to say no to temptations arising from my own desires. Remind me that even when the small lie reaches my inner ear, I must say no to what could become a crack in the dam of recovery. Strengthen me, Lord, as I fight the destruction of addiction in my life.***

The temptation once yielded to gains power. The crack in the embankment which lets a drop or two ooze through is soon a hole which lets out a flood.

ALEXANDER MACLAREN (1826–1910)

You can find today's Scripture passage on page 1601 of *The Life Recovery Bible*.

The Way Out

The temptations in your life are no different from what others experience. And God is faithful. He will not allow the temptation to be more than you can stand. When you are tempted, he will show you a way out so that you can endure.

1 CORINTHIANS 10:13

WHEN WE'RE NOT BEING TEMPTED, we can readily believe we will have a way of escape. But then, when temptation comes, that escape seems invisible. Living by faith during the hour of temptation is a matter of keeping our eyes open to God's promise of an escape and then fixing our eyes on that door out of destruction. Though temptation will be with us always, God's way of escape is also always with us. If tempted today, watch for your route out of harm's way.

† *God, I trust you in all things. In my temptations, I trust you for that door of escape. Please make it clear to me because I'm so often slow to see what's right before me in the way of blessing. I thank you that my every temptation is also a summons to draw closer to you.*

Temptation may even be a blessing to a man when it reveals to him his weakness and drives him to the almighty Savior. Do not be surprised, then, dear child of God, if you are tempted at every step of your earthly journey, and almost beyond endurance; but you will not be tempted beyond what you are able to bear, and with every temptation there will be a way of escape.

F. B. MEYER (1847–1929)

You can find today's Scripture passage on page 1467 of *The Life Recovery Bible.*

Riding Out the Storm

He calmed the storm to a whisper
and stilled the waves.

PSALM 107:29

WE'RE MISTAKEN IF WE BELIEVE THE recovery journey is a short hop, skip, and jump to permanent sobriety. We will encounter storms along the way. Hurricane-force winds, earthquakes that shake the ground under our feet, and tornadoes that set themselves down in our path unexpectedly are par for the course. And when the storms come, we can ride them out if we set our eyes on God's sovereignty coupled with his great compassion and zeal for us personally.

✝ *Praise you, Lord. I'm thankful that when storms come, they also are simply passing through. Every storm may rage for a short season but will eventually—and sometimes quickly—move on. Keep me strong as I ride out the storms. Help me become very good at watching and waiting.*

Let this encourage those of you who belong to Christ: the storm may be tempestuous, but it is only temporary. The clouds that are temporarily rolling over your head will pass, and then you will have fair weather, an eternal sunshine of glory.

WILLIAM GURNALL (1617–1679)

You can find today's Scripture passage on page 757 of *The Life Recovery Bible*.

Escaping Evil

Stay away from every kind of evil.

1 THESSALONIANS 5:22

DO WE SEE OUR ADDICTION as simply a "mistake" on our part? Simply bad decision-making during a time when our resistance was low?

It helps immensely to know that addiction is an evil and that we are commanded to abstain from evil for our own good. Many fail at recovery because they dabble at recovery or reject the idea of ending their dependency altogether. Those who are most successful see addiction for what it is and become determined to have a better, safer, sober life.

A benefit of labeling addiction as evil is that God spells out remedies for evil in his Word. The most important remedy is simply *training* ourselves to abstain by essentially rewiring our brains to respond differently to our addiction. This, with God's help, we can do. We can do it today . . . and tomorrow . . . and every day after that.

† ***Father, in The Lord's Prayer, you have encouraged me to pray, "Rescue us from the evil one." I know there are many possible labels for addiction, and the one I find most true is that addiction is indeed "evil." So, yes, Lord, I do echo that prayer that you would today and always deliver me from the evil of addiction.***

Many have puzzled themselves about the origin of evil. I am content to observe that there is evil, and that there is a way to escape from it, and with this I begin and end.

JOHN NEWTON (1725–1807)

You can find today's Scripture passage on page 1542 of *The Life Recovery Bible*.

Treasure Your Deliverance

He sent out his word and healed them,
snatching them from the door of death.

PSALM 107:20

WE KNOW THAT DESTRUCTION COMES to many addicted lives. We've seen it in friends. We've grieved over the losses—and at some point, we may have surrendered all hope that our fate would be any different. But God has sent his Word to heal us. He has sent his Spirit to deliver us from the destruction we've feared for so long. This great deliverance is what we can treasure daily. Thank God at all times for our recovery.

✝ *Father, deliverance from addiction is no small thing. It has taken and is taking a miracle to bring it all to pass. This deliverance is one I will never take for granted. You have done miracles in my life, and each one is worthy of a lifetime of thanks. I take nothing you've done for granted. And I never will.*

How quickly we forget God's great deliverances in our lives.
How easily we take for granted the miracles he performed in our past.

DAVID WILKERSON (1931–2011)

You can find today's Scripture passage on page 756 of *The Life Recovery Bible*.

The Support of Others

Two people are better off than one, for they can help each other succeed. If one person falls, the other can reach out and help. But someone who falls alone is in real trouble.

ECCLESIASTES 4:9-10

A SUPPORT SYSTEM DURING RECOVERY—and most likely after—is a huge asset. The right person or persons can be not just a friend in need but an accountability partner, an adviser, a comforter, and more. The one thing they cannot be is an enabler. They must be willing to take their role seriously—perhaps more seriously than even you do. Such a person may be rare and hard to find. Pray for the right person. It could be someone from your church, a fellow traveler on the sobriety journey, or a willing medical professional. It's best to choose someone the same gender as you. If the person is also overcoming addiction, it would be wise for them to be further along than you are. At some point, you may be the supporter of someone who needs your help.

✝ *Father, you know the people in my life who are concerned for me and praying for me. I do need their support in overcoming addiction. If there's one particular person I can add to my support team, I pray you will reveal him or her to me. Bring me into contact with one or more persons who will uphold me in prayer and offer to be my accountability partner in a crisis. And, Father, may I in turn become part of another struggler's support team.*

He is your friend who pushes you nearer to God.

ABRAHAM KUYPER (1837–1920)

You can find today's Scripture passage on page 828 of *The Life Recovery Bible*.

When You're Worried

Don't worry about anything; instead, pray about everything.
Tell God what you need, and thank him for all he has done.

PHILIPPIANS 4:6

DURING RECOVERY, and especially during withdrawal, we may experience an intense sense of worry and anxiety. Of course, at that point, sadly our desired remedy will be our addiction. But it need not be. Going without our addictive substance or behavior will be painful, but God will be there, expecting us to stand firm, to pray, and to thank him for pulling us through until the waves subside.

At particularly hard times, we're invited to "tell God what [we] need." When we do, we need to keep in mind the power of our God. We are not talking to the air. Our prayers do not stop at the ceiling. God, in all his might, hears and will answer. Faith it through the trial.

† *Father, I do have seasons of worry and anxiety about all sorts of things. My addiction, the future, the past. . . . You know better than I do the causes of my down times. Please hear my needs as I pray. When I'm tempted again to worry, I'll choose instead to rejoice in you, dispelling the poison of worry and anxiety.*

> Begin to rejoice in the Lord, and your bones will flourish like an herb, and your cheeks will glow with the bloom of health and freshness. Worry, fear, distrust, care—all are poisonous! Joy is balm and healing, and if you will but rejoice, God will give power.
>
> **A. B. SIMPSON (1843–1919)**

You can find today's Scripture passage on page 1525 of *The Life Recovery Bible*.

There *Is* a Future

Surely there is a future,
and your hope will not be cut off.

PROVERBS 23:18, ESV

DURING THE LOWEST DAYS OF OUR ADDICTION, we were well aware of how without hope we were. We *wanted* to hope. We were desperate for hope. But from where would the hope come? How could we ever have a happy future unless we had hope?

But God says *surely* there is a future for us. Our hope is as present with us as God himself is present. It will not be cut off. *Ever*. Our hope in God is secure.

If we pursue our future with the hope of God, we will find a post-addiction, God-designed life perfect for each of us.

✝ *God, at my bleakest, I saw no future for myself. But in recovery, I now know beyond a shadow of a doubt that I do have a future and that my hope will not be cut off. Lord, I release my addictive past into your hand and walk forward into my invincible future.*

Leave the broken, irreversible past in God's hands, and step out into the invincible future with Him.

OSWALD CHAMBERS (1874–1917)

You can find today's Scripture passage on page 811 of *The Life Recovery Bible*.

Forgive One Another

Get rid of all bitterness, rage, anger, harsh words, and slander, as well as all types of evil behavior. Instead, be kind to each other, tenderhearted, forgiving one another, just as God through Christ has forgiven you.

EPHESIANS 4:31-32

MANY OF US CAN REMEMBER PAST OFFENSES committed against us, perhaps associated with our addiction or maybe preceding our addiction. Abuse, self-hatred, wrongs committed against us . . . whatever the offense, we must pray to be healed from the hurts and wrongs no one ever apologized for—and never will.

It's hard to let go of bitterness and wrath. Harder still to be kind to those who have wronged us. But once we experience the power that forgiveness brings, we understand. We see how our own offenses against God have wounded our relationship with him, and yet he is quick to forgive us. So must we forgive others in order to be healed.

✝ ***Father, there are people from my past I need to forgive. It doesn't matter if they wronged me or if I was at fault. In recovery, you have forgiven me, and so I, too, take the step of faith and forgive the ones I've harbored ill-will toward. Forgive us all our trespasses, Lord.***

Whenever I see myself before God and realize something of what my blessed Lord has done for me at Calvary, I am ready to forgive anybody anything. I cannot withhold it. I do not even want to withhold it.

MARTYN LLOYD-JONES (1899–1981)

You can find today's Scripture passage on page 1515 of *The Life Recovery Bible.*

Dealing with Residual Effects

In his kindness God called you to share in his eternal glory by means of Christ Jesus. So after you have suffered a little while, he will restore, support, and strengthen you, and he will place you on a firm foundation.

1 PETER 5:10

LIKELY, WE WILL EXPERIENCE THE RESIDUAL effects of our addiction for some time. In fact, those residual effects are often triggers to resume our addiction. Or sometimes they're simply obstacles to resuming our normal life post-addiction. We will need to anticipate the residual effects of a broken relationship, financial strain, loss of employment opportunities, and others unique to each person—but anticipate them with a promise from God to see these effects lessen as we move on to wholeness. Expect them, but don't let them bring you down. Find the promises of God for your residual effects, and cling to them.

✝ *God, I know that not every aspect of my addiction will be healed at once. You are aware of the residual effects I'm experiencing. Give me strength to wade through these weeds and come out on the other side. Father, please diminish the residual effects of my addiction as part of your healing plan for me. May your promises see me through.*

The promises of God are an inexhaustible mine of wealth to the believer. Happy is it for him if he knows how to search out their secret veins, and enrich himself with their hidden treasures.

CHARLES SPURGEON (1834–1892)

You can find today's Scripture passage on page 1617 of *The Life Recovery Bible*.

How Do We Make It?

When you go through deep waters,
I will be with you.
When you go through rivers of difficulty,
you will not drown.
When you walk through the fire of oppression,
you will not be burned up;
the flames will not consume you.

ISAIAH 43:2

HOW DO WE MAKE IT THROUGH DEEP WATERS, overwhelming rivers, and blazing fire? By knowing that the Lord our God, the Holy One of Israel, our Savior is *with* us. No matter the depth of our recovery pain or any longing we may have to go back, God's hand is upon us. He will save us. He will gather us unto himself. He will allow nothing to prevent our destiny if we will but stay the course. We need not fear for he has redeemed us. He has called us by name. Fear not!

✝ *Father, because you are with me through every trial, I will not fear. You are with me in my recovery, you know my desires and my weaknesses, and through it all, you're still with me. No flame of temptation shall consume me. No rivers of difficulty shall overwhelm me. I am yours. You have called me by name.*

Dear friend, Jesus finds His delight in you, if you are His redeemed child. True, His love commenced as the love of compassion. He found us wandering; but now that love has mellowed into one of infinite satisfaction. He not only refreshes—but he is refreshed by communion with His people.

ARCHIBALD G. BROWN (1844–1922)

You can find today's Scripture passage on page 895 of *The Life Recovery Bible.*

Cultural Resistance

We know that we are from God, and
the whole world lies in the power of the evil one.

1 JOHN 5:19, ESV

ONE REASON ADDICTION IS AN EPIDEMIC is that, slowly through the years, our culture has lost its resistance to what used to be inappropriate behaviors. Much of what was known as wrong or sinful a generation ago has become routinely accepted today. With little cultural resistance, addictions will abound. But where addiction abounds, so does grace. Not grace to continue in addiction but grace to overcome.

A vital mistake we make is to give our addiction a free pass simply because others tolerate it. We must never lose the perspective that any addiction is dangerous and to be avoided. In that sense, we're restoring a cultural resistance to addiction, even if only in our own circle of acquaintances.

The world may continue to accommodate substances and behaviors that lead to addiction, but we must not.

† *Father, the ease with which one can become addicted today bothers me. In my own case, it wasn't hard to get pulled into a habit that could be lethal to me. Lord, help me be a warning sign to others that addictive substances and behaviors are not to be toyed with. I pray you would restore a strong cultural resistance to addictions of any kind. Especially among young people.*

In such a world as this, with such hearts as ours, weakness *is* wickedness in the long run. Whoever lets himself be shaped and guided by anything lower than an inflexible will, fixed in obedience to God, will in the end be shaped into a deformity, and guided to wreck and ruin.

ALEXANDER MACLAREN (1826–1910)

You can find today's Scripture passage on page 1634 of *The Life Recovery Bible*.

The Beauty of the Lord

One thing have I asked of the LORD,
that will I seek after:
that I may dwell in the house of the LORD
all the days of my life,
to gaze upon the beauty of the LORD
and to inquire in his temple.

PSALM 27:4, ESV

HAVE WE OFTEN CONSIDERED THE BEAUTY of the Lord? His beauty is so dazzling that humans cannot be in his presence and live. But one day, in eternity, we shall gaze upon his beauty and, in a moment's time, be changed by what we see. If we were to seek just this one thing—to dwell with God all our days and to behold his beauty—we would need nothing else.

Today, by faith, behold his beauty. Whatever you picture as his beauty can only pale in comparison to the reality. But in that, rejoice. Gain strength today by imagining that great day ahead when we shall forever dwell with him and gaze at his beauty.

† ***Lord, I can barely imagine your beauty. It transcends anything I see or can imagine on earth. Father, I long to gaze on your beauty and behold your magnificence. Just a glimpse of you in my imagination can get me through this life. Lord, I praise you for inviting me to dwell in your house forever to gaze upon your beauty.***

The man who gazes upon and contemplates day by day the face of the Lord Jesus Christ, and who has caught the glow of the reality that the Lord is not a theory but an indwelling power and force in his life, is as a mirror reflecting the glory of the Lord.

ALAN REDPATH (1907–1989)

You can find today's Scripture passage on page 696 of *The Life Recovery Bible*.

God Is Happy to Provide for Us

Don't be afraid, little flock. For it gives your Father
great happiness to give you the Kingdom.

LUKE 12:32

A RELUCTANCE TO BELIEVE THAT GOD WILL help us in our recovery—in other words, *doubt* about his ability or care—makes it very hard to move the bricks from the wall that must come down. We must know that it gives God happiness to bring us healing. He delights in providing for us, if we will only look to his hand to feed and care for us. How then can we have any doubt?

† ***God, sometimes I'm unaware of just how deeply you're committed to my recovery. You're in my corner all the way. It brings you happiness to walk through this journey with me. By knowing you, I have the key to my own happiness. I have fulfillment in living as part of your Kingdom.***

You may have lost much that you once possessed. You may have failed to have all that you desired, or expected to have. But, child of God, think what it is to have the Kingdom of Heaven!

Who is rich—if you are not rich!
Who is happy—if you are not happy!
Who is honorable—if you are not glorious!
Fear not, child of God! Fear not poverty. Fear not trial.
Fear nothing which makes you feel your dependence upon God.

LOUIS GEORGE MYLNE (1843–1921)

You can find today's Scripture passage on page 1314 of *The Life Recovery Bible*.

God's Prescription

A cheerful heart is good medicine,
but a broken spirit saps a person's strength.

PROVERBS 17:22

WE HAVE BEEN GIVEN A PRESCRIPTION FOR our healing, and that prescription is to have a cheerful heart—no matter what. Yes, the enemy will always try to take down our joy. He knows a broken spirit will sap our strength. But we can and must displace him from having any say about our emotions. Joy is ours. We will not let the enemy rob us of this vital medicine.

✝ *Lord, I receive your prescription of joy as medicine for my soul. For a long time, my crushed spirit has dried up my bones, leaving me feeling lifeless. But you are renewing me. Each day is a different step forward in the healing journey. Brick by brick, the wall is coming down. I have joy—deep joy that heals my crushed spirit.*

> You may have strong corruptions, powerful inbred sins, severe temptations, deep trials, heavy afflictions, yet if you know Christ, and have Christ in the midst of all, you have ground for the deepest, holiest joy.
>
> **OCTAVIUS WINSLOW (1808–1878)**

You can find today's Scripture passage on page 805 of *The Life Recovery Bible.*

Be Still

Be still in the presence of the LORD,
and wait patiently for him to act.

PSALM 37:7

STILLNESS IS NOT USUALLY THE LOT of the addict. Restlessness, impatience, mood swings are more likely. But by bringing ourselves into God's stillness, we find relief from the symptoms of our addiction. Perhaps not at first. But are we willing to practice stillness in God's presence until it becomes natural to us? If we're patient, we will find strength in stillness. Never rush from the presence of the Lord, even if you feel compelled to. Wait patiently instead.

† *God, sometimes being still is hard for me. My mind races. My body wants to move. My soul isn't at rest. Yet you call me to stillness, and so I submit my active mind, body, and soul to you in the best way I know. In this stillness, I find peace. I call to mind that you never lose sight of me and that you're working all things for my own good. Thank you for the quiet, Lord.*

> Be still, for though painful at present—your trial will soon be over. Know that God is supreme and works all things after the counsel of His own will. Know that God never loses sight of you, or forgets your frame and your weakness. Exercise patience, relieve your burdened heart by prayer—and wait in full expectation of a blessing.
>
> JAMES SMITH (1802–1862)

You can find today's Scripture passage on page 704 of *The Life Recovery Bible*.

JUNE 7

The Adrenaline Rush

[Jesus said,] "Remain in me, and I will remain in you. For a branch cannot produce fruit if it is severed from the vine, and you cannot be fruitful unless you remain in me. Yes, I am the vine; you are the branches. Those who remain in me, and I in them, will produce much fruit. For apart from me you can do nothing."

JOHN 15:4-5

WHO, HAVING ONCE EXPERIENCED THE adrenaline rush of addiction, can ever forget it?

In addiction, we have allowed either a substance or at the very least adrenaline to course through our veins like sap in a grapevine. As Christians, we have the opportunity to have the life of Christ coursing through our veins by abiding in Christ. Compare the two options: Abiding in addiction kills us. Abiding in Christ allows us to bear good fruit, not the least of which is our sobriety.

✝ ***Father, you ask me to abide in you and allow the life of Christ to bring forth fruit in my life. For a long time, I have abided in addiction. But I've now exchanged that addiction for the life of abiding in Christ, the true Vine. I choose daily to live in union with Christ and bear the good fruit his life brings to me.***

> Let [man] choose Life; let him daily nourish his soul; let him forever starve the old life; let him abide continuously as a living branch in the Vine, and the True-Vine Life will flow into his soul, assimilating, renewing, conforming to Type, till Christ, pledged by His own law, be formed in him.
>
> **HENRY DRUMMOND (1851–1897)**

You can find today's Scripture passage on page 1366 of *The Life Recovery Bible*.

Contentment

I have learned how to be content with whatever I have.
I know how to live on almost nothing or with everything.
I have learned the secret of living in every situation, whether
it is with a full stomach or empty, with plenty or little.

PHILIPPIANS 4:11-12

IN RECOVERY, WE LEARN CONTENTMENT. At first, we may be restless and discontent. But God's recipe for healing from addiction is learning to be content in every situation . . . including sobriety. The apostle Paul knew how to be brought low, and so do we, though his lowness is not our lowness. He also knew how to abound—and either way, he was content.

Our contentedness is found only in abstinence from the source of our addiction and embracing God's power to deliver us. A sure sign of active recovery is the ability to see God in our daily circumstances and to be content with what he provides, not what our flesh craves.

✝ *Lord, contentment is what I love about my new life. I no longer ache for momentary pleasures. I'm pleased and grateful for what you're bringing into my life. I let you choose what's best for me and am thankful.*

Whatever He gives us—let us thankfully receive it.
Whatever He denies us—let us be satisfied without it.
Whatever He takes from us—let us uncomplainingly part with it.
Whatever trial He lays on us—let us endeavor patiently to bear it.

JOHN MACDUFF (1818–1895)

You can find today's Scripture passage on page 1526 of *The Life Recovery Bible*.

JUNE 9

Resisting the Enemy

Don't sin by letting anger control you. Don't let the sun go down while you are still angry, for anger gives a foothold to the devil.

EPHESIANS 4:26-27

FROM OUR INITIATION INTO ADDICTION and through our deepest involvement, even now to any current temptations, Satan gains a wedge (a foothold) into our lives should we give him the opportunity to have a say.

Anger, for instance, is an emotion that can draw us back into addiction by giving the enemy such a foothold. Victory in recovery comes from firmly learning to give our enemy no opportunity through anger or any other emotion. Satan and his addiction trap must be gone forever. This means severe resistance on our part. Resistance that overcomes the compulsion to relapse. Resistance that closes the door on future acting out. Resistance to anger or any other emotion that gives the enemy an opportunity to have at us.

Nothing less than continued firm resistance to Satan and his "opportunities" will do.

† *God, surely recovery from addiction includes a healing of my emotions. My tendency to let certain emotions have their way with me has been one of Satan's most effective strategies. Help me say no to his every attempt at exploiting my emotions, particularly anger. Instead of giving way to anger, teach me to have joy in the situations that would tempt me to anger.*

We sin in anger when its root is self, when our anger is directed not so much against the sin as the sinner, and because of some personal hurt. . . . To be angry and sin not, we must be angry at nothing but sin.

RUTH PAXSON (1875–1949)

You can find today's Scripture passage on page 1514 of *The Life Recovery Bible*.

The Idolatry of Addiction

Put to death the sinful, earthly things lurking within you. Have nothing to do with sexual immorality, impurity, lust, and evil desires. Don't be greedy, for a greedy person is an idolater, worshiping the things of this world.

COLOSSIANS 3:5

WE OFTEN THINK OF IDOLS AS GRAVEN images or totems . . . any object that receives worship. But Paul named several human activities as idolatry. Would he not also label addiction as idolatry? In the midst of our addiction, if someone urged us to turn to Christ, didn't we ignore that suggestion at first? Wasn't the idol of our addiction more attractive than what we perceived as a faraway Christ? Remember that as long as we want anything more than we want Jesus, it is an idol. Be done with any remaining idols in your life.

✝ *Lord, in my addiction, I have created an idol that received my "worship" through my continued attention and consecration to it. I have repented of that idolatry and receive your forgiveness. I have no other gods before you, Father.*

Whatsoever we have over-loved, idolized, and leaned upon, God has from time to time broken it, and made us to see the vanity of it; so that we find the readiest course to be rid our comforts is to set our hearts inordinately upon them.

JOHN FLAVEL (1627–1691)

You can find today's Scripture passage on page 1534 of *The Life Recovery Bible*.

Obstacles

Turn my eyes from worthless things,
and give me life through your word.

PSALM 119:37

ARE THERE OBSTACLES TO RECOVERY? Of course there are. We continue to face temptations, loss of friends, challenges in finding a new way to live, possible job or relational obstacles, and more. But obstacles are there for us to overcome. We become stronger by facing barriers and making our way past them. Visualize Christ on the other side of every obstacle you face. With each hurdle you jump, you're that much closer to the goal.

✝ *Father, all of us overcoming addiction face obstacles to full recovery. I have my own set of stumbling blocks I try to avoid. You, though, are familiar with each of them and have a remedy that turns those stumbling blocks into stepping-stones leading to the goal of a fully recovered life. You go first along the path, Lord; I'll follow, stepping-stone by stepping-stone, my eyes fixed on the goal.*

Obstacles are those frightful things you see when
you take your eyes off the goal.

HANNAH MORE (1745–1833)

You can find today's Scripture passage on page 764 of *The Life Recovery Bible.*

Satanic Attack

We would not be outwitted by Satan;
for we are not ignorant of his designs.

2 CORINTHIANS 2:11, ESV

OUR MONTHS OR YEARS UNDER THE HEAVY hand of addiction have made us aware of the enemy's designs on us. We are no longer ignorant as we were in the beginning. We know his faulty reasoning, his rationalizations, his accusations, his condemnation. We have become wise to them all. And with the truth of God and the power of his Word as our weapons, we need not ever be outwitted again. For every evil plan Satan has designed for us, we have the power to say no—and mean it. Consider, too, that we are also not ignorant of God's designs for our happiness.

✝ *Lord, I see how my addiction has eroded my ability to say no, not just to my addiction but to other temptations from the enemy that have kept me from your perfect will. After my sojourn on the painful path, I'm no longer ignorant of Satan's designs on me. With your help, and the knowledge of your designs for me, I'm learning once again how to say no—and mean it. I'm also learning how to say yes and receive all that comes with agreeing with you about my valuable life.*

> If the Lord has taught thee not to be ignorant of Satan's devices, as soon as the thought arises, whether thou art in Christ, because of such failings, thou wilt know from what quarter it comes, and will immediately resist it: so that the temptation will make thee stand faster; it will drive thee closer to Christ; make thine dependence stronger on his blood and righteousness; put thee upon making more use of him as thine intercessor and advocate with the Father, and help thee to live more out of thyself by faith upon him. Thus Christ becomes precious, thou art more humble, the snare is broken, and thou art delivered.
>
> **WILLIAM ROMAINE (1714–1795)**

You can find today's Scripture passage on page 1482 of *The Life Recovery Bible.*

JUNE 13

Christ Lives in Me

My old self has been crucified with Christ. It is no longer I who live, but Christ lives in me. So I live in this earthly body by trusting in the Son of God, who loved me and gave himself for me.

GALATIANS 2:20

FOR THE RECOVERING ADDICT, it's a glorious thing to consider one's self to be crucified with Christ. But thank God that, though we are dead, we still live because of the risen Christ who lives in us. We live daily in the flesh by our faith in the Son of God, who loves us and who gave himself for us. To be emptied of self is to be filled with Christ. And Christ is always victorious over any addiction.

✝ *Praise God for my death! Lord, what a great thought—that in Christ's death, I, too, died and yet I now live by faith in the Son of God, who loved me and gave himself for me. What a miracle! The heavy load of life is lifted by knowing Christ in me can meet any need, any temptation, or any trial I face.*

> Christ living in us, ourselves living upon Christ, and our union to Christ being visibly maintained by an act of simple faith in him, this is the true Christian's life.
>
> CHARLES SPURGEON (1834–1892)

You can find today's Scripture passage on page 1500 of *The Life Recovery Bible.*

To Live Forever

This world is fading away, along with everything that people crave. But anyone who does what pleases God will live forever.

1 JOHN 2:17

IT'S A WONDERFUL FACT THAT, ONE DAY, addiction will be no more. It simply won't exist. The world will pass away and with it all the petty but devouring desires that held us captive. Though addiction passes away along with the world, we who tend to the will of God will live forever.

To be in recovery is to allow the future passing away of addiction to become a present reality. We don't have to wait. We can enjoy our own personal experience of addiction's passing away now as we recover.

In addiction's place there stands the sanctifying door of God's perfect will for each of us. To desire, to receive, to abide in the will of God is to enjoy life's greatest pleasure.

† ***God, living forever in your presence is surely your greatest promise. Living in a new world where addiction and human cravings have all passed away sounds like a great future, but even better is that I don't have to wait. I can enjoy addiction's passing away now. Lord, thank you for how you brought me to pursue recovery and have led me along the way. It has made all the difference in my life.***

What is this world, and all things in it, if a man does not have God for his friend? All things around us remind us that we are nothing better than grass, and are like a fleeting shadow. And if we are void of saving grace, awful is our state, whether we feel it so or not. But we find that the Lord must make us view things in their true colors. And if He favors us with a few breathings after the "heavenly manna," it will stop us from so earnestly seeking that "bread which perishes."

WILLIAM TIPTAFT (1803–1864)

You can find today's Scripture passage on page 1630 of *The Life Recovery Bible.*

The Patience of God

The Lord isn't really being slow about his promise, as some people think. No, he is being patient for your sake. He does not want anyone to be destroyed, but wants everyone to repent.

2 PETER 3:9

HAVE YOU EVER QUESTIONED WHY GOD sometimes seems to move so slowly in your recovery? One of God's great attributes is his patience. And anyone who is patient moves most effectively in the perfect time required for the task. God has chosen the speed with which to bring about full recovery for each of us. Let him decide the swiftness or the slowness of healing. He is not unaware of your desire to be healed quickly. But just remember that the wall of your addiction was built brick by brick, not in a day. The tearing down of the wall must also be brick by patient brick.

† *Father, you know how often I have wished for a speedy recovery. But faith in you requires patience from me. Many are the people in the Bible who waited until the fullness of time to see their complete victory. As I wait, may I wait in faith and trust, never wavering, never questioning your timetable. May my patience be a reflection of my trust in you.*

Wait for the Lord. Behave yourself manfully, and be of good courage. Do not be faithless, but stay in your place and do not turn back.

THOMAS À KEMPIS (1380–1471)

You can find today's Scripture passage on page 1625 of *The Life Recovery Bible*.

Healing Happens Best in Community

Whoever isolates himself seeks his own desire;
he breaks out against all sound judgment.

PROVERBS 18:1, ESV

GOD GAVE US THE CHURCH TO FELLOWSHIP together in the worship of our Lord and as an encouragement to each other. It's no wonder that so many effective recovery ministries and organizations promote meeting together regularly and developing relationships with others who know our history. *Healing happens best in community*. Sadly, the opposite is also true: Isolation breeds more misery and brings healing to a halt. Be part of a community of those being healed. It will strengthen you, and you will have a role in strengthening others.

✝ *God, thank you for the church, literally your "called out" ones according to the Greek text. You desire for each of us to be planted in a fellowship of other redeemed sinners who have overcome or are overcoming as many problems as there are people. When I begin to isolate, Lord, call me out of my aloneness and into greater intimacy with others. Teach me how to do this, Lord.*

Aloneness can lead to loneliness. God's preventative for loneliness is intimacy—meaningful, open, sharing relationships with one another. In Christ we have the capacity for the fulfilling sense of belonging which comes from intimate fellowship with God and with other believers.

NEIL T. ANDERSON (1942–)

You can find today's Scripture passage on page 806 of *The Life Recovery Bible*.

Recovery Is God's Will

We are confident that he hears us whenever we ask for anything that pleases him. And since we know he hears us when we make our requests, we also know that he will give us what we ask for.

1 JOHN 5:14-15

IT SHOULD BE OBVIOUS THAT IT IS GOD'S WILL for us to be set free from our addiction. According to the apostle John, this brings us great confidence as we make prayer a major part of our recovery. We know God surely hears us, and knowing his will in the matter, we can be confident of his affirming answer. Pray with assurance today, knowing his will is for your continued recovery.

✝ *God, sometimes my prayers for healing have been embarrassingly meager. I underestimate your power to change, your power to open my eyes to the reality of the free, unadulterated life without addiction. Lord, I pray today with assurance that you are fully for my recovery and fully able to bring about every aspect of my freedom. I'm asking large, Lord. Please answer large!*

Our God has boundless resources. The only limit is in us. Our asking, our thinking, our praying are too small. Our expectations are too limited.

A. B. SIMPSON (1843–1919)

You can find today's Scripture passage on page 1634 of *The Life Recovery Bible.*

The Giver of Spiritual Life

Humans can reproduce only human life, but
the Holy Spirit gives birth to spiritual life.

JOHN 3:6

THE TRUTH IS THAT ETERNAL VALUES AND God himself cannot be accessed through our flesh. It's just not possible. Our fleshly body, with all its senses, is useful in navigating this world, but it can't get us through spiritual battles—and addiction, at its root, is a spiritual battle. Through the Holy Spirit, we can become strong spiritually and battle successfully, overcoming the whimpering of the flesh, including its demand for satisfying our addiction.

Today, strengthen your spirit by taking in God's Word, by earnest prayer, and by fellowship with other strong-in-the-Spirit Christians.

† *Lord, my spirit is growing stronger every day as I walk out by faith the victory you provide for my addiction. The flesh still wants pampering, but its voice is becoming softer and softer as I put down strong spiritual roots. Father, continue the work in me that urges me forward from strength to strength and victory to victory.*

> The pampering of the flesh is the quenching of God's Spirit. The flesh chokes and stifles holy motions—the flesh sides with Satan. There is a party within us, which will not pray, which will not believe. The flesh inclines us more to believe a temptation than a promise. The flesh is so near to us, its counsels are more attractive. There is no chain of adamant which binds so tightly as the chain of lust.
>
> THOMAS WATSON (1620–1686)

You can find today's Scripture passage on page 1344 of *The Life Recovery Bible*.

Denial

We are instructed to turn from godless living and sinful pleasures. We should live in this evil world with wisdom, righteousness, and devotion to God, while we look forward with hope to that wonderful day when the glory of our great God and Savior, Jesus Christ, will be revealed.

TITUS 2:12-13

EARLY ON IN OUR RECOVERY, we may go through a phase of denial. We may say to ourselves or to others that we can handle our addiction. "I don't need outside help," we claim—when, in fact, that's exactly what we need. A huge early (and ongoing) step in recovery is getting past denial by admitting our helplessness and our need for God's intervention. We must learn to turn from our addiction and embrace "wisdom, righteousness, and devotion to God." All of which are polar opposites of denial. And if tomorrow we find ourselves back in denial, we must deal with it firmly again. The only type of denial that serves a purpose in recovery is self-denial—living for others.

† *Father, you know the truth about my temptations. You know when I stumble, and you know when I succeed. Lord, help me always see my situation as you see it—clear and transparently, with no room for denial. No room for lies to myself or to others. May I always be honest in my assessment of my ongoing recovery. Remind me that denial is a roadblock to recovery and honesty is an express lane to full sobriety.*

The astonishing paradox of Christ's teaching and of Christian experience is this: if we lose ourselves in following Christ, we actually find ourselves. True self-denial is self-discovery. To live for ourselves is insanity and suicide; to live for God and for man is wisdom and life indeed. We do not begin to find ourselves until we have become willing to lose ourselves in the service of Christ and of our fellows.

JOHN STOTT (1921–2011)

You can find today's Scripture passage on page 1570 of *The Life Recovery Bible.*

The God Who Completes His Work in Us

I am certain that God, who began the good work within you, will continue his work until it is finally finished on the day when Christ Jesus returns.

PHILIPPIANS 1:6

GOD ALWAYS COMPLETES WHAT HE STARTS. He has started a work of recovery in us and will not fail to see it to completion. Through hard times, good times, setbacks, and advances, we make our way down the recovery road. There are no off-ramps, no detours, no U-turns, or shortcuts on this road. It is God's road, and he will see that you arrive at the destination of full recovery.

✝ *God, I've seen others who started the recovery journey only to eventually turn back to their preferred poison of addiction. Some were even far down the road and threw it all away. Father, I won't have that happen to me. I'm trusting you not for a partial work but for a total work of freedom. You began a good work in me, and you will bring it to completion. I will not turn back.*

Behold therefore thy God at work, and promise thyself that what he is about, will be an excellent piece.

WILLIAM GURNALL (1617–1679)

You can find today's Scripture passage on page 1520 of *The Life Recovery Bible*.

JUNE 21

Rivers of Living Water

On the last day, the climax of the festival, Jesus stood and shouted to the crowds, "Anyone who is thirsty may come to me! Anyone who believes in me may come and drink! For the Scriptures declare, 'Rivers of living water will flow from his heart.'" (When he said "living water," he was speaking of the Spirit, who would be given to everyone believing in him. But the Spirit had not yet been given, because Jesus had not yet entered into his glory.)

JOHN 7:37-39

THE CHRISTIAN LIFE IS *SO* GOOD; we don't want to allow anything in our lives that will mess it up. While we once thirsted after our addictive substance or behavior of choice, we have now accepted Christ's invitation to come to him.

The living waters he promises are far more rewarding than the stagnant water of addiction. Christ spoke of the Holy Spirit as the one who would dispense the rivers of living water. We need only ask and believe in order to receive, even if the waters begin as only a stream, ever increasing as we rely on him day by day.

✝ ***Father, while I once craved the object of my addiction, now I crave the living waters of the Holy Spirit. I crave the joy, wholeness, and the sheer satisfaction of a life free from slavery. Bring forth the flow, Lord. I'm so ready, for without your living water, there is no life in me.***

If a spring has not been opened in a soul, a spring of living water from God's own Son, no waters can flow and there is no life in you.

G. V. WIGRAM (1805–1879)

You can find today's Scripture passage on page 1352 of *The Life Recovery Bible.*

Hesed

Give thanks to the Lord, for he is good!
His faithful love endures forever.
Cry out, "Save us, O God of our salvation!
Gather and rescue us from among the nations,
so we can thank your holy name
and rejoice and praise you."
Praise the Lord, the God of Israel,
who lives from everlasting to everlasting!

1 CHRONICLES 16:34-36

THE HEBREW WORD *HESED* OCCURS SEVERAL times in the Old Testament and is always a reference to God's loyalty. In the passage above, the word *faithful* is the English translation of *hesed*. We have a God who is good to us (always!) and whose *hesed* toward us lasts forever. Oh, let us give thanks to our *hesed* Lord![1]

† *Lord, I love the word* hesed. *You are so very loyal to anyone addicted who wants to be free, including me. Father, I lean hard into your loyalty to me. I treasure that attribute of your being. In turn, may I always be* hesed *to you.*

> All God's giants have been weak men and women who have gotten hold of God's faithfulness.
>
> HUDSON TAYLOR (1832–1905)

---

[1] For further reading, you'll enjoy Michael Card's excellent book, *Inexpressible: Hesed and the Mystery of God's Lovingkindness*.

You can find today's Scripture passage on page 525 of *The Life Recovery Bible*.

God Is in the Small Things Too

The very hairs on your head are all numbered. So don't be afraid; you are more valuable to God than a whole flock of sparrows.

LUKE 12:7

ADDICTION IS SUCH A BIG THING, we may forget that God is intricately involved in the very small things of our lives, some of which may contribute to addiction . . . or contribute to recovery. Look for God in every aspect of life. He is there attending to both small *and* large. How then can we doubt him? How then can we not trust the keeper of our souls?

† *God, sometimes I forget to see you in every aspect of my life, especially the small things that might seem insignificant. But to you, there is nothing in my life that's insignificant. All is important. Even the very hairs on my head. Lord, I cannot doubt such deep guardianship of my life. All is entrusted to you.*

> Bring God into everything. The very least anxiety that weighs upon you—you may roll upon Him. He will not despise it. The very least ache or pain of mind or body is a part of His loving discipline—and will do its work the better if brought to Him. The heaving of a sigh, the dropping of a tear, the unuttered desire and longing of the heart—He marks and considers.
>
> GEORGE EVERARD (1828–1901)

You can find today's Scripture passage on page 1312 of *The Life Recovery Bible.*

The Kudzu of Addiction

Everyone has sinned; we all fall short
of God's glorious standard.

ROMANS 3:23

KUDZU IS A WILD PLANT THAT, though now in the United States, was native to Asia. It has a reputation of being a wild and fast-growing weed that chokes out whatever lies in its path. In that way, it's sort of like addiction. Addiction spreads quickly and leaves a mean path wherever it grows. Controlling kudzu requires always dealing with it quickly and firmly—again like our addiction or any sin that's trying to overtake us.

Inspect your life for any wild kudzu springing up. Deal with it now before it takes hold of you, choking your inner life.

† *Father, please inspect the garden that is my life. Remove any weed that, though small now, would entangle everything in its path. Keep the seeds of kudzu far from me. Tend well to the garden of my life with care. Bring forth a healthy harvest of spiritual nutrition.*

As in a plot of ground which lies untilled, among the great variety of weeds, there is usually some master-weed, which is more plenteous and more repulsive than all the rest. So it is also in the souls of men—though there be a general mixture and medley of all evil and corrupt qualities; yet there is some one sin which is usually paramount, which is most powerful and prevalent—which sways and manifests itself more eminently and evidently than any other of them do.

THOMAS BROOKS (1608–1680)

You can find today's Scripture passage on page 1435 of *The Life Recovery Bible.*

Taste and See!

Taste and see that the LORD is good.
Oh, the joys of those who take refuge in him!

PSALM 34:8

IF WE WOULD BE BLESSED, IF WE WOULD BE FREE, if we would have joy in our lives, we must taste and see that the Lord is good! What an invitation to the recovering addict! What a blessing we have by taking refuge in him. As we grow in our relationship with Christ, we find the sweet taste of our Lord takes away the bitter taste of our addiction. This invitation is, of course, renewable, day by day. Today and every day, taste the Lord. Savor him!

✝ *Father, we who have tasted of addiction know that, at first, the taste is pleasant, pulling us back for another taste . . . and then another . . . until we are captured by the poisonous taste that so quickly turns sour. But you, Lord, invite me to taste of you and see that you are good. Not just momentarily good, but every taste with you is only better than the one before. Father, I do taste again today and see that you are good indeed. I am blessed!*

> He only designs to wean you from all others—that you may be satisfied and filled with Himself! He wishes to be your portion, your comfort, and your all. He desires that you should make a God of Him. He is ready to save you, able to deliver you, willing to bless you.
>
> JAMES SMITH (1802–1862)

You can find today's Scripture passage on page 702 of *The Life Recovery Bible*.

Unshakable

I know the LORD is always with me.
I will not be shaken, for he is right beside me.

PSALM 16:8

OUR PAST IS EVIDENCE OF JUST HOW SHAKABLE we've been. We were shaken to the core by our addictions until we lost hope of regaining our stability. But, thank God, there is a cure for those of us who have been shaken. By setting the Lord always before us—by acknowledging him at our right hand, by knowing he is always with us—we become unshakable. God's presence ensures our stability in a world shaken by addiction. Gaze on the Lord. Set him always before you. You shall not be shaken.

✝ *Father God, you promise that, as I acknowledge your presence is always with me, I shall not be shaken. With you beside me, I can withstand trials, wavering emotions, recurring temptations—and all else that would threaten my sobriety. Lord, as a mighty tree sends down roots that keep it unshakable in storms, so, too, do I send down spiritual roots that will withstand the fiercest storms. I am unshakable.*

> However far you have gone from God and however stiff may be the tempest that blows about you, if you get this promise under your feet all the storms that hell can let loose against a human soul will leave you unshaken. But you must keep a firm stand on the promise.
>
> CLOVIS G. CHAPPELL (1882–1972)

You can find today's Scripture passage on page 688 of *The Life Recovery Bible*.

Wonderfully Complex

You made all the delicate, inner parts of my body
and knit me together in my mother's womb.
Thank you for making me so wonderfully complex!
Your workmanship is marvelous—how well I know it.

PSALM 139:13-14

THOUGH OUR BODY MAY NOW BE WORSE FOR the wear, it was not created that way. God was there when we were conceived. He knit us together in our mother's womb. He formed our inner parts. Truly, we were created wonderfully complex, and for that we praise our Creator. We can easily believe that he so cared for us in creation, that he now cares for us daily in our recovery: body, soul, and spirit.

† *Father, the intricacy with which you made me speaks of your attention to the details that form me. Even now, you are aware of every aspect of my being. Your creative power is on display daily in my body. Lord, may your divine skill continue to bring healing to the innermost being of both my soul and my body.*

> God's thorough knowledge of us and all our ways is patent from His creative power. Before we breathed, His will arranged our incipient being. What mechanism can be more exquisite in all its parts than the formation of our bodies! Divine skill is manifested in the design of its innumerable members. Wonder is exhausted in the contemplation. Select any part, it proclaims that infinite wisdom devised the plan, and infinite power brought it to perfection. Can this great Creator not have most intimate acquaintance with the beings which He thus formed?
>
> **HENRY LAW (1797–1884)**

You can find today's Scripture passage on page 775 of *The Life Recovery Bible*.

Transformation

Don't copy the behavior and customs of this world, but let God transform you into a new person by changing the way you think. Then you will learn to know God's will for you, which is good and pleasing and perfect.

ROMANS 12:2

WHAT DOES IT MEAN TO BE CONFORMED TO this world? It means we allow the current culture to define our lives. We devour movies, television, books, and other aspects of culture to so wire our brains as to accept as true what the culture deems is true.

To be transformed by the renewal of our minds is to allow our brains to be rewired by God's Spirit. It means to avoid compromise with the dangers that would take us under—just as our addiction once did. As people in recovery, we must discern the good and pleasing will of God—and transformation of our minds is the only way that can happen. Watch for misguided opportunities to be conformed to this world. When those opportunities conflict with God's will, refuse them and choose God's will instead.

✝ *Lord, I'm daily besieged with this present world and its value judgments. Even my addiction was from this world. In recovery, you are transforming me, essentially rewiring my brain day by day. Help me avoid the deceptive values of this world in its attempts to keep me wired to it and to addictive substances and practices. Remind me of all the joy and happiness to be found only in your Kingdom and only accessible to me as I choose your ways over my own natural inclinations.*

We must not conform to the spirit of the world. As believers, we are strangers and pilgrims upon earth. Heaven is our country, and the Lord is our King. We are to be known and noticed as His subjects; and therefore it is His desire, that we do not adopt the sinful customs of the land in which we sojourn.

JOHN NEWTON (1725–1807)

You can find today's Scripture passage on page 1447 of *The Life Recovery Bible.*

The Fear of Death

Even though I walk through the valley of the shadow of death,
I will fear no evil,
for you are with me; your rod and your staff,
they comfort me.

PSALM 23:4, ESV

DEATH LURKS SILENTLY BEHIND THE SCENES in every addict's life. It stalks us as prey. We have witnessed this in the loss of friends or loved ones who never made the escape from death's trap. For we who are believers in Christ, death is not a stalker, nor do we fear it. God has intervened in our lives and will call us home in his good time. We no longer need to fear a shortened life. We have traded death's scythe for God's rod and staff.

† *God, death pursued me through my addiction. And yet you allowed me to outrun that fierce enemy. Now I know that not only my life but my eventual death is in your hands. While I yet live, may I live in Christ. I shall then fear no evil. Your rod and staff comfort me.*

Live in Christ, live in Christ, and the flesh need not fear death.

JOHN KNOX (1514–1572)

You can find today's Scripture passage on page 694 of *The Life Recovery Bible.*

The Majesty of God

The gods of other nations are mere idols,
but the LORD made the heavens!
Honor and majesty surround him;
strength and joy fill his dwelling.
O nations of the world, recognize the LORD,
recognize that the LORD is glorious and strong.

1 CHRONICLES 16:26-28

DURING THIS EARTHLY LIFE, we do not see God with our physical eyes. What we know of God is through his Word and is received by faith. We know of his splendor and majesty. We know of his power and his love. And because of who God is, we can fully trust him. We can also draw our own strength and joy from him. Like the sun gives off light to all who see it above, so, too, does God give light to those who look to him.

✝ *Father, just a glimpse of your majesty causes me to bow down in worship. You are the God of glory and strength. Your power is beyond my comprehension. You love is endless. Your desire for me as your child is astonishing. You give light to all who seek you. Your delivering power from addiction is freeing. How then can I not worship your majesty?*

Happy the soul that has been awed by a view of God's majesty.

A. W. PINK (1886–1952)

You can find today's Scripture passage on page 525 of *The Life Recovery Bible.*

We Are His Children

See how very much our Father loves us,
for he calls us his children, and that is what we are!

1 JOHN 3:1

IT WOULD BE RARE FOR A PERSON DEEPLY rooted in the love of God to begin and then continue in addiction. Why? Because the love of God fills all the nooks and crannies that we thought our addiction would fill. If we have not fully grasped the magnitude of this love, we still have time to do so now. Ask God to reveal through his Word, through your prayers, or through another person the kind of love he has for us that allows us to be called children of God. That single revelation of our Father-child relationship will hasten our recovery. And, as all children grow into maturity, so shall we, free from all addiction.

✝ ***Lord, your love is the great healer of all ailments, especially those of the soul. Father, all those things I longed for sent me searching in all the wrong places for what can only be found in a true relationship with you. Thank you that you have called me your child.***

> The single desire that dominated my search for delight was simply to love and to be loved.
>
> SAINT AUGUSTINE OF HIPPO (354–430)

You can find today's Scripture passage on page 1631 of *The Life Recovery Bible*.

God Intends It for Good

[Joseph said,] "You intended to harm me, but God intended it all for good. He brought me to this position so I could save the lives of many people."

GENESIS 50:20

IT'S AMAZING HOW GOD IS ABLE TO TAKE WHAT is meant for our harm and turn it into something good. In the case of Joseph in Egypt, all the evil that befell him worked for the eventual good of him, his family—and even all of Egypt. Though he was innocent, he suffered unjustly—but God had a purpose in mind, even when it was not discernible to Joseph. Addiction means to harm us, but is there a way it can be redeemed and turned into good? That's left up to God, but Joseph would tell us, yes, it can happen in our lives too. Just trust God, and see what happens.

† *Father, I don't think Joseph had any idea that you could intend what happened to him in slavery and in prison for good, but you did. I, too, have been in slavery and in a prison of addiction. As I recover, I pray for a good end for this hell I've gone through. Lord, make it all turn out with the best resolution possible.*

God will turn all evils to our good. He will make a healing potion, from poison. Joseph's imprisonment was a means for his advancement. Out of the bitterest drug—he will distill his glory and our salvation. In short, he will be our guide to death, our comfort in death, and our reward after death.

THOMAS WATSON (1620–1686)

You can find today's Scripture passage on page 73 of *The Life Recovery Bible*.

Longing

We are looking forward to the new heavens and new earth he has promised, a world filled with God's righteousness. And so, dear friends, while you are waiting for these things to happen, make every effort to be found living peaceful lives that are pure and blameless in his sight.

2 PETER 3:13-14

ADDICTION HAD BECOME FOR US A FORM of longing. When sober for a time, we would once again yearn for our comforting "friend." Now, as we recover, we may become aware of just how full this present world is of vices meant to entrap us by appealing to our sense of longing. If we have an addictive personality, we may even stop one habit and pick up another. A cure for this longing is to replace it with the deep desire for the presence of God and, eventually, heaven, where we will find the ultimate security and safety from the ills of this fallen world. Heaven is not here on this earth. It's there—and it awaits us.

† *Lord, I have to believe you created longing in our hearts. It's not wrong to yearn for fullness and satisfaction. But when a legitimate need is known, it seems the enemy has a counterfeit offer to meet the need. Father, keep me longing, but keep me longing for the right things. Fill me, Lord, so I won't be drawn away by Satan's fool's gold.*

Heaven is not here, it's There. If we were given all we wanted here, our hearts would settle for this world rather than the next. God is forever luring us up and away from this one, wooing us to Himself and His still invisible Kingdom, where we will certainly find what we so keenly long for.

ELISABETH ELLIOT (1926–2015)

You can find today's Scripture passage on page 1625 of *The Life Recovery Bible*.

Declaration of Dependence

The Lord himself watches over you!
The Lord stands beside you as your protective shade.
The sun will not harm you by day,
nor the moon at night.
The Lord keeps you from all harm
and watches over your life.
The Lord keeps watch over you as you come and go,
both now and forever.

PSALM 121:5-8

DEPENDENCY, CODEPENDENCY, ENABLING, and self-medicating are all bricks in the wall separating us from our true life in Christ. But on the Fourth of July, we should celebrate not only our nation's independence but also our own independence from our addiction, having replaced it with dependence on God who is our Keeper, our protective shade. He will keep us from evil. He will protect our going out and coming in, both now and forever.

† *Father, I was dependent on my addiction for so long that ending it has been painful. My relationship with you is rightly transferring my dependence from my addiction to you. I know you accept me and welcome me as your dependent child. I find safety in your care. Lord, keep watch over me, both now and forever.*

My Christian friend, we shall need keeping in the future; never let us forget this. Let us make sure that the Lord is our keeper. Let us daily seek his keeping; never going out into the world—until we have put ourselves into his hand, by a solemn act of faith and prayer. Never let us, for one moment, trust to our own vigilance, power, or sagacity; for if we do, we shall certainly fall. Self-dependence always procures a fall.

JAMES SMITH (1802–1862)

You can find today's Scripture passage on page 769 of *The Life Recovery Bible*.

Time, God's Gift

My future is in your hands.
Rescue me from those who hunt me down relentlessly.

PSALM 31:15

TIME IS A PRECIOUS GIFT OF GOD. We've been robbed of this gift all through our days of addiction. But now, in recovery, we place our time firmly in God's hands. We allow him to rescue us from our addiction and to redeem the time we have left on this earth. May he bring healing to give us extra years, certainly far beyond the shortened lives we would have had if we had remained in our addiction. The time ahead is indeed a gift. Make sure it is in God's hands.

† *Father, help me forget the time I've lost in addiction. I know I have no way to bring it back. You can, however, be Lord of my future. You can help me make the time useful to myself and to you. Lord, I ask you for a healing that enables me to be more productive in the years ahead.*

> There is just enough time for you to live your life well if you spend every moment of it in earnest, faithful duty. A life thus lived in unbroken diligence and faithfulness, will have no regrets when the end comes. Its work will be completed.
>
> J. R. MILLER (1840–1912)

You can find today's Scripture passage on page 699 of *The Life Recovery Bible*.

God Uses Flawed People

It was by faith that Rahab the prostitute was not destroyed
with the people in her city who refused to obey God.
For she had given a friendly welcome to the spies.

HEBREWS 11:31

GOD USES FLAWED PEOPLE WHO BELIEVE HIM. These people believe their present weaknesses and past failures can be overcome, even used to their advantage. Rahab didn't consider her past or even her present. She simply allowed God to use her. She had *faith* in the God of flawed people.

We must not limit what God can do through our flawed lives, our many weaknesses, our often-minimal faith, or regardless of our many shortcomings. Instead, we must see past all those and focus on God who *chooses* to display his strength through our individual human weaknesses. The greater our weaknesses, the greater the opportunity for God's strength to be on display. Just ask the flawed people of the Bible: Abraham, Jacob, Rahab, David, Peter, Mary Magdalene, and Thomas, to name a few.

✝ ***Lord, I am so very flawed. But I won't let that stop me from pursuing you or your will for my life. Just as Rahab looked past her flaws and by faith became one of the Bible's heroines, so do I reckon my flaws as not fatal but redeemable. Father, increase my faith so that, like Rahab and others in the Bible, I will make the right choices, even when they're not the popular choices.***

When we take the history of a child of God, compressed within the short period of a single day—mark what flaws, what imperfections, what fickleness, what dereliction in principle, what flaws in practice, what errors in judgment and what wanderings of heart make up that brief history—how we are led to thank God for the stability of the covenant, . . . which provides for the full redemption of all believers, which from eternity secures the effectual calling, the perfect keeping and certain salvation of every chosen vessel of mercy!

OCTAVIUS WINSLOW (1808–1878)

You can find today's Scripture passage on page 1592 of *The Life Recovery Bible.*

Stick to the Fundamentals

Seek the Kingdom of God above all else, and live righteously,
and he will give you everything you need.

MATTHEW 6:33

THE FOOTBALL GAME WAS LOST. The weary team entered the locker room with their heads hanging. The coach gathered the players around and asked the obvious question: "Why did we lose this game? A game we should have won." When no one answered, the coach said, "We lost because we didn't stick to the fundamentals." It was that simple.

That's likely the reason some of us fail or have setbacks in our recovery. We don't stick to the fundamentals of recovery: grounding our lives in the Word of God, finding fellowship in a strong church, and becoming answerable to another person or accountability group. In addition to those fundamentals, we need to focus on telling ourselves and others the truth about our dependence, learning to say no to our temptations, and removing ourselves from an enabling environment.

Stick with what works. Stick with the fundamentals of recovery, seeking first God's Kingdom and his righteousness.

† ***Father, I know the fundamentals of following you, and I infuse them into my life. I practice them over and over, even when I think I know them well enough to lighten up. Lord, I want to win the game; therefore, I will stick with what I know works: the fundamentals.***

> The [Christian] who seeks first God's kingdom shall never lack anything that is for his good. He may not have so much health as some. He may not have so much wealth as others. He may not have a richly spread table, or royal dainties. But he shall always have enough.
>
> **J. C. RYLE (1816–1900)**

You can find today's Scripture passage on page 1206 of *The Life Recovery Bible*.

Self-Forgiveness

Immediately the rooster crowed. Suddenly, Jesus' words flashed through Peter's mind: "Before the rooster crows, you will deny three times that you even know me." And he went away, weeping bitterly.

MATTHEW 26:74-75

ONE OF THE VILEST OBSTACLES FOR US TO overcome is forgiving ourselves for our addiction. The guilt can be overwhelming as we ask ourselves over and over, *Why did I allow this to happen?*

For an answer, we have the apostle Peter and his betrayal of the Lord—something he had vowed he'd never do. And yet, after Peter betrayed the Lord and found forgiveness, God used him greatly, commissioning him to "feed my lambs" (John 21:15).

Few people have been used as mightily as this great denier of Christ. But for that to happen, Peter had to confront his failure and come to a place of self-forgiveness. And so must we. Enough crying over what we've lost. We have much to gain in our sober future. We must never let unresolved guilt erode our confidence that God has forgiven us and, like Peter, will use us for his Kingdom.

✝ ***Father, like Peter, I have wept bitterly over the wrong decisions that have taken me far away from the life you've called me to. But also like Peter, after I sorrow about my past, I then forgive myself—just as you've forgiven me—and I move on to be used in whatever way you choose for me. Lord, may I often be reminded of Peter's story—and my story of restoration.***

Peter, who wept so bitterly for denying Christ, never denied him again, but confessed him often in the face of danger. True repentance for any sin will be shown by the contrary grace and duty; that is a sign of our sorrowing not only bitterly, but sincerely.

MATTHEW HENRY (1662–1714)

You can find today's Scripture passage on page 1240 of *The Life Recovery Bible*.

The Humility of Addiction

Humble yourselves before the Lord,
and he will lift you up in honor.
JAMES 4:10

WHEN WE FINALLY CAME TO A PLACE OF admitting our addiction, it was most likely humbling. To admit how weak we are assaults our very personhood. But we know that humbling ourselves in the light of addiction actually aids our recovery. The Christian life is, after all, a life not of pride but of humility.

If you have been embarrassed by your weakness, the reluctant humbling of yourself, take heart. You've taken a huge step in your recovery. Never despise humility in yourself or others. Humility and meekness were aspects of Christ's character while here on earth. He would have us follow in his steps. And for one who follows Christ, the way up is down.

✝ ***Lord, I'm humbled by my past failures to overcome addiction on my own. Thank you that, in humbling myself, I'm able to appreciate the humbling of Jesus at the hands of angry sinners . . . like me. I praise you that humbling is an act of growth and maturity. I'm growing in my faith, Lord, as I'm willing to be humbled.***

I used to think that God's gifts were on shelves one above the other; and that the taller we grew in Christian character the easier we could reach them. I now find that God's gifts are on shelves one beneath the other; and it is not a question of growing taller but of stooping lower; that we have to go down, always down, to get His best gifts.

F. B. MEYER (1847–1929)

You can find today's Scripture passage on page 1605 of *The Life Recovery Bible*.

Great Expectations

All praise to God, the Father of our Lord Jesus Christ. It is by his great mercy that we have been born again, because God raised Jesus Christ from the dead. Now we live with great expectation.

1 PETER 1:3

THE TRUEST THING ABOUT US TODAY IS THAT we are each a new person, full of light—God's light—having been born again to live with great expectation of the future. This happened according to his "great mercy."

It has been wisely said that grace is giving us what we *don't* deserve while mercy is not giving us what we *do* deserve. Consider now how merciful God has been with us. And then consider that his great mercy never ends. It's always there, always available—and always necessary.

† *God, without your grace and mercy, I'm done for. And yet there* is *grace and mercy for me. It is my privilege as your child to enjoy the fullness of your gifts. I have now all the mercy you have to give. I need it now, and I will need it every day. Thank you for your overflowing mercy.*

Our mind cannot find a comparison too large for expressing the superabundant mercy of the Lord toward his people.

DAVID DICKSON (1583–1663)

You can find today's Scripture passage on page 1610 of *The Life Recovery Bible.*

Building for the Bright Future

Wisdom is sweet to your soul.
If you find it, you will have a bright future,
and your hopes will not be cut short.

PROVERBS 24:14

TIMEWISE, THERE ARE TWO PARTS TO RECOVERY. Dealing with the past and building a new post-addiction future.

Many of us spend a lot of time regretting our past and trying to cut off that era of our lives. We spend too little time planning and building and praying about our future without addiction. Some who relapse do so because their addiction is their default behavior without a vision for the future—even if it's only tomorrow's future.

Take time to write down goals. Don't list too many, because that's a recipe for defeat. Then write down some doable steps you can begin to take to reach those goals. Bring your accountability partner or a loved one into your plans—as long as you know this person will be supportive (no naysayers allowed). Ask God to give you the strength to reach your goal. Pray for open doors and new relationships that will help get you farther down the road. Think positively about the future. Think less about the past.

✝ ***Father, there were times when I didn't think I had much of a future. My addiction seemed to control my life. Now, though, I know you're working out a God-designed future that will satisfy me and be useful to you. In the time of rough seas ahead, help me to remember that when the storm is past, the seas will calm. Until then, I am safe.***

Nothing but Christian faith gives to the furthest future the solidity and definiteness which it must have if it is to be a breakwater for us against the fluctuating sea of present cares and thoughts.

ALEXANDER MACLAREN (1826–1910)

You can find today's Scripture passage on page 812 of *The Life Recovery Bible.*

Consider Jesus

Since he himself has gone through suffering and testing,
he is able to help us when we are being tested.

HEBREWS 2:18

IF WE THINK RECOVERY MEANS AN END to temptation, we're setting ourselves up for failure. What, then, is our response to ongoing temptations? Consider Jesus. He knew temptation and *suffered*, just as we do. But in so doing, he understands our severe temptations and is able to help us. After he had passed through the temptations to appease his hunger, to cast himself down from the pinnacle of the temple, and to bow down to Satan, we're told that "the devil went away, and angels came and took care of Jesus" (Matthew 4:11). It's interesting to note that in every temptation, Jesus quoted God's Word back to Satan. The end result was that Satan went away and angels ministered to Jesus. We, too, can overcome temptation and see the enemy flee when we meet our temptations with the Word of God.

† *God, I know temptation will be part of my life until I die. But that's okay. Everyone is tempted. The secret is that you will also be part of my life, even past death. When I'm tempted to think you don't know the pull of temptation, remind me of the suffering and testing of Jesus who endured temptations far more persuasive than mine. Lord Jesus, you are qualified to help when I'm tested and to bring me through. You do understand after all.*

> We must expect to be tempted by [Satan] in some degree or another, all of our lives, because this life is a continual warfare. We must never expect to have rest from our spiritual adversary the devil, or to say, our combat with him is finished. Our fight with the evil one will continue until we bow our heads and our spirit is removed from our body and is brought into the presence of our dear precious Savior Jesus Christ!
>
> GEORGE WHITEFIELD (1714–1770)

You can find today's Scripture passage on page 1580 of *The Life Recovery Bible*.

Resist Evil in Its Many Forms

Let love be genuine. Abhor what is evil;
hold fast to what is good.

ROMANS 12:9, ESV

A HEALTHY ABHORRENCE OF OUR ADDICTION aids us in tearing down the brick wall separating us from the man or woman God plans for us to be. We abhor not just the addiction, but we especially abhor what it does to us and to our friends. There are only a few things in life we are called to abhor, but for us, addiction is at the top of the list.

In contrast, we're to hold tightly to that which is good. In our case, we hold fast to sobriety. We hold fast to abstinence. We hold fast to all aspects of recovery. Most of all, we hold fast to Christ.

† *Lord, I abhor all evil, especially evil in the form of addiction. I hold fast to all the good I see. I hold fast to sobriety, recovery, encouraging others, giving instead of taking, and most of all, I hold fast to you. Father, hold fast to me.*

Resist with the utmost abhorrence anything that causes you to doubt God's love and his lovingkindness toward you. Allow nothing to make you question the Father's love for his child.

A. W. PINK (1886–1952)

You can find today's Scripture passage on page 1448 of *The Life Recovery Bible.*

The Knowledge of God Changes Us

This is the way to have eternal life—to know you, the only true God, and Jesus Christ, the one you sent to earth.

JOHN 17:3

WHEN WE RELAPSE OR EXPERIENCE FAILURE in some aspect of our recovery, we may want to consider what we think about God. Too often, we recall our early childhood images of God as an old man with a white beard spoiling all our fun, keeping track of our every wrong move. When we start to see God for who he is and begin to experience his love, we find change easier.

So who is God if not the old man with the white beard? God is best seen in his incarnation of Jesus Christ. If we see Jesus by studying his life in the Gospels, we see God. And so, in Jesus, we see God as Healer, Deliverer, Redeemer, Lover of sinners, Forgiver, Warner, Promise Keeper, and, ultimately, King of kings, Lord of lords, Alpha and Omega. When we see God in Christ, we get a glimpse of the kind of power that changes us.

† *Lord, knowing you is life changing. You are my Healer, Restorer, and Recovery Captain. In Jesus I see the traits that identify him as your Son. I see you in Christ, and I long for Christ to be seen in me. I pray you will bring to mind other aspects of who you are in my life. May I keep learning of you by studying your Word and living the life of sobriety you've called me to.*

One encounter with Jesus Christ is enough to change you, instantly, forever.

LUIS PALAU (1934–2021)

You can find today's Scripture passage on page 1368 of *The Life Recovery Bible*.

The Cumulative Effect of Sin

The wages of sin is death, but the free gift of God
is eternal life through Christ Jesus our Lord.

ROMANS 6:23

WE MAY LIVE AN ADDICTED LIFE AND REAP the consequences quickly (for example, if you're addicted to sex, you may contract an STD) or we may reap consequences more slowly (such as suffering financial ruin after years of gambling). Years of addiction will reap a regrettable crop one way or another. But the moment we choose to live God's way, that decision also brings both an immediate and cumulative effect. The immediate effect of coming to Christ is an instant forgiving of all our sins and the assurance of eternal life, starting now. The cumulative effect of sobriety is found in the fruits of right living according to God's Word. These effects can include restored health, renewed relationships, and confidence in our long-term future. Don't give up on what may be cumulative effects just because they're not immediate effects.

† *Father, I know only too well both the immediate and cumulative effects of addiction. I pray that, through my recovery, I'll enjoy the immediate effects of sobriety and be patient as the cumulative effects become apparent. Thank you for every positive change in my life.*

> The covenant of works provided no restoration for the soul that departed from God under the first testament. But the covenant of grace has this distinction, this glorious feature—it places before the penitent backslider, the contrite child, an open door of return, a way of restored pardon, joy, and peace—and bids him enter. The Lord Jesus is this open door.
>
> OCTAVIUS WINSLOW (1808–1878)

You can find today's Scripture passage on page 1439 of *The Life Recovery Bible*.

Union with Christ

Don't you realize that if a man joins himself to a prostitute, he becomes one body with her? For the Scriptures say, "The two are united into one." But the person who is joined to the Lord is one spirit with him. Run from sexual sin! No other sin so clearly affects the body as this one does. For sexual immorality is a sin against your own body.

1 CORINTHIANS 6:16-18

THINK OF IT—HE WHO IS JOINED TO THE LORD becomes one spirit with him! That one biblical truth is enough to bring us the change we need. It demonstrates how close we are to Christ as believers. How much closer can one get than to be "joined" with another? And by being joined to the One who enables us to overcome our addictions, we have a huge advantage in moving through our recovery. Take in the vital truth of your union with Christ. Ponder it, accept it, and allow your union with Christ to be your life's center on your journey toward recovery.

✝ *Father, one of the most healing truths about Christian recovery is that every believer is united to you as "one spirit." From this one truth we draw every supply we need not just for our recovery but for our entire life's needs. I praise you that you have joined me to yourself as part of the body of Christ. May I continue to be strengthened by being united to you.*

Christian, rejoice in your union with Jesus!
The changes of time cannot touch it!
The storms of life cannot injure it!
The sword of persecution cannot sever it!
The damps of death cannot affect it!
The malice of hell cannot move it!

JOHN MACDUFF (1818–1895)

You can find today's Scripture passage on page 1462 of *The Life Recovery Bible.*

The Divine No

Jesus left them a second time and prayed, "My Father! If this cup cannot be taken away unless I drink it, your will be done."

MATTHEW 26:42

JESUS, IN HIS HUMANITY, prayed the cup called crucifixion might pass from him. But in his divinity, he accepted it as that which must be done to accomplish the Father's plan. When God says no to us, we sometimes balk. "But God . . ." we begin before offering up our reasons.

God listens to those prayers, but he still may overrule them with a divine no. When this happens, we need to lean into our faith and say, "Your will be done." For those who have been caught up in addiction, our prayers are many. And no is sometimes the answer we hear. That's when we learn we must trust.

✝ *Lord, like most believers, I want a divine yes to all my prayers. But more than that, I want your will to be done. So I lay down my need for a yes, and I will by faith accept the times I must drink from the cup of acceptance, remembering how Jesus' acceptance of your will accomplished my freedom.*

You may not know why it is that he deals so strangely with you, but oh! never think that he is unfaithful for an instant, or that he has broken his word. Continue still to trust him.

CHARLES SPURGEON (1834–1892)

You can find today's Scripture passage on page 1239 of *The Life Recovery Bible*.

God Is Always for Us

The LORD says, "I will rescue those who love me.
I will protect those who trust in my name."

PSALM 91:14

WE MAY OCCASIONALLY HAVE DOUBTS AS to whether God is really for us in our recovery journey. Yet God's Word is clear on this question. God will rescue and protect those who hold fast to him in love . . . those who trust in his name. Never again doubt that God is entirely *for* you.

✝ ***Father, I know the enemy's desire is for me to return to my addiction. But with you, Lord, in my corner, I willingly stay the course. You really are my only option for I know from bitter experience there'd be nothing for me if I were to return to my former life. Protect me, Father. Keep me holding fast to you in all my ways.***

> Those who rightly know God, will set their love upon him. They by prayer constantly call upon him. His promise is, that he will in due time deliver the believer out of trouble, and in the meantime be with him in trouble.
>
> MATTHEW HENRY (1662–1714)

You can find today's Scripture passage on page 744 of *The Life Recovery Bible.*

God Is Not Tempting Us

Remember, when you are being tempted, do not say, "God is tempting me." God is never tempted to do wrong, and he never tempts anyone else.

JAMES 1:13

GOD'S PURITY AND RIGHTEOUSNESS LEAVE no room for him to be a tempter. Even in the garden of Eden, when Adam and Eve were tempted, it was Satan, not God, involved in the lie that brought about the fall of humanity. Today, it's still true that God's hands are clean when it comes to our temptations to addiction. He did not cause those temptations, and even now, in our recovery, when we experience residual temptations from our past, God is there as a Helper, Healer, and Comforter, never as the source of our temptation.

Never pray, "God, why are you tempting me?" Only pray, "God, use this temptation to strengthen me."

✝ *God, it's freeing to realize that you are not the source of my temptations. You are, however, the source of my resistance to temptation. As I continue in my recovery, I will draw my strength from you but will never assign the blame for my temptations to you.*

To realize God's presence is the one sovereign remedy against temptation.

FRANÇOIS FÉNELON (1651–1715)

You can find today's Scripture passage on page 1601 of *The Life Recovery Bible.*

Remain in Me

If you remain in me and my words remain in you,
you may ask for anything you want, and it will be granted!

JOHN 15:7

THE PROMISE OF GOD TO ANSWER OUR PRAYERS has a condition. That condition is that we remain in him and allow his words to remain in us. Of course, the enemy wants to keep us ignorant of the Word—he certainly doesn't want God's Word to remain in us. But we must always stay with what God has said. No compromise, no letting up on building our future on the solid rock of the Bible. All else—especially addiction—is nothing but sand.

✝ ***God, you have made it plain that your Word is paramount in living successfully and in having my prayers answered. It's your Word that sustains me through the day. It keeps me from temptation and encourages me to stay the course. Father, increase my hunger for the Bible. Rebuild my inner life through an absorption of it. As I do, hear and answer my many prayers, Lord.***

God is a Father to all who love him, and as certainly as the sun rises, he hears them when they pray. Do believe him. Never regard the feeling, the emotions; stagger not at the promise of God through unbelief. You can be strong; you can triumph; you can rise and live above the clouds on the wings of believing prayer. Your prayer has gone up to the throne of God, where it is kept in memorial, and some time, somewhere it will be answered. Be encouraged and pray on, believing. You will find an answer. Be childlike, and God will lead you safely. Do not fear to trust him. Look above the circumstances surrounding, and see the promise and believe it. It will never, never, *never* fail.

CHARLES ORR (1844–1913)

You can find today's Scripture passage on page 1366 of *The Life Recovery Bible*.

Obedience

You were cleansed from your sins when you obeyed the truth, so now you must show sincere love to each other as brothers and sisters. Love each other deeply with all your heart.

1 PETER 1:22

GOD REQUIRES OBEDIENCE FROM EVERY believer. Obeying God isn't difficult. Disobeying and reaping the results—now *that's* difficult. The benefits of obedience will include healing from our addiction, the ability to more fully love others, and a brighter future. Though obedience isn't difficult, it is costly. Jim Elliot was one of five men who obeyed the call to reach the Huaorani people of Ecuador. That obedience cost him his life. Though it's likely God is asking less than physical death from each of us, he *is* asking for an obedience that is total. His commitment to us is total, and so must our commitment to him be total.

What is God asking of you today? Whatever it is, obey, knowing his power to obey is in you.

✝ ***Father, sometimes I find it hard to obey unless I understand why I should. That can only be a lack of trust on my part. Help me trust in you so firmly that I instantly obey whether I understand or not. I do believe that I will see the fruits of my obedience eventually, but if I don't, I still will trust and obey.***

Rest in this: It is His business to lead, command, impel, send, call or whatever you want to call it. It is your business to obey, follow, move, respond, or what have you.

JIM ELLIOT (1927–1956)

You can find today's Scripture passage on page 1612 of *The Life Recovery Bible.*

The Sovereignty of God

Remember the things I have done in the past.
For I alone am God!
I am God, and there is none like me.
Only I can tell you the future
before it even happens.
Everything I plan will come to pass,
for I do whatever I wish.

ISAIAH 46:9-10

IN CONSIDERING GOD'S PRESENCE IN our recovery, we must never overlook his sovereignty. God's counsel *will* stand. He *will* accomplish all his purposes. All that remains of our future is in God's sovereign hands. What he has brought us through so far is but a means to an end filled with blessing.

God does not curse us. He blesses us, and doing so is his sovereign choice and desire. Praise God for his sovereignty. Rely on it as you pray. God hears and God acts. We are blessed to be a praying part of bringing about his perfect will.

† ***Lord, you are sovereign over all, including me. Yet in your sovereignty, you ask me to pray your will be done on earth as it is in heaven. And so I do. Daily, I pray your will, accept your will, and implement what I know to be your will in my life. Thank you for allowing me to be part of accomplishing your sovereign will through my prayers.***

To the one who delights in the sovereignty of God the clouds not only have a "silver lining" but they are silver all through, the darkness only serving to offset the light!

A. W. PINK (1886–1952)

You can find today's Scripture passage on page 900 of *The Life Recovery Bible*.

Sorrow

It was our weaknesses he carried;
it was our sorrows that weighed him down.

ISAIAH 53:4

RECOVERY USUALLY INCLUDES A SEASON of sorrow over lost years, time, relationships, and money. We have lost much through addiction. But even in our sorrow, God has a plan for our recovery. In Christ, we find a Savior who has carried our weaknesses and been weighed down by our sorrows. Why then should we continue to be weighed down by past sorrows?

Have you any sorrows yet undealt with? Surrender them now, lest they continue to be a burden on your recovery. Recovery from addiction must include recovering from your griefs and sorrows.

✝ *Father, I have sorrows that have weighed me down. Some are related to my past addiction; some are related to other aspects of my life and even my failures. I now lay all my griefs and sorrows on Jesus, who bore them for me. I will not take them up again, knowing they are now deposited on my Savior and Burden-Bearer.*

How fast we learn in a day of sorrow! Scripture shines out in a new effulgence; every verse seems to contain a sunbeam, every promise stands out in illuminated splendor; things hard to be understood become in a moment plain.

HORATIUS BONAR (1808–1889)

You can find today's Scripture passage on page 907 of *The Life Recovery Bible.*

He Cares for Us

When I look at the night sky and see the work of your fingers—
the moon and the stars you set in place—
what are mere mortals that you should think about them,
human beings that you should care for them?

PSALM 8:3-4

IS IT NOT A WONDER THAT THE GOD OF all creation is mindful of mere mortals? Mindful of us, despite our many failings? The truth is that God not only is mindful of us to the extent that there is no time—none, zilch, nada—when we're not on his mind, but he also cares for us. He knows our longings, our best hopes, our failures, our sorrows, and he is with us in all of them.

✝ *Lord, I echo the psalmist in asking this question: What are mere mortals like me that you should think about us—and should care for us? Yet you do! I am on your mind all the time. You have arranged a life for me that surpasses the life I would live left to my own devices. Father, when I look at the night sky and see the work of your fingers, may I be reminded that you are mindful of mere mortals, including me.*

Prayer turns ordinary mortals into men of power. It brings power. It brings fire. It brings rain. It brings life. It brings God.

SAMUEL CHADWICK (1840–1932)

You can find today's Scripture passage on page 684 of *The Life Recovery Bible*.

Holiness

You must be holy in everything you do, just as God who chose you is holy. For the Scriptures say, "You must be holy because I am holy."

1 PETER 1:15-16

HOLINESS GETS A BAD RAP. It's too often associated with what we *can't* do. Some interpretations of holy living even border on legalism. The truth is that God's holiness is something we're to embrace and enjoy, not endure or resent.

Know that your holiness originates in God's holiness. His holiness is your holiness. And God cannot be unholy. Neither can you if your holiness is his holiness imputed to you and lived out by you. As we reflect on holiness, we can't help but note how incompatible addiction is with holiness.

† *God, you are holy. All that is about you is holy and righteous. In my natural self, I'm far from holy. I need your imputed holiness in my life to replace all the unholiness in me. I need a holiness that is joy-filled, not one that is manmade and joyless. Do this work in me, Lord. Create a greater degree of hunger for holiness in my life.*

Holiness is not something we are called upon to do in order that we may become something; it is something we are to do because of what we already are.

MARTYN LLOYD-JONES (1899–1981)

You can find today's Scripture passage on page 1611 of *The Life Recovery Bible.*

Our Truest Need

[Jesus said,] "I have loved you even as the Father has loved me. Remain in my love."

JOHN 15:9

WE WERE CREATED TO BE LOVED BY GOD. We must accept the fact that no human on earth can fill the place in us that God means to occupy. Human love, as much as we value it, is but a foretaste of the love God has for each of us. But *only* a foretaste. We err greatly and invite heartache when we consciously or unconsciously expect a person to meet our need for divine love. When that need is not met by a person (for it cannot be), we may seek counterfeit ways of feeling loved and accepted. Human love is only meant to be a shadow of divine love. God's love is vastly more than what we know when we think of human love.

† ***Lord God, I believe that your love—your perfect agape, divine love—is the great healer of all maladies. As I learn to accept more of your love, may it lead me into a stronger walk with you. A walk that overcomes every wrong desire and sidesteps every obstacle in my recovery path.***

Divine love is perfect peace and joy, it is a freedom from all disquiet, it is all content and happiness; and makes everything to rejoice in itself.

WILLIAM LAW (1686–1761)

You can find today's Scripture passage on page 1366 of *The Life Recovery Bible.*

Lament

Rise during the night and cry out.
Pour out your hearts like water to the Lord.

LAMENTATIONS 2:19

WE DON'T HEAR MUCH ABOUT THE BIBLICAL call to lament. According to one dictionary, a *lament* is "a passionate expression of grief or sorrow." We may lament at the loss of a loved one or when suffering some other profound loss. In our recovery, we may lament the entire portion of our lives given over to our addiction. God is fully in favor of such lament. In fact, God wants us to cry out to him when we are so grieved that we are moved to lament. At any point in recovery, feel free to lament. But don't wallow. Rise up in victory and move ahead.

✝ *Father, I have much to lament about. I know you hear my every cry and every sigh. You are aware of the pain and disappointment that prompt my lamentations. You, too, have lamented over your fallen creation, of which I'm a part. As you hear, Lord, may you also heal. Comfort me as a true father would do.*

> We, the children of God; we, who each knows his own plague and his own sore; we, who carry about with us day by day a body of sin and death, that makes us lament, sigh, and groan; we who know painfully what it is to be encompassed with infirmities; we, who come to His feet as being nothing and having nothing but sin and woe; "we do not have a High Priest who is unable to sympathize with our infirmities," but One who carries in His bosom that sympathizing, merciful, feeling, tender, and compassionate heart.
>
> J. C. PHILPOT (1802–1869)

You can find today's Scripture passage on page 1008 of *The Life Recovery Bible.*

Heaven, Our Eternal Home

He will wipe every tear from their eyes, and there will be no more death or sorrow or crying or pain. All these things are gone forever.

REVELATION 21:4

WHILE IN RECOVERY, we may wish for God to wipe away our tears, but we must wait until eternity for that. What a promise to hold in our hearts now while we wait! In that day, neither addiction nor temptation of any kind will be in our presence. All evil shall be finished and forgotten. Though we cannot experience it now, we can long for it and count it as a future treasure awaiting us.

✝ *Father, I know heaven is my home, and I long for that day when I'm no longer plagued by the attractions of earth—including addiction. Until then, I pray to be useful and to learn to see things here as you see them. I pray to see my trials and temptations through the eyes of one whose affections are already in heaven. Lord, thank you for providing an eternal home for all who believe.*

We must learn to live on the heavenly side and look at things from above. To contemplate all things as God sees them, as Christ beholds them, overcomes sin, defies Satan, dissolves perplexities, lifts us above trials, separates us from the world and conquers fear of death.

A. B. SIMPSON (1843–1919)

You can find today's Scripture passage on page 1669 of *The Life Recovery Bible*.

Helping Others

Don't look out only for your own interests,
but take an interest in others, too.

PHILIPPIANS 2:4

THERE'S NOTHING BETTER TO TAKE OUR MINDS off ourselves than looking for ways to help others. Seek opportunities to serve in your church, at your local pregnancy crisis center, or at the local rescue mission where you may be able to encourage others still in their addiction. Consider this not just a momentary add-on to your recovery but a lifelong admonition. You are needed somewhere, even if in a small way. Be available. God will open doors.

✝ *Father, as I practice sobriety, I know it will help to have a place to give of myself. I pray for open doors and creative ways for me to look out for the interests of others, not just myself. Lord, there is so much need in the world! Allow me to be part of the healing process for others in need.*

> What does love look like? It has the hands to help others. It has the feet to hasten to the poor and needy. It has eyes to see misery and want. It has the ears to hear the sighs and sorrows of men. That is what love looks like.
>
> SAINT AUGUSTINE OF HIPPO (354–430)

You can find today's Scripture passage on page 1522 of *The Life Recovery Bible.*

Freed from the Judgment of Others

Do not judge others, and you will not be judged. Do not condemn others, or it will all come back against you. Forgive others, and you will be forgiven.

LUKE 6:37

WHEN WE SEE A CHRISTIAN WHO'S JUDGMENTAL toward others, we can wonder if they've ever really taken stock of their own situation and need for mercy, not judgment. Because to know our own frailty—as we who understand addiction do—is to be merciful and without judgment of others. A benefit is that, when we become less judgmental, others' judgment toward us becomes like water off a duck's back. Thank God, as we live in his freedom, we can be free from the judgment of others and free from God's judgment of us . . . because of Christ.

✝ *Lord, I have no place to judge others. It's enough for me to mind my own failures rather than judge the shortcomings of others. Keep me free from a critical spirit, Lord. May I become a more merciful and forgiving person. Blind me to the faults of others, and open my eyes to my own need.*

While we are looking after the faults of others, we are in danger of neglecting the care of our own life!

J. R. MILLER (1840–1912)

You can find today's Scripture passage on page 1299 of *The Life Recovery Bible.*

Accepting Incremental Change

Though our bodies are dying,
our spirits are being renewed every day.
2 CORINTHIANS 4:16

SOME GIVE UP ON RECOVERY BECAUSE THE process often seems too slow. They want immediate sobriety and instant maturity. But it doesn't work that way. We are being renewed incrementally, day by day. We must accept God's timeline in our recovery and rejoice that he knows far better than we do. So do not lose heart. Your recovery is still on God's schedule.

✝ ***Lord, addiction is so consuming; it's only natural that I want drastic and speedy change. But I know you bring recovery in your own way and your own time. Still, I pray for as quick a recovery as is your will for me. And when it seems like the changes are happening too slowly, give me patience to trust and keep walking the road to recovery, content with your timetable.***

> Gradual growth in grace, growth in knowledge, growth in faith, growth in love, growth in holiness, growth in humility, growth in spiritual-mindedness—all this I see clearly taught and urged in Scripture, and clearly exemplified in the lives of many of God's saints. But sudden, instantaneous leaps from conversion to consecration I fail to see in the Bible.
>
> J. C. RYLE (1816–1900)

You can find today's Scripture passage on page 1485 of *The Life Recovery Bible*.

The Blood of Christ

He is so rich in kindness and grace that he purchased our freedom with the blood of his Son and forgave our sins.

EPHESIANS 1:7

HOW ARE WE REDEEMED FROM OUR SINS, our addictions, ourselves? It all happens because Christ shed his blood on our behalf. We must never underestimate what happened at the Cross. There, we were freed from condemnation for yesterday, empowered to live for today, and given hope for an even better tomorrow.

Being saved by the shedding of innocent blood wasn't just a New Testament event. In the Old Testament, we read that the Hebrews, God's chosen people, were saved during the first Passover by smearing blood of a lamb on their doorposts. So, too, are we saved and protected by the blood of the Lamb. The Jews will never forget the night of the Passover, and neither must we ever forget our deliverance is because of the blood of the Lamb.

† *Jesus, you are the Lamb of God sacrificed for me. Thank you for the kindness and grace you exhibited when you purchased my freedom. May I never forget the great Passover in my life when the blood saved me. May it always avail for me as the cleansing agent for my sins.*

The blood is everything to us—it is everything to God. He provided it, is satisfied with it, beholds it, and when He sees it on the soul, that soul becomes a living and a lovely soul in His sight. May our meditation on atoning blood exalt our views of its dignity, increase in us its power, and endear to our hearts the preciousness of Him who shed it!

OCTAVIUS WINSLOW (1808–1878)

You can find today's Scripture passage on page 1510 of *The Life Recovery Bible*.

AUGUST 2

A God of Peace

God is not a God of disorder but of peace.

1 CORINTHIANS 14:33

WHAT DOES A RECOVERED life look like? For one thing, confusion and mind-numbness are replaced with peace. The road that was bumpy with ruts is now paved smoothly. Where once there was chaos, now there is order—even what can be called *artistry*—in our new lives. For this to happen, we must invite our heavenly Father to take the canvas we've nearly destroyed and allow him to make the masterpiece he has in mind for us.

Living according to God's Word brings artistry and order into our lives.

✝ *Father, you see me as an ordered work of art. I often see myself as a disordered lump of clay. I ask you to mold that clay, Lord, into the image you see in me. Smooth away the rough edges, chip away at the pieces that don't belong, remove the small imperfections that mar the sculpture. Bring order into my life, Lord, and thus a work of art.*

Never be in a hurry; do everything quietly and in a calm spirit. Do not lose your inner peace for anything whatsoever, even if your whole world seems upset.

FRANCIS DE SALES (1567–1622)

You can find today's Scripture passage on page 1473 of *The Life Recovery Bible.*

Overflowing Joy

When you obey my commandments, you remain in my love, just as I obey my Father's commandments and remain in his love. I have told you these things so that you will be filled with my joy. Yes, your joy will overflow!

JOHN 15:10-11

WHEN JESUS TAUGHT DURING HIS EARTHLY ministry, what was his goal? John records that Jesus' goal was that our joy may be full. Think of it: Jesus' desire for us is that *his* joy may be in us and that our joy will overflow. A heart full of joy need not roam to seek artificial pleasures. It's only when our joy is not full that we seek carnal pleasures. Be assured today of Christ's joy. May it be in you, and may it fill you to overflowing.

✝ ***Lord, you want me to be filled with your joy—and so do I! Father, may I know today the overflowing joy that silences all desires for carnal pleasures and addictions. Today, I trade my restlessness for your abundant joy.***

Man cannot live without joy; therefore when he is deprived of true spiritual joys it is necessary that he become addicted to carnal pleasures.

THOMAS AQUINAS (1225–1274)

You can find today's Scripture passage on page 1366 of *The Life Recovery Bible.*

The Power of Friendship

Confess your sins to each other and pray for each other so that you may be healed. The earnest prayer of a righteous person has great power and produces wonderful results.

JAMES 5:16

GOD NEVER MEANS FOR US TO WALK THROUGH recovery alone. We need friends on the journey. At the beginning, we need the oversight of someone who knows the ropes of recovery. Along the way, we need someone who is farther down the road than us. And some blessed day, we will be that person for someone just starting their recovery journey. At every point along the way, we all need someone to hear our sins, listen to our story, and pray on our behalf prayers that bring healing. Don't try to walk the recovery road alone.

† *Father, one thing about addiction: After a season of recovery, it produces some of the most compassionate friends and protectors of my soul. While addiction itself hardens me, recovery, day by day, softens me. Thank you for those whom I call friends and who are friends indeed. Bring me into a closer relationship with my brothers and sisters in recovery. Our prayers for each other will bring wonderful results. Lord, guide me into these deeper friendships.*

Let those be thy choicest companions who have made Christ their chief companion.

THOMAS BROOKS (1608–1680)

You can find today's Scripture passage on page 1607 of *The Life Recovery Bible*.

The Pathway through the Wilderness

I am about to do something new.
See, I have already begun! Do you not see it?
I will make a pathway through the wilderness.
I will create rivers in the dry wasteland.

ISAIAH 43:19

WE SPENT OUR ADDICTED LIVES EITHER IN the wilderness or in the desert. Sometimes it seemed like both. Then God stepped in and began a new thing in our lives. There appeared rivers where there was desert. The wilderness gave way to a path forged by God. Now our post-addiction lives are secure as we stay on that path. We never long to be in the desert again. The fountains we thought were there were mere mirages. The wilderness is no longer our home; therefore, we will stay on course and enjoy the true waters of the river of recovery.

✝ *Father, I know the dry life of the desert only too well. I know the way of the wilderness. In my thirst for living water, I've turned to you. I've forsaken the old worn path of desolation and traded it for the path where the oases abound. I drink from the cup of living waters and am satisfied. You quench my thirst.*

There is water in it—the water of spiritual life. I am dying of thirst in the desert—the desert of my sin and guilt. But He puts the cup to my lips, and I live. It brings me pardon, the remission of all my transgressions, His own favour and fellowship, the assurance that He is pacified toward me. It is a new discovery in the divine resources. It is the dawning of a happy day.

ALEXANDER SMELLIE (1857–1923)

You can find today's Scripture passage on page 896 of *The Life Recovery Bible*.

Second Wind

Don't you realize that in a race everyone runs, but only one person gets the prize? So run to win! All athletes are disciplined in their training. They do it to win a prize that will fade away, but we do it for an eternal prize.

1 CORINTHIANS 9:24-25

THE RECOVERY RACE WE'RE IN IS A LONG COURSE, not a sprint. But we find we always have a second wind waiting for us when we need it most. So on we run, picking ourselves up if we fall, straining confidently ahead, knowing the prize is ours if we simply move ahead toward the finish line. There we claim our eternal prize.

† *Lord, sometimes this race, though glorious, is hard. Yet today I push ahead despite any obstacles to deter me or trip me up. Father, be sure to have that second wind ready for me when I need it—better include a third and fourth wind too.*

Run each day's race with all your might, so that at the end you will receive the victory wreath from God. Keep on running even when you have had a fall. The victory wreath is won by him who does not stay down, but always gets up again, grasps the banner of faith, and keeps on running in the assurance that Jesus is Victor.

BASILEA SCHLINK (1904–2001)

You can find today's Scripture passage on page 1466 of *The Life Recovery Bible.*

Confident Hope

I pray that God, the source of hope, will fill you completely with joy and peace because you trust in him. Then you will overflow with confident hope through the power of the Holy Spirit.

ROMANS 15:13

WE WERE MADE—DESIGNED—to need a connection with God to complete us. And only when we are thus connected are we complete. Too often, we try to complete ourselves through appeals to the flesh, but they can never deliver the right and permanent connection we need. God, by his Holy Spirit indwelling us, *is* a permanent and complete connection. But in order to live this out, we must forsake all appeals to the flesh with the hope that comes from God himself, causing us to overflow with this divine and confident hope by which we live and are healed.

† *Father, having the Holy Spirit within me makes me overflow with confident hope. Fill me, Lord, with true joy and peace as I continue this recovery journey. May I always rely on the knowledge that I was designed specifically for connection with you. May my restlessness cease as I rest in you.*

You have made us for yourself, and our hearts are restless,
until they can find rest in you.

SAINT AUGUSTINE OF HIPPO (354–430)

You can find today's Scripture passage on page 1451 of *The Life Recovery Bible*.

Contentment in Christ

When you ask, you don't get it because your motives are all wrong—
you want only what will give you pleasure.

JAMES 4:3

WHAT WAS IT WE SOUGHT TO CURE our discontent with when we began our addictions? We sought pleasure. Surely pleasure would bring us contentment. It didn't deliver on the promise, though—far from it. It made our discontent even deeper. We learned there is no lasting pleasure in addiction. But God sees our need for contentment and offers it to us in the person of Christ. We can find more contentment in him than in all the supposed comforts of this world. But when we ask, we must ask with a pure motive, not for another dose of momentary pleasure.

✝ *God, my motives have not always been right. Sometimes, I've prayed in the wrong spirit. But please know that, ultimately, I want your will for my life and the lives of those I love. Therefore, I pray for the contentment that comes from praying rightly and boldly for what your will is for me. The pleasure I now seek in prayer is fully answered in your will.*

There is more good in contentment, than there is in the thing that you would fain have to cure your discontent.

JEREMIAH BURROUGHS (1599–1646)

You can find today's Scripture passage on page 1605 of *The Life Recovery Bible.*

The Life of God Is in You

Living means living for Christ,
and dying is even better.
PHILIPPIANS 1:21

MANY OF US REMEMBER THE DAYS WHEN living meant living for our addiction. Those days have passed and are still passing as we are recovering. Now we live for Christ, empowered by the realization that the life of God himself dwells in us. His indwelling Holy Spirit enables us to endure suffering, overcome temptation, conquer our selfish desires, and bring a profit to the investment God has made in us. No matter what happens today, rely not on yourself but on Christ in you, for to live means living for Christ.

✝ *Father, for me to live is Christ and dying is better. But before you call me to that better life in eternity, you have an assignment for me here. So while I live, let me be part of your plan to bring healing to others. Help me make a better life for others by encouraging them to trust in you. Thank you for your indwelling Holy Spirit that guides my every step.*

> It was a blessed strait which Paul was in, not between two evil things, but between two good things . . . living to Christ, and being with him. . . . In this world we are compassed about with sin . . . but, if we come to be with Christ, farewell sin and temptation, farewell sorrow and death, for ever. . . . Those who have most reason to desire to depart should be willing to continue in the world as long as God has any work for them to do. Paul's strait was not between living in this world and living in heaven; between these two there is no comparison: but his strait was between serving Christ in this world and enjoying him in another.
>
> MATTHEW HENRY (1662–1714)

You can find today's Scripture passage on page 1521 of *The Life Recovery Bible.*

AUGUST 10

On Being a Chosen People

You are a chosen people. You are royal priests, a holy nation, God's very own possession. As a result, you can show others the goodness of God, for he called you out of the darkness into his wonderful light.

1 PETER 2:9

LET'S NEVER FORGET WHO WE ARE AND to whom we belong. We are a chosen people, a royal priesthood, members of a holy nation. We each are God's own possession. We each have been called out of our darkness into his marvelous light so that we can proclaim his goodness. This, our true calling, is easy to overlook or to put on the back burner of our minds. Never let that be the case. Always know that you are part of a chosen people. You belong to God.

✝ ***Father, I know I've been called out twice. As a Christian, I've been called out of the world into your holy nation. But I've also been called out of addiction through my recovery protocol. In both cases, I've been called out of darkness into your wonderful light. I am no longer my own but am now called out to belong to you. I am your possession.***

To think that you are your own, or at your own disposal, is as absurd as to think that you created and can preserve yourself. It is as plain and necessary a first principle, to believe you are thus God's, that you thus belong to Him.

WILLIAM LAW (1686–1761)

You can find today's Scripture passage on page 1612 of *The Life Recovery Bible.*

Give God Room

O Sovereign LORD! You made the heavens and
earth by your strong hand and powerful arm.
Nothing is too hard for you!

JEREMIAH 32:17

WE ARE SO PRONE TO ASSUME WHAT GOD should do about our addiction and when he should do it. And so often, we're dead wrong. God's miracles usually happen in unexpected and often untimely ways. Regardless of how God chooses to bring our recovery, we must know that our addiction is no match for his strong hand and powerful arm. Our brains are no match for his wisdom. We must stop anticipating how God will work and just give him room to do the impossible. Remember, nothing is too hard for God.

✝ *Father, it gives me great confidence to know that you're in charge of my recovery. You are here, poised to help me, eagerly watching over me, seeking my best. Though hard for me, recovery is as nothing to you. You are my mighty God with a strong hand and powerful arm. Nothing is too hard for you!*

We cannot ask God to do greater things than he has already done, or than he has promised to do in his blessed word. His loving heart is larger than our most extensive wishes. His promises go beyond our expectations. His power to discover what we want, and to do what he discovers to be necessary, ought to fill us with joy and peace. We have to do with a God who is at peace with us, whose love is fixed upon us, who rejoices in opportunities to do us good, and who has all power over all worlds.

JAMES SMITH (1802–1862)

You can find today's Scripture passage on page 975 of *The Life Recovery Bible.*

The Proof of New Life

Now repent of your sins and turn to God, so
that your sins may be wiped away.

ACTS 3:19

YES, WE MUST REPENT OF OUR PAST SINS. But then, because we're forgiven, we become thankful that God can now use our past sins and failures as a marker pointing to a positive future. We must praise God for his ability to turn the ashes from a bitter past into a thing of beauty. Our abandoned addiction now has no other purpose than to be the marker reminding us where we have come from. It's never a signpost for where we want to go.

✝ *Lord, I see repentance as a good friend, urging me to leave behind the past that has done such harm in my life. Repentance is my way of saying, "I'm done with my self-destruction." From that declaration, Father, allow me to bring forth the fruit of true repentance. May my life now prove the reality of a changed life.*

To do so no more is the truest repentance.

MARTIN LUTHER (1483–1546)

You can find today's Scripture passage on page 1384 of *The Life Recovery Bible.*

The Holy Spirit as Advocate

I will ask the Father, and he will give you another Advocate, who will never leave you.

JOHN 14:16

OF ALL THE TITLES GIVEN TO THE HOLY SPIRIT (Teacher, Helper, Counselor, Comforter), perhaps the most meaningful to us is Advocate. We who are in recovery need advocates—people who will be on our side and root for us in our struggle. What better advocate than God himself in the person of the Holy Spirit? He advocated for us yesterday, he advocates for us today, and he will advocate for us tomorrow. Why is he so persistent in this role? Because he loves us and genuinely cares about what happens to us. Today, as you pray, thank God for the Holy Spirit's presence in our lives to advocate for us. He knows there are times we can't muster up the faith to advocate for ourselves.

† *Holy Spirit, thank you for your roles in my life, particularly that of an advocate. You know how I need someone in my corner who believes in me and seeks the best for me. I take by faith your leading role in my life as Advocate. Thanks for always being for me.*

The neglect of one day, of one duty, of one hour, would undo us, if we had not an advocate with the Father. Those years, months, weeks, days, and hours that are not filled up with God, with Christ, with grace, with duty, will certainly be filled up with vanity and folly.

THOMAS BROOKS (1608–1680)

You can find today's Scripture passage on page 1365 of *The Life Recovery Bible*.

A Brilliant Future

"I know the plans I have for you," says the LORD.
"They are plans for good and not for disaster, to give you a future and a hope."

JEREMIAH 29:11

GOD HAS PLANS FOR EACH OF US. *Good* plans that will bring us to a place of hope and happiness. The wall that separates us from those plans—and that person we're meant to be—is being torn down brick by brick as we move on through the recovery process. Keeping ourselves focused on not just recovery but the great fruit of recovery (happiness, security, health, and a God-designed future) motivates us to go full steam ahead. We can trust this promise of God. It's gold for us.

✝ *Father, I praise you that your thoughts are always directed toward me. In return, may my thoughts become more focused on you. For you have the best plans and the best future for every person, including me. By faith, I walk daily in the footsteps that lead me straight into that promised future. I will allow nothing to deter me from living your best life for me.*

> We often do not know our own thoughts, nor know our own mind, but God is never at any uncertainty within himself. We are sometimes ready to fear that God's designs concerning us are all against us; but he knows the contrary concerning his own people, that they are thoughts of good and not of evil; even that which seems evil is designed for good. His thoughts are all working towards the expected end, which he will give in due time.
>
> MATTHEW HENRY (1662–1714)

You can find today's Scripture passage on page 970 of *The Life Recovery Bible.*

Springs of Water

He also turns deserts into pools of water,
the dry land into springs of water.

PSALM 107:35

WHEN A PATIENT FINISHES THEIR PRESCRIBED antibiotic treatment for an infection, their recovery is complete, and they need not return to the medicine that healed them. Not so with addiction. We must always be drinking from the springs of water God provides for the parched land of our life, and if ever the springs stop flowing, recovery stops. That, of course, need never be because, with God, the springs keep flowing for the rest of our lives. We will never outgrow the need for the springs of God's living water.

† *God, I have permanently moved from the dry desert into the land where I find continual springs of water. You, Lord, are the spring from which the waters come. You refresh me as I come to you again and again. I never find that the spring has run dry. I never will.*

> To be filled with Christ . . . is not a reservoir but a spring. It is a life which is continual, active and ever passing on with an outflow as necessary as its inflow, and if we do not perpetually draw the fresh supply from the living fountain, we shall either grow stagnant or empty. It is, therefore, not so much a perpetual fullness as a perpetual filling.
>
> A. B. SIMPSON (1843–1919)

You can find today's Scripture passage on page 757 of *The Life Recovery Bible*.

AUGUST 16

Our Constant Intercessor

Therefore [Jesus] is able, once and forever, to save those who come to God through him. He lives forever to intercede with God on their behalf.

HEBREWS 7:25

IT'S GREAT TO KNOW WE HAVE EARTHLY FRIENDS who pray for us, but how much greater the joy in knowing that Christ lives to intercede with God on our behalf? He who saves us from addiction to the uttermost invites us to come near to him. This we do by faith. The great reward is that he also draws near to us. In his presence, we dwell safely.

✝ *Jesus, you are now and forever interceding to the Father on my behalf. May I enjoy the security and safety in knowing you have my back. While I thank you for the many earthly friends who are interceding for me, their prayers, though powerful, pale in contrast to your advocating for me. Thank you for this grand assurance, Lord.*

> Oh, what an unspeakable comfort it is to remember that we have an High Priest in heaven, who never forgets us night or day, and is continually interceding for us, and providing for our safety. . . . That great High Priest who died for us and intercedes for us, will never forget His people, or allow one lamb of His flock to perish.
>
> J. C. RYLE (1816–1900)

You can find today's Scripture passage on page 1585 of *The Life Recovery Bible.*

Just Ask Job

When Job prayed for his friends, the LORD restored his fortunes. In fact, the LORD gave him twice as much as before!

JOB 42:10

IS IT POSSIBLE FOR GOD TO SO RESTORE US AFTER addiction that we have twice as much as we once had? There's no guarantee of how many restored blessings we'll receive—only that our sobriety brings as much restoration of goods, relationships, and prosperity as God will measure out. And it will be more than we expect. We must always keep in mind that God definitely knows *how* to restore fortunes. Just ask Job.

† *Lord, throughout the Bible, I see story after story of restoration. Most remarkable is Job's restoration to twice what he lost in the tragedy of his early years. Father, you know I've lost much in my addiction. But I call on you as my great Restorer to bring blessing upon blessing in my recovered life. Every restored blessing will glorify you and be a testament to your forgiveness and power.*

Despair not! He that turned the captivity of Job can turn thine as the streams in the south. He shall make again thy vineyard again to blossom, and thy field to yield her fruit. Thou shalt again come forth with those that make merry, and once more shall the song of gladness be on thy lip.

CHARLES SPURGEON (1834–1892)

You can find today's Scripture passage on page 675 of *The Life Recovery Bible.*

Making God Laugh

Commit your actions to the LORD,
and your plans will succeed.

PROVERBS 16:3

THE JOKE IS OFTEN TOLD, "IF YOU WANT TO make God laugh, tell him your plans." The truth is that our so-called plans often derail at some point along the way. Sometimes, addiction stalls our plans or even puts an end to them. The good news is that we're the ones who can laugh with joy at the plans God has for us post-addiction. Our recovery is based on committing all our actions to the Lord, so we should expect him to establish our plans as they also reflect his plans—and not ours alone. And rest assured, there will be a difference between what we may have planned and what God unfolds as his plan for our future.

✝ *Lord, I commit my actions to you. I commit my plans and my life to you. I pray for my will to bow to your designed plan for me. I cast aside all my attempts to maneuver the future into my own design. I leave it to you, Father. You know best.*

Faith spreads the need before God, rolls the burden upon Him,
and calmly leaves the solution to Him.

ARTHUR PINK (1886–1952)

You can find today's Scripture passage on page 804 of *The Life Recovery Bible*.

Self-Pity

Their insults have broken my heart,
and I am in despair.
If only one person would show some pity;
if only one would turn and comfort me.

PSALM 69:20

WE MAY BE TEMPTED TO LOOK AT FRIENDS OR relatives who are living the good life, never having faced the trials we've endured, and find ourselves at a self-pity party. The danger is that self-pity can be a trigger that causes us to once again resort to self-medicating, thus getting us back on the very treadmill we need to stay away from.

Turn any attempts at self-pity inside out by remembering that God's plan for you is very personal. It's not your rich brother's plan. It's not your healthy father's plan. It's not your business executive sister's plan. Trade your self-pity for biblical self-care. Try putting on compassion for yourself instead of self-pity. Trade any low self-esteem for the knowledge of who you are in Christ. Stand firm when the enemy whispers his lies about you. You are of great value to God. There is no room for self-pity.

✝ *God, forgive the times I've felt sorry for myself. I know it's not healthy and can even trigger a relapse. Help me see again what you've done so far in my recovery and the good things that remain ahead for me. Show me ways to infuse some good biblical self-care into my life in place of any remaining self-pity.*

Self-pity is a death that has no resurrection, a sinkhole from which no rescuing hand can drag you because you have chosen to sink.

ELISABETH ELLIOT (1926–2015)

You can find today's Scripture passage on page 727 of *The Life Recovery Bible*.

Foolish Comparisons

Oh, don't worry; we wouldn't dare say that we are as wonderful
as these other men who tell you how important they are!
But they are only comparing themselves with each other,
using themselves as the standard of measurement. How ignorant!

2 CORINTHIANS 10:12

IT'S ALWAYS A MISTAKE TO COMPARE OUR personalities or our addictions or our recoveries to someone else's. Comparison will make us either proud when we see we're better off or ashamed when we see we're not doing as well as someone else. We are all unique, and God's plans for us aren't God's plans for them. Have confidence that God is working just as lovingly on your behalf as on your neighbor's. Set aside your judgment of others. Let God be their God just as he is your God.

† *Lord, I commit to not judging others or comparing my situation with what I see happening in someone else's life. Your plan for me is just that. It's not your way of working with everyone. Thank you for the unique way you're working with me, and thank you for your plan for the recovery of others.*

Comparison, more than reality, makes men happy and
can make them wretched.

OWEN FELLTHAM (1602–1668)

You can find today's Scripture passage on page 1491 of *The Life Recovery Bible.*

We Must Allow God to Change the Way We Think

God has not given us a spirit of fear and timidity,
but of power, love, and self-discipline.

2 TIMOTHY 1:7

REWIRING OUR BRAINS, POST ADDICTION, is no small feat. Our flesh will often question why the brain is denying our usual cravings. But the healing brain knows best, as it is being renewed by the power of the Holy Spirit, enriched by the love of God, giving us self-control.

Be patient with yourself as your brain rewires. Time is on your side. Don't expect an overnight zap from God. He will renew your mind and rewire your brain with delicacy and precision. Tell your flesh to be patient, and follow the brain's wise pursuit of renewal.

✝ *Lord, I know my behavior flows out of how my brain perceives a situation. In my addiction, my brain was wired to desire dangerous pleasures that ended up being anti-pleasures. In my recovery, help me be patient as my brain renews itself and rewires in a healthy way.*

> To renew your mind is to involve yourself in the process of allowing God to bring to the surface the lies you have mistakenly accepted and replace them with truth. To the degree that you do this, your behavior will be transformed.
>
> CHARLES STANLEY (1932–)

You can find today's Scripture passage on page 1561 of *The Life Recovery Bible.*

More Than Conquerors

Who shall separate us from the love of Christ? Shall tribulation, or distress, or persecution, or famine, or nakedness, or danger, or sword? . . . In all these things we are more than conquerors through him who loved us.

ROMANS 8:35-37, ESV

IF WE START OUT BELIEVING WE CAN'T, then we can't. If we start out believing we can, then we can. Paul tells us that we are more than conquerors through Christ who loved us. *More* than conquerors.

Daily, we must make sure our minds are set on the truth that we *can* do this—and that we *must* do this. We must bolster our attitude by reminding ourselves every day that we have great security in knowing that nothing can defeat us.

† *God, your perfect will for me is to know and experience daily victory over addiction. That is the normal experience of a solid Christian. Today, may I walk out the very real truth that, in Christ, I'm more than a conqueror. Any desires relating to addiction must bow before the Christ in me. Nothing, therefore, can defeat me. Praise God!*

Victory is the normal experience of a Christian;
defeat should be the abnormal experience.

WATCHMAN NEE (1903–1972)

You can find today's Scripture passage on page 1442 of *The Life Recovery Bible*.

Remember Not

Remember not the former things,
nor consider the things of old.

ISAIAH 43:18, ESV

WHY ARE WE SO OFTEN PLAGUED BY MEMORIES of events that God himself has chosen to forget? Why can't we accept God's directive to "remember not the former things"?

It may take practice, but it can be done. At every remembrance of troubling things in the past, make a conscious decision to let them go. Don't even take time to regret them again. Even to despise our past is to give it more control in our lives than it should have. Let only the future be your rudder in life.

† *God, sometimes my memory is my worst enemy. It dredges up images from my past life in addiction that cause fresh regret. Yet you, Lord, have forgotten all that and command me to forget it too. There is, therefore, renewed strength in my ability to choose to forget "the former things." Help me, Father, as I practice letting go of all those painful memories.*

> It is well to forget the things which are behind. If I remember too vividly former failures, the recollection will depress my soul and hamper my movements. If I remember too often former attainments, I shall grow contented and make no further progress.
>
> ALEXANDER SMELLIE (1857–1923)

You can find today's Scripture passage on page 896 of *The Life Recovery Bible.*

Walking on Water

Peter called to him, "Lord, if it's really you, tell me to come to you, walking on the water." "Yes, come," Jesus said. So Peter went over the side of the boat and walked on the water toward Jesus. But when he saw the strong wind and the waves, he was terrified and began to sink. "Save me, Lord!" he shouted. Jesus immediately reached out and grabbed him. "You have so little faith," Jesus said. "Why did you doubt me?"

MATTHEW 14:28-31

THE RECOVERY PROCESS AND ITS GOAL—long-term sobriety—is a gift of God that he is pleased to give us. Eager, in fact. But like all of God's gifts, it comes through faith in what God has said. This faith then leads us to live out that God-given gift. It's not unlike Peter stepping out of the boat at Jesus' invitation and, by faith, walking on water—a seeming impossibility. But, also like Peter, when we look around at the swirling sea below and take our eyes off the promised gift of sobriety, we, too, are sunk. At that point, Jesus would ask us, "Why did you doubt me?"

How would we answer?

✝ ***Lord, your gift of sobriety is one I treasure. I thank you daily for my victory over addiction, though sometimes my faith seems to waver—just like Peter's faith when he walked on the water. Father, keep that invitation always open. I vow not to climb back in the boat but to walk on the waves with Jesus. Thank you for the invitation with no expiration date.***

[Peter was] invited to walk where none but the feet of faith dare go. The Christian's walk is a supernatural one. He walks by faith. This, in the eyes of the wise men of the world, is like walking on the sea. They cannot understand it. Every believer is invited by Christ to walk with Him on the deep as He walked.

JAMES SMITH (1802–1862)

You can find today's Scripture passage on page 1220 of *The Life Recovery Bible.*

A Holy Violence

Praise the LORD, who is my rock.
He trains my hands for war
and gives my fingers skill for battle.

PSALM 144:1

ADDICTION INVOLVES A BODILY CRAVING FOR A particular wrong response resulting in an artificial high. Having been trained to receive that wrong response over time, we find we're now physically (and mentally) dependent on it. Recovery involves reversing the response—and there's the rub.

Our bodies, our brains, seemingly our very beings screaming for satisfaction, find themselves at war with our desire to be free. War involves violence, and to subdue our body with its desires will take the strength of an army battalion. But we have one who trains us in this war. He even transforms our hands for war (and how many of us have addictions that require the use of our hands?) and our fingers for battle.

Praise the Lord, who is our Rock!

† *Father, my hands have been part of my problem. You've seen how my hands have been used to further my addiction. In your wonderful way of redeeming and restoring the lost, I pray you'll redeem and restore my hands by training them for war against the enemy. Use my redeemed fingers to win the battle.*

They that would keep themselves pure must have their bodies in subjection, and that may require, in some cases, a holy violence.

THOMAS BOSTON (1676–1732)

You can find today's Scripture passage on page 778 of *The Life Recovery Bible*.

AUGUST 26

Reaping What We Sow

Don't be misled—you cannot mock the justice of God.
You will always harvest what you plant.

GALATIANS 6:7

SOMETIMES OUR WRONG CHOICES set in motion circumstances we must simply ride out. But even then, when those consequences are surrendered fully to God, he is able to work them out for our good.

Our addiction may have set in motion consequences we would not have chosen. We may now feel that those unwanted consequences are unredeemable. *But God!*

Yes, we may have to suffer an unwanted harvest due to the seeds we planted, but we will survive. God will see to it, and he may even bring something of value from it.

✝ *Father, I've sown some seeds that have produced a bad harvest in my life. Though I regret having to live through the consequences, I will do so, realizing that now, in my new life, you are able to work out that bad harvest so as to minimize the damage. I now plant new seeds that will also produce a harvest—but a harvest of good works and a satisfied life.*

Sow a thought, and you reap an action;
sow an act, and you reap a habit;
sow a habit, and you reap a character;
sow character, and you will reap a destiny.

UNKNOWN

You can find today's Scripture passage on page 1506 of *The Life Recovery Bible.*

God, the Great Giver

It is impossible to please God without faith. Anyone who wants to come to him must believe that God exists and that he rewards those who sincerely seek him.

HEBREWS 11:6

TO BE REWARDED BY GOD IS THE GREATEST aspiration for any Christian. And there's a simple way to get this reward: Believe God exists and seek him in faith. That's it! Faith pleases God. Our problem may be with unexpected obstacles that seem to keep us from seeking him. Are we too busy with our jobs? Are there people who seem to roadblock our seeking God? Do we expect too little from God? The Christian who will be rewarded is the Christian who will remove the obstacles, jump the hurdles, and press on to the finish line.

Today, a reward awaits us as we sincerely seek him.

✝ *Father, I draw near to you, knowing you exist and reward me as I seek you. I invite you anew to have access to every part of my life, especially the part that is so easily attracted to addiction. Give me, Lord, of yourself as I give all of myself to you.*

The righteous do not indeed deserve any good thing, yet of his mercy and grace God will at last reward them, as though they deserved much.

WILLIAM S. PLUMER (1802–1880)

You can find today's Scripture passage on page 1590 of *The Life Recovery Bible*.

The Fruit of the Spirit

The Holy Spirit produces this kind of fruit in our lives: love, joy, peace, patience, kindness, goodness, faithfulness, gentleness, and self-control. There is no law against these things!

GALATIANS 5:22-23

WHAT WAS THE "FRUIT" OF OUR ADDICTION? How does it compare with the fruit of the Spirit? Fruit doesn't just appear. Fruit grows on trees or vines. We nourish the apple tree, the grapevine, in order to reap the fruit. We reap the fruit of the Spirit, too. But we must be sure of the Holy Spirit's presence and work in our lives. We do this by asking, receiving, and yielding. We do all three through faith.

Have as your goal to bear much fruit.

✝ *Praise you, Father, for the new fruit in my life that's supplanting the former bitter fruit of my addiction. Your Holy Spirit is the producer of this fruit, and as I grow closer to you, I'll reap more of his fruit and less of the soured fruit of the flesh. I'm thankful that the fruit is from you, not something I work up on my own.*

We shall never bear fruit to God, until we are brought to see that our fruit comes from God.

J. C. PHILPOT (1802–1869)

You can find today's Scripture passage on page 1505 of *The Life Recovery Bible*.

A Quieted Soul

Instead, I have calmed and quieted myself,
like a weaned child who no longer cries for its mother's milk.
Yes, like a weaned child is my soul within me.

PSALM 131:2

WHEN WE'VE GONE WITHOUT OUR ADDICTION for a brief time, many of us get fidgety and restless, seeking our calming agent of addiction. What if, instead, we could learn to calm and quiet our souls, like a weaned child in its mother's arms? When we rest in Christ, the result is the same.

In addiction, we have become used to the pattern of restlessness followed by our need to self-medicate. Recovery is, in part, unlearning that restlessness and relearning how to calm and quiet our souls by resting in Christ.

✝ *Lord, my soul gets so restless. I want to find a way to calm it down; otherwise, I can be tempted to self-medicate again. Help me relearn how simply to rest my soul in quietness and there find strength so that I no longer seek an artificial soother of my soul. Let me find the joy of a calm and quiet spirit, Father.*

It is not necessary to maintain a conversation when we are in the presence of God. We can come into His presence and rest our weary souls in quiet contemplation of Him. Our groanings, which cannot be uttered, rise to Him and tell Him better than words how dependent we are upon Him.

OLE HALLESBY (1879–1961)

You can find today's Scripture passage on page 771 of *The Life Recovery Bible*.

Loving Ourselves as Christ Loved Us

Jesus replied, "'You must love the LORD your God with all your heart, all your soul, and all your mind.' This is the first and greatest commandment. A second is equally important: 'Love your neighbor as yourself.'"

MATTHEW 22:37-39

JESUS TEACHES US THAT LOVING OURSELVES AS we love our neighbors is equally important to loving God. Self-love can, of course, be a selfish concept . . . or it can be, as God means it to be, a healthy concept. If we love ourselves in the right way, we will treat ourselves—our entire selves—with respect and honor. This self-love will be reflected in how we treat our bodies, our minds, and our spirits. It's not wrong to love ourselves. It's only wrong to exalt ourselves as if we were God. We're not.

† *Father, I've not always loved myself the way I should. At times, I've not seen how great a creation of yours I am. You have designed me to be more than I am. Help me to establish a love for my life that is biblical. A love that honors the creation that you, my Creator, have made.*

There is a self-love which is corrupt, and the root of the greatest sins, and it must be put off and mortified; but there is a self-love which is the rule of the greatest duty: we must have a due concern for the welfare of our own souls and bodies. And we must love our neighbour as truly and sincerely as we love ourselves; in many cases we must deny ourselves for the good of others. By these two commandments let our hearts be formed as by a mould.

MATTHEW HENRY (1662–1714)

You can find today's Scripture passage on page 1232 of *The Life Recovery Bible*.

Sin or Disease?

Let all that I am praise the LORD;
may I never forget the good things he does for me.
He forgives all my sins
and heals all my diseases.

PSALM 103:2-3

IS ADDICTION SIN OR A DISEASE? Does it really matter, since God offers a remedy for both? In the case of disease, God offers healing. For sin, he offers forgiveness. No matter how we choose to label our addiction, God has the definitive answer. We are, therefore, with no excuse for not continuing our pursuit of healing from our disease or our sin.

✝ ***Lord, my addiction puzzles me. Some say it's a disease, and others say it's sin. Either way, God, I know you provide the remedy in Christ. He takes away my sin, and on the cross, he bore my addiction as a disease. Thank you, Lord, for your provision for healing from my addiction.***

The believer, though heir of forgiveness, is ever prone to fall into unhealthy malady. It is a true description, The whole head is sick—and the whole heart faint—from the sole of the foot to the crown of the head there is nothing in us but wounds and bruises and putrefying sores. Can these diseases be all healed? Jesus is full remedy. He gives health and a cure. He is Jehovah-Rophi. To Him, also, we may bring every malady of our sickly frames.

HENRY LAW (1797–1884)

You can find today's Scripture passage on page 750 of *The Life Recovery Bible.*

Addiction Always Works against Us

You can enter God's Kingdom only through the narrow gate. The highway to hell is broad, and its gate is wide for the many who choose that way. But the gateway to life is very narrow and the road is difficult, and only a few ever find it.

MATTHEW 7:13-14

ADDICTION ALWAYS WORKS AGAINST US, never for us. Sobriety is just the opposite. Living soberly opens doors that addiction closes. Doors marked "happiness," "wholeness," "freedom," prosperity," and much more.

The doors of addiction are marked, too. Marked by "depression," "remorse," "dependence," and "slavery." You may be able to identify some of the names you've noticed on the door of addiction. The good news is that we never have to walk through them again. To be sure, the door of recovery we're choosing is a narrow gate, but it leads to life. We can be among the few to find freedom, not the many who remain behind the closed doors of addiction. As it has been said, "Addiction is giving up everything for one thing. Recovery is giving up one thing to gain everything."

† *God, I know the door marked "happiness" for me is not on the wide road but on the more obscure, less-traveled road that few seem to find. And yet here I am, choosing that very narrow and difficult road and the door that, to many, is hidden. Keep me on that road, Lord. Keep me walking through the happiness door that leads to life.*

O what a narrow way is that which leads to life!

WILLIAM TIPTAFT (1803–1864)

You can find today's Scripture passage on page 1206 of *The Life Recovery Bible.*

Don't Be Defined by Your Failures

At that moment the Lord turned and looked at Peter. Suddenly, the Lord's words flashed through Peter's mind: "Before the rooster crows tomorrow morning, you will deny three times that you even know me." And Peter left the courtyard, weeping bitterly.

LUKE 22:61-62

I DOUBT THERE HAS BEEN A MORE MISERABLE personal failure than that of Peter, who denied the Lord and, upon realizing the gravity of his denial, wept bitterly. Most addicts—especially those in recovery—can well remember days and nights of weeping bitterly. Peter, though, rose from his misery and later was used mightily by God, writing two inspired books of the New Testament, until his own martyr's death.

Don't be defined by your past. You've wept bitterly. Now it's time to dry the tears, rise, and meet your better destiny.

† *God, you've seen my tears. You've heard my cries. Now, though, the time for tears has passed. It's time for me to move on into the better era of my life. Guide me, Father, into a destiny marked by productivity and joy that only you can give. Thank you for loving and saving broken people.*

Men want only the strong, the successful, the victorious, the unbroken, in building their kingdoms; but God is the God of the unsuccessful, of those who have failed. Heaven is filling with earth's broken lives, and there is no bruised reed that Christ cannot take and restore to glorious blessedness and beauty.

J. R. MILLER (1840–1912)

You can find today's Scripture passage on page 1331 of *The Life Recovery Bible*.

The Exchanged Life

His divine power has granted to us all things that pertain
to life and godliness, through the knowledge of him
who called us to his own glory and excellence.

2 PETER 1:3, ESV

IT IS *ALWAYS* GOD'S DIVINE POWER THAT GRANTS us all things that pertain to life and godliness. We, of all people, know that it *must* be his divine power for natural power has failed us so fully in the past. This divine power comes through the knowledge of Christ who called us (called *us*!) to his own glory and excellence. Can I get a shout of victory?

✝ *God, your divine power has granted me all I need! You have called me out of addiction into restoration and healing. May I never take for granted all your provision, and may I continue to chase down your every promise to me in order to live out the productive life you see in me.*

> It is through knowing God that we realize that "his divine power hath [granted] to us all things that pertain unto life and godliness," for all these things are in him; and as we know him, trust him, love him, and become like him, we also come to possess all these precious things in him.
>
> CHARLES SPURGEON (1834–1892)

You can find today's Scripture passage on page 1622 of *The Life Recovery Bible*.

The Implanted Word

Get rid of all the filth and evil in your lives, and humbly accept the word God has planted in your hearts, for it has the power to save your souls.

JAMES 1:21

WE TAKE A HUGE STEP FORWARD IN RECOVERY by implanting God's Word in our hearts. At times of temptation or loneliness or feeling misunderstood, you will find comfort and direction in God's Word.

We implant the Word in part by memorizing it so we can easily bring it to mind when needed. But memorizing is only a part of implanting. The next part is meditating on the Word as we're going about our day.

If you've not implanted the Word, start now. Choose three "go-to" verses that have helped you in your recovery. Commit them to memory. Meditate on them throughout the day. Don't stop at three, though. Keep implanting Scriptures so your collection will be ready to bring up at a moment's notice.

✝ *Lord, your Word is now my guide. As I read, show me insights that will help me in my recovery. Prepare my mind to be able to commit specific verses to memory. As I implant the Word in my mind and heart, teach me to call up the appropriate Scriptures when I need them. Soften my heart to better receive your Word. Make the truths of Scripture the anchor of my life.*

Without meditation, the truths of God will not stay with us. The heart is hard, and the memory slippery, and without meditation all is lost! Meditation imprints and fastens a truth in the mind. Serious meditation is like the engraving of letters in gold or marble which endures.

THOMAS WATSON (1620–1686)

You can find today's Scripture passage on page 1601 of *The Life Recovery Bible*.

Dwelling in God's Presence

Because of Christ and our faith in him, we can now come boldly and confidently into God's presence.

EPHESIANS 3:12

SPIRITUAL REST FOR THE ADDICT IS always needed. Rest from the focus of our addiction. Rest from compulsive behavior. Rest from self-condemnation. Rest from perceived failure.

Rest comes to us by learning to dwell in God's presence. That is, becoming more and more aware that he is always with us, never leaving us for a second. Dwelling in God's presence not only gives us rest; it gives us confidence, comfort, fellowship with our heavenly Father, and, over the course of time, freedom from addiction's magnetic pull. To be strong in God's presence is to see our dependence on our addiction weakened.

† *Father, it's a great realization to know that you're with me now, will be with me in the future, and were even with me in my past. I long to make your presence my moment-by-moment experience. You know I need the rest that comes with your presence. Stay, Lord, by my side always. Remind me often that you're there for me in my every move and thought.*

> To realize His presence, to abide continually under His eye, to recognize our Father as close by our side, is the secret of much peace. We must ever regard Him, not as if He were far away in some inaccessible abode, but nearer to us than our nearest friend. In our chamber, by the wayside, at our work, in our recreation, when mingling with others, or all alone we must see One whom the world sees not, we must hear a voice that the world hears not.
>
> GEORGE EVERARD (1828–1901)

You can find today's Scripture passage on page 1513 of *The Life Recovery Bible.*

Confidence in God's Work

Those who fear the LORD are secure;
he will be a refuge for their children.

PROVERBS 14:26

IF OUR RECOVERY IS SLOW, we may be tempted to lose confidence in God's work in us. When that happens, it helps to remind ourselves that strong confidence in God comes as we fear the Lord. Fear him not just in awe, as is commonly thought, but fear him as we would fear a loving father whom we would hate to disappoint, remembering that a loving father is also a disciplining father. When we fear God rightly, we can be confident (and patient) in God's work in us, and we will have a refuge.

✝ *Father, I know that you work on your timetable, not mine. If I consider your work in me as too slow, just remind me of how diamonds are made—from being pressured over a long period. Remind me often that fearing you is not a cowering fear but a fear that comes with love attached to it. In the confidence of that fear, I will trust in you, my Refuge.*

Faith is a living and unshakable confidence, a belief in the grace of God so assured that a man would die a thousand deaths for its sake.

MARTIN LUTHER (1483–1546)

You can find today's Scripture passage on page 801 of *The Life Recovery Bible*.

More Joy

You have put more joy in my heart
than they have when their grain and wine abound.
In peace I will both lie down and sleep;
for you alone, O LORD, make me dwell in safety.

PSALM 4:7-8, ESV

DID OUR ADDICTION PRODUCE JOY? It produced a temporary high, but we always experienced the inevitable letdown. Joy is different from a "high." And the joy God gives exceeds the "high" of "grain and wine" or whatever the source of our addiction was.

When we want joy, we don't need to turn to our addiction. We can turn to the Lord. When we want *more* joy, he supplies an abundance. We can rest in peace, knowing he is our provider, who makes us dwell in safety.

✝ *Father, the joy you give is more than I had in my addiction, and yet I crave even more. I pray you will continue to bring into my life fountains of joy that overflow. I don't need to have constant emotional highs, but even the quiet, subdued joys of knowing your ownership of me will do. Pour out the joy, Lord. More joy.*

I sometimes wonder whether all pleasures are not substitutes for Joy.

C. S. LEWIS (1898–1963)

You can find today's Scripture passage on page 682 of *The Life Recovery Bible.*

Encouraging Words

Don't use foul or abusive language. Let everything you say be good and helpful, so that your words will be an encouragement to those who hear them.

EPHESIANS 4:29

AS OUR BRAINS REWIRE IN RECOVERY, positive affirmations reinforce the creation of new neural pathways. The way we think, talk, and act all contribute to the new mind of our post-addictive selves. Paul tells us to end all corrupting talk and to speak only of that which builds up. When negative thoughts yield the fruit of corrupt talk, it's time to help our brains in creating those new neural pathways by thinking and speaking words of encouragement to ourselves or to others.

✝ *Lord, when you saved me, you saved all of me, including my mouth. Help me guard my speech, keeping my words positive and helpful to myself and others. I trust you with the necessary rewiring of my brain. I pray for your healing hand to be constantly renewing my mind, producing affirming words and attitudes.*

In our manner of speech, our plans of living, our dealings with others, our conduct and walk in the church and out of it—all should be done as becomes the gospel.

ALBERT BARNES (1798–1870)

You can find today's Scripture passage on page 1515 of *The Life Recovery Bible*.

Weaning Ourselves from Temptation

Don't let us yield to temptation,
but rescue us from the evil one.

MATTHEW 6:13

SOME RELAPSES OR OUTRIGHT FAILURES in addiction recovery occur because we don't wean ourselves from the sources of our temptations. We may regret our slow progress and give in to a trigger or to an invitation to indulge with a friend once again. This may happen, too, because we have forgotten that part of our long-term recovery will include a maintenance plan.

Failure happens when we think we're strong enough to simply nibble at the attractive bait. That nibble turns into a relapse unless we're involved in a plan to maintain our sobriety. At all times during recovery and maintenance, we must wean ourselves from every form of temptation as we also count on God to rescue us.

† *Father, I pray in accordance with the prayer Jesus taught his disciples that you would not let me yield to temptation and would rescue me from the evil one. Lord, you know relapses take their toll. So much so that I really want to be done forever with the flirtations of my addiction that lead to cheating on my recovery. You are fully capable of delivering me, God. My addiction, severe to me, is as nothing to you. I call on you for your help in keeping me clean.*

I do not know what your particular sorrow or hardship may be, but I do know that, whatever its nature—cruel, or bitter, or hopeless—it is as nothing to Him! He is able to deliver you as easily as you can call upon Him for support and help.

SUSANNAH SPURGEON (1832–1903)

You can find today's Scripture passage on page 1205 of *The Life Recovery Bible.*

Firmly Established

Establish your hearts,
for the coming of the Lord is at hand.

JAMES 5:8, ESV

A TREE WITH SHALLOW ROOTS IN POOR SOIL will topple during a storm. A Christian caught up in addiction must be firmly grounded (or planted) in Christ to endure the storm of addiction recovery, which is often fraught with overpowering temptations and illicit desires. Our hearts *must* be established. If we are not grounded in Christ, we will return once again to our addiction. We are grounded in either Christ or our addiction, but we can never be grounded in both.

✝ *Father, the storms still occasionally rage. The winds of temptation can be fierce. Still, I remain established firmly in you. I will never again be the person I once was in the worst of my addiction. I may grow slowly, but I will grow surely. The storms will not prevail as they pass through my life.*

> There is only one secure foundation: a genuine, deep relationship with Jesus Christ, which will carry you through any and all turmoil. No matter what storms are raging all around, you'll stand firm if you stand on His love.
>
> CHARLES STANLEY (1932–)

You can find today's Scripture passage on page 1606 of *The Life Recovery Bible.*

God's Rest for Our Souls

Jesus said, "Come to me, all of you who are weary and carry heavy burdens, and I will give you rest. Take my yoke upon you. Let me teach you, because I am humble and gentle at heart, and you will find rest for your souls. For my yoke is easy to bear, and the burden I give you is light."

MATTHEW 11:28-30

THE YOKE OF ADDICTION IS HARD. It bears down like a merciless weight. Jesus has an invitation for us, though: an offer to trade yokes. For our heavy burden, he offers his light load. For our furious, restless addiction, he offers rest for our souls. He offers an easy yoke and a light burden. As always, he favors us with his great gifts.

† *Lord, I'm amazed at your open offer to trade yokes, to trade burdens. I do very much want rest for my soul. Therefore, I accept your offer of a trade. I lay down my heavy load at your feet for you to pick up and bear. In exchange, I take your light burden and your easy yoke. Thank you for the rest that results from this awesome trade.*

What can be lighter than a burden which takes our burdens away, and a yoke which bears up the bearer himself?

BERNARD OF CLAIRVAUX (1090–1153)

You can find today's Scripture passage on page 1214 of *The Life Recovery Bible*.

Gracious Provision

He who did not spare his own Son but gave him up for us all,
how will he not also with him graciously give us all things?

ROMANS 8:32, ESV

WE ERR WHEN THINK THAT GOD HAS NOT provided all we need in recovery. More likely, we need to learn to be satisfied with God's provision. He who loves us and has brought us this far will not desert us. He will graciously give us all things we need. Has he not shown this already by giving up his Son for our sins? If we ever question God's love and provision for us, we need only look at the Cross. God will not and *cannot* show his love by any greater means than Calvary.

† *Lord, you have demonstrated your intense love for me in the most graphic way possible—you gave up your Son on the cross for my sake. The effects of that history-changing day are with us still. The power released in the resurrection of Christ is how I now live today. It is my provision for a recovered life. Thank you, Lord.*

God knows what each one of us is dealing with. He knows our pressures. He knows our conflicts. And He has made a provision for each and every one of them.

KAY ARTHUR (1933–)

You can find today's Scripture passage on page 1442 of *The Life Recovery Bible*.

SEPTEMBER 13

There's Power in Rejoicing

Whatever happens, my dear brothers and sisters,
rejoice in the Lord. I never get tired of telling you these
things, and I do it to safeguard your faith.

PHILIPPIANS 3:1

THERE IS GREAT POWER IN REJOICING IN the Lord—whatever happens. One of the many benefits of rejoicing is that it reinforces our new life. Another benefit is that our mental and even physical health can once again flourish if we make rejoicing a priority—rejoicing not in ourselves and our accomplishments but rejoicing in the Lord for who he is and what he's done. Rejoicing calls to mind the idea of bringing joy to the forefront of our thoughts and expressing that joy through words, song, or in the silence of our own minds.

Such rejoicing is an antidote to the weariness and discouragement we may find in the world. Spend time rejoicing now before you move on in your day—and whatever happens today, rejoice in the Lord.

✝ *Lord, sometimes I can't rejoice in myself, but I can always rejoice in you. Nothing about you ever changes. You are always generous, merciful, faithful, and loving to me. No matter what happens, I can always find cause for great rejoicing. Today, my weapon against whatever comes against me will be my ability to rejoice in you—and to take joy in you.*

When you cannot rejoice in feelings, circumstances or conditions, rejoice in the Lord.

A. B. SIMPSON (1843–1919)

You can find today's Scripture passage on page 1524 of *The Life Recovery Bible.*

Persecution

Everyone who wants to live a godly life in
Christ Jesus will suffer persecution.

2 TIMOTHY 3:12

AT SOME POINT, IF YOU SHARE YOUR RECOVERY journey with friends still enslaved to addiction, you may be taunted for your decision. You'll hear, "I tried recovery, and it doesn't work." Or: "Oh, so you've 'got religion' now?" Or you just may become an outcast among former friends. That's part of the price of following Christ. But if you'll stay on the recovery road, you'll find new friends as you sadly watch your former friends stay in their addictions. Live right, and allow them to see a recovery that does work.

† *Father, you have changed my life. I've already seen the difference you've made, and I know you have many more plans for my future. My hope now is that friends who have known me in my addiction will see the changes you're making and they'll want to give up their dependency for the freedom I've found in you. Lord, they know, and I know, that "religion" isn't what brings about change. Only a relationship with you, the living God, can work the miracle of recovery.*

Let me beg you, not to rest contented with the commonplace religion that is now so prevalent.

ADONIRAM JUDSON (1788–1850)

You can find today's Scripture passage on page 1564 of *The Life Recovery Bible*.

"What If . . . ?"

All who listen to me will live in peace,
untroubled by fear of harm.

PROVERBS 1:33

OUR LIVES ARE FULL OF "WHAT IFS." What if this happens, or what if that should happen? What would we do? How could we bear it? But if we're living in close fellowship with God, all these "what ifs" will drop out of our lives. Worry accomplishes nothing. Besides, studies have shown that up to 85 percent of the things we worry about never come to pass. Even philosopher Michel de Montaigne noted, "My life has been filled with terrible misfortune; most of which never happened."[2]

Be done with the "what if" whispers of the enemy. Refuse the fear they attempt to lay on you. Remember that God does not acknowledge our "what ifs."

✝ ***Lord, so many times I've played the "what if" game, fearful of what might happen to bring me down. But, God, you don't play that game. You offer me peace and a life untroubled by fear of what might happen. Nothing can penetrate your surrounding presence.***

> We shall be quiet from the fear of evil, for no threatenings of evil can penetrate into the high tower of God.
>
> **HANNAH WHITALL SMITH (1832–1911)**

---

[2] Don Joseph Goewey, "85 Percent of What We Worry About Never Happens," *HuffPost*, December 6, 2017, https://www.huffpost.com/entry/85-of-what-we-worry-about_b_8028368.

You can find today's Scripture passage on page 788 of *The Life Recovery Bible*.

Forsaking the Right Way

Forsaking the right way,
they have gone astray.
2 PETER 2:15, ESV

IN OUR PRESENT DAY, the black and white of right and wrong have become gray. What was once known as an evil is now tolerated or even celebrated. But to do that requires forsaking the right way for the wrong way. Those who choose to do that have gone astray.

Our first indulgence in what would become our addiction was a step leading us astray. Recovery is simply reversing the process: Forsaking the wrong way and choosing the right way. Therein lies our happiness.

✝ ***God, the way to life and happiness is narrow but right. For a long time, I had forsaken the right way and went astray. Now, though, I'm back on the right way. I follow your lead on the journey ahead. Instead of accepting the gray choice of what's permissible, I now choose to see the clear-cut choices of right and wrong. It will make all the difference!***

> The Narrow Way must be followed, no matter how much it may militate against my worldly interests. It is right here that the testing point is reached: it is much easier (unto the natural man) and far pleasanter to indulge the flesh and follow our worldly propensities. The Broad Road, where the flesh is allowed "liberty" under the pretense of the Christian's not "being under the law" is easy, smooth, and attractive; but it ends in "destruction!" Though the "Narrow Way" leads to life, only few tread it.
>
> A. W. PINK (1886–1952)

You can find today's Scripture passage on page 1624 of *The Life Recovery Bible*.

The Fleeting Pleasures of Sin

It was by faith that Moses, when he grew up, refused to be called the son of Pharaoh's daughter. He chose to share the oppression of God's people instead of enjoying the fleeting pleasures of sin.

HEBREWS 11:24-25

WE CAN REMEMBER THE EARLY DAYS of our addiction. We remember anticipating the promised pleasure. The offered candy was sweet, and it quickly drew us in. But it wasn't long before we understood that the candy was poison and it could kill us—*wanted* to kill us. By then, it seemed too late. Though the pleasure was there, it was "fleeting," leaving us unfulfilled . . . until the next time. Over and over, the process repeated. The lure of the candy, the sweet taste, then the letdown, the depression, the guilt.

By faith, Moses escaped the lure of the candy. And it's by faith that those of us who have tasted the candy must also escape to find our freedom. We do this as we become unwilling to enjoy the poisonous candy, despite the alluring taste, and instead, choose the joys of sobriety. Joy, love, peace, which can be found in recovery, all become antidotes to the poison of addiction.

† *Father, I well remember the lure of the candy. I remember, too, how quickly it turned to poison and affected every aspect of my life. Now, with Moses as an example of one who gave up the fleeting pleasures of sin, I, too, refuse to return to the poisoned candy of addiction. I do this knowing that I won't really be giving up something; I'll be gaining something—a blessed life that far exceeds the alluring taste of poisoned candy.*

Faith in the blessing of God on the people of God; union in spirit with the Christ of God; the assurance of a coming world, with its reversal of the judgments of earth—no wonder that all this guided and strengthened [Moses] to the choice he made, the good part never to be taken away.

ANDREW MURRAY (1828–1917)

You can find today's Scripture passage on page 1591 of *The Life Recovery Bible.*

Pressing On

Since we are surrounded by such a huge crowd of witnesses to the life of faith, let us strip off every weight that slows us down, especially the sin that so easily trips us up. And let us run with endurance the race God has set before us.

HEBREWS 12:1

WHEN WE COME TO CHRIST, WE MUST, of necessity, lay aside the heavy weight of addiction. We must cast off the sin that so easily trips us up. Then we "run with endurance the race God has set before us." We each have our own laps to run, but we have the love of God urging us on—and the crowd of witnesses who have gone on before. We can do this.

† *Lord, the weight is heavy, but it is set aside so I can run my race with endurance, nothing holding me back. I know a crowd of witnesses has gone on this road before me—many of them knowing my struggle. Thank you for their encouragement. Thank you for the love that urges me on. I will finish this race with joy.*

There is usually one sin that is the favorite—the sin which the heart is most fond of. . . . A godly man will not indulge his darling sin. . . . A godly man fights this king sin. . . . If we would have peace in our souls, we must maintain a war against our favorite sin, and never leave off until it is subdued.

THOMAS WATSON (1620–1686)

You can find today's Scripture passage on page 1592 of *The Life Recovery Bible*.

Holiness Is Happiness

God has called us to live holy lives, not impure lives. Therefore, anyone who refuses to live by these rules is not disobeying human teaching but is rejecting God, who gives his Holy Spirit to you.

1 THESSALONIANS 4:7-8

***HOLINESS* CAN SOUND LIKE SUCH** a religious word. We think of the teasing accusations of being "holier than thou." Holiness has been given a bad rap in some circles. But the truth is that holiness brings happiness to the one who lives it. That's why God calls us to holiness, not impurity, which leads only to misery and unhappiness. Make "Holiness Is Happiness" one of your mottoes. Pursue the holiness that comes from the residence of the *Holy* Spirit within.

✝ *Lord, I look at my life and wonder how you can consider me holy. And yet that is the life you've called me to. You even reckon me as holy now, based on my faith in Christ. Thank you for the happiness I find in holiness. It sure beats the unhappiness I found in living an unholy life.*

Holiness is not something we are called upon to do in order that we may become something; it is something we are to do because of what we already are.

MARTYN LLOYD-JONES (1899–1981)

You can find today's Scripture passage on page 1540 of *The Life Recovery Bible.*

The Cards Are Stacked

You bless the godly, O LORD;
you surround them with your shield of love.

PSALM 5:12

THOSE WITH A GAMBLING ADDICTION KNOW THAT, in a casino, the cards are stacked against them. So, too, in any addiction are the cards stacked against us. There's simply no way to win in life as an addict. The payoff for the addict eventually becomes death itself.

However, in righteousness, in recovery, the cards are stacked in our favor. A repentant addict who enters recovery has all the forces of God himself now aligned to work in his or her favor. In recovery, the casino of sin is shut down forever.

✝ *God, in walking away from the casino of addiction, I walk into a life where the "cards" are in my favor. I leave behind a pair of threes for a Royal Flush. Loving you and serving you is the best wager I can make. The pot is mine!*

Belief is a wise wager. Granted that faith cannot be proved, what harm will come to you if you gamble on its truth and it proves false? . . . If you gain, you gain all; if you lose, you lose nothing. Wager, then, without hesitation, that He exists.

BLAISE PASCAL (1623–1662)

You can find today's Scripture passage on page 682 of *The Life Recovery Bible.*

Escaping the Pit of Depression

Answer me quickly, O LORD!
My spirit fails!
Hide not your face from me,
lest I be like those who go down to the pit.
Let me hear in the morning of your steadfast love,
for in you I trust.
Make me know the way I should go,
for to you I lift up my soul.

PSALM 143:7-8, ESV

HAVE YOU BEEN THERE? HAS YOUR SPIRIT FAILED? Have you been in "the pit"? That was the case with David as he wrote Psalm 143. He was so desperate, his request to God was for a quick answer. To have God's face hidden was sheer misery. So what was David's remedy? He wrote, "To you I lift up my soul" (verse 8). That's the mark of absolute surrender. That's the response we all must have when in the pit of despair, depression, a failing spirit. Surrender it all to God and come out of the pit.

✝ ***Lord, I've often been in the pit of depression. Some of it was due to my circumstances, some was due to the choices I made, and some was due to a cause unknown to me. But in every pit I've been in, you've been with me, even though I didn't realize it. Father, let's be done with the pit. Let's fill it in, cover it, make it disappear, supplant it with a fresh trust in you and the power of the Holy Spirit.***

> I find myself frequently depressed; perhaps more so than any other person here. And I find no better cure for that depression than to trust in the Lord with all my heart, and seek to realize afresh the power of the peace-speaking blood of Jesus, and His infinite love in dying upon the cross to put away all my transgressions.
>
> CHARLES SPURGEON (1834–1892)

You can find today's Scripture passage on page 777 of *The Life Recovery Bible.*

Prosperity

They are like trees planted along the riverbank,
bearing fruit each season.
Their leaves never wither,
and they prosper in all they do.

PSALM 1:3

PROSPERITY IS OFTEN TAKEN TODAY AS RELATING to finances. But Merriam-Webster defines *prosperity* as "thriving." And for the Christian, that's the biblical connotation of prosperity. We may or may not be financially prosperous, but we can all be spiritually prosperous. We can all *thrive* in life. This happens by being planted where God wants us—by the streams of water. When we're where God wants us—and recovery *is* where God wants us—we yield good fruit, and our leaves do not wither. In all we do, *we shall proper.*

✝ *Father, prosper me! Not so much financially but spiritually, mentally, and physically. Plant me along the riverbank. Set my roots deep. Bring forth fruit for every season. May my blessings overflow in all I do.*

Let us carefully avoid everything that would hinder our prosperity. . . . Let us not only carefully avoid everything likely to *hinder*—but let us diligently employ every means to *secure* it. Prosperity flows from God: it is a free-grace blessing; but it flows in a certain channel, and is generally attracted by certain means.

JAMES SMITH (1802–1862)

You can find today's Scripture passage on page 680 of *The Life Recovery Bible*.

Laughter

We were filled with laughter,
and we sang for joy.
And the other nations said,
"What amazing things the Lord has done for them."

PSALM 126:2

HAVE YOU LAUGHED AT YOUR SITUATION? We've all mourned over our addiction, but have we laughed with joy at the goodness of God in unlocking our chains? Have we laughed at the defeat of the enemy who kept us captive for so long?

God invites us to laugh because of the "amazing things the Lord has done." Has God done great things for you? Yes, he has. Then use your tongue to sing for joy, and fill your mouth with godly laughter. Yes, it sounds like an odd part of recovery, but oh what a release it is to laugh with shouts of joy because of the amazing things God has done for us! Replace your mourning with the kind of laughter God loves to hear from his redeemed ones.

† *God, thank you for laughter. As tragic as addiction is, I need to be able to laugh as therapy in my recovery. You have surely done amazing things in my life, and I know that, as I continue to trust you, more amazement lies ahead for me. Lord, I sing for joy, and I laugh for the great victory you have brought into my life.*

The most beautiful and beneficial therapy God ever granted humanity: laughter.

CHARLES SWINDOLL (1934–)

You can find today's Scripture passage on page 770 of *The Life Recovery Bible*.

Live According to Truth

Teach me your ways, O LORD,
that I may live according to your truth!
Grant me purity of heart,
so that I may honor you.

PSALM 86:11

WE MUST LIVE ACCORDING TO WHAT IS TRUE. Truth must be *in* us, not simply as an add-on to who we are but basic to our very core. Addiction is the opposite of truth. Addiction is built on lies. Recovery is tearing down those lies one at a time and, in their place, establishing our lives on the truths of God's Word. We rely on God teaching us his way so that we can live according to truth.

✝ *Lord Jesus, you are the truth. You are the way. You are life itself. I pray that you grant me purity of heart so I honor you. Teach me your ways as I forsake my own devices and designs. Bring me into more truth that will enable me to walk closer to you.*

The gospel is not speculation but fact. It is truth, because it is the record of a Person who is the Truth.

ALEXANDER MACLAREN (1826–1910)

You can find today's Scripture passage on page 740 of *The Life Recovery Bible*.

Clothed in His Righteousness

I no longer count on my own righteousness through obeying the law;
rather, I become righteous through faith in Christ.
For God's way of making us right with himself depends on faith.

PHILIPPIANS 3:9

RIGHTEOUSNESS—RIGHT STANDING with God—is, like salvation, a gift of God we receive by faith. We have no other way to righteousness than by faith. Self-righteousness is as filthy rags (see Isaiah 64:6). God "reckons" us as righteous the moment we believe in Christ and receive him as Savior. We must then reckon ourselves as God reckons us: righteous by faith.

✝ *Father, by faith, I am saved. By faith, I am righteous with the righteousness of Christ. I lay aside my own perceived righteousness made of filthy rags. I trust that you will credit my account with Christ's obedience and his righteousness. I choose to reckon myself righteous because that's how you reckon me, regardless of how I feel. Thank you, righteous Lord, for the free gift of righteousness.*

> Christ took our sins and the sins of the whole world as well as the Father's wrath on his shoulders, and he has drowned them both in himself so that we are thereby reconciled to God and become completely righteous.
>
> MARTIN LUTHER (1483–1546)

You can find today's Scripture passage on page 1524 of *The Life Recovery Bible*.

Child of God

To all who believed him and accepted him,
he gave the right to become children of God.

JOHN 1:12

TRUE HAPPINESS IS BEING FAITHFUL TO WHO God says we are, not to who we think we are or who we wish we were. Happiness comes from receiving Christ and believing in his name. Our happiness, then, is rooted in our relationship to Christ.

Think of a parent's love for their child—if you're a parent, think of your love for your child. Magnify that love an infinite number of times, and you'll approximate God's love for you.

† *God, my so-called adulthood hasn't always been so great. It is far better to be recognized as your child, with all the accrued benefits. Thank you for being a true Father to me and for treating me as would a faithful parent. You bless me but never spoil me. You discipline me but never harm me. You're sometimes silent, but you never leave me. The right to become your child has been my greatest blessing.*

I wonder many times that ever a child of God should have a sad heart,
considering what the Lord is preparing for him.

SAMUEL RUTHERFORD (1600–1661)

You can find today's Scripture passage on page 1341 of *The Life Recovery Bible.*

Living in Triumph

The sin of this one man, Adam, caused death to rule over many. But even greater is God's wonderful grace and his gift of righteousness, for all who receive it will live in triumph over sin and death through this one man, Jesus Christ.

ROMANS 5:17

TO "LIVE IN TRIUMPH" IS TO BE IN CHARGE of one's life rather than a victim of circumstances or an addiction. Because of God's grace, we have moved from being "under the pile" to being apart from the pile. Where we once had surrendered our freedom and become subjects to our slave master addictions, we now have received the abundance of grace that is freely ours—and we triumph as though royal monarchs.

† *Father, it seems like a long trip from where I was—under the reign of the enemy—to where I am now—reigning in life. In your love for me, you have not only restored me but are allowing me to triumph in life—giving me the ability not simply to exist or go through life's motions but to be out from under the bottom of the pile. For this, I praise you.*

The riches of His free grace cause me daily to triumph over all the temptations of the wicked one, who is very vigilant, and seeks all occasions to disturb me.

GEORGE WHITEFIELD (1714–1770)

You can find today's Scripture passage on page 1438 of *The Life Recovery Bible.*

God Our Rock

No one is holy like the LORD!
There is no one besides you;
there is no Rock like our God.

1 SAMUEL 2:2

ADDICTION BREEDS INSECURITY. During our addiction days, we were standing on sand. Our emotions ran hot and cold. Our ability to trust was diminished as our fears increased. Our instability caused us to make wrong decisions. But trusting in the Lord brings security to the recovering addict. We move from sinking sand to standing on a solid Rock—the Rock that is our God. Regain your sense of security by clinging to the "Rock of ages."

✝ *Wow, Lord. I remember so well the shifting sands of my addiction. I could practically feel my feet slip from under me. But then I found stability in you. Thank you for setting me on a Rock that cannot crumble or erode with the passage of time. Father, there is no rock like you. Safe, stable, and sure. What security I find when I trust in you!*

> Take your stand on the Rock of Ages. Let death, let the grave, let the judgment come: the victory is Christ's and yours through Him.
>
> D. L. MOODY (1837–1899)

You can find today's Scripture passage on page 346 of *The Life Recovery Bible*.

Nothing Can Separate Us

I am convinced that nothing can ever separate us from God's love. Neither death nor life, neither angels nor demons, neither our fears for today nor our worries about tomorrow—not even the powers of hell can separate us from God's love. No power in the sky above or in the earth below—indeed, nothing in all creation will ever be able to separate us from the love of God that is revealed in Christ Jesus our Lord.

ROMANS 8:38-39

"NOTHING IN ALL CREATION WILL EVER be able to separate us from the love of God." What beautiful words they are considering our addiction falls under the umbrella of "all creation." Even addiction cannot separate us from the love of God in Christ Jesus our Lord.

To not be separate is to be joined. We who believe in Christ are *joined* to the Lord—and are never separated from his love. Because of this, we are fearless in the face of all the things that we've imagined could separate us from our Lord.

† *God, though you were present with me in my addiction, I still felt separated, and I know that it was I who did the separating. But in Christ, there is no separation, perceived or otherwise. You have joined me to yourself in a way that is impossible to sever. No power in the sky above or on the earth below nor anything in all creation can divide me from you. This is pure love of your part. Thank you, Father.*

None can take Christ from the believer: none can take the believer from Him; and that is enough.

MATTHEW HENRY (1662–1714)

You can find today's Scripture passage on page 1442 of *The Life Recovery Bible.*

Guarding Our Eyes

I will set nothing wicked before my eyes.

PSALM 101:3, NKJV

ONE OF THE MOST DANGEROUS PARTS OF a recovering addict's physical self is our eyes. Our eyes are the entry point into our bodies. What we see will have an effect on what we do. This is the reason behind the many appeals to the eyes in advertising campaigns.

Guarding our eyes will save us from many a blunder, many a sin. Assaults to our eyes come through innocent means every day, but the most dangerous temptations come when we see an attraction and invite it into our lives by acting as if it were of little consequence. We must take care of our eyes, for every time we resolve to set no wicked thing before them, we remove another brick from the wall that addiction built.

† *Father, my eyes are inlets to my being—for good or for bad. As I resolve to guard my eyes, help me to quickly reject tempting images by bouncing my gaze off the offending sight and onto something more edifying. Help me escape the corruption that sometimes comes through sight.*

> The eyes have a great influence upon the heart either to good or evil—but chiefly to evil. In this corrupt state of man, by looking—we come to liking, and are brought inordinately to love what we behold.
>
> THOMAS MANTON (1620–1677)

You can find today's Scripture passage on page 748 of *The Life Recovery Bible*.

OCTOBER 1

Rebuilding

I will restore the fortunes of Judah and
Israel and rebuild their towns.

JEREMIAH 33:7

WHEN THERE IS DESTRUCTION AMONG God's people, God's goal is to rebuild, whether the fortunes of Judah and Israel or a man or woman caught up in addiction.

So much of recovery is rebuilding what was lost during addiction. We often see on the news victims of floods, fires, and earthquakes who have lost everything. In almost every case, they shed their tears and then vow to rebuild. They will not let tragedy dictate their futures. We must be like-minded. Yes, rebuilding may seem daunting, but it's doable. God is with us every step of the way. If we are obedient to God and rebuild, he will work with us.

† *Lord, you are the Great Rebuilder of lives. My own life is in your hands. You can tear down the shambles that need to be removed and, in their place, build the solid, restored life I prize. Just as victims of natural disasters rebuild, so I, too, shall rebuild—and the latter dwelling, built on a surer foundation, will stand the test of time.*

> When disaster has come to us . . . [w]e should not waste a moment in grieving over the ruin—but should quickly begin to rebuild our place with joy and trust.
>
> J. R. MILLER (1840–1912)

You can find today's Scripture passage on page 976 of *The Life Recovery Bible.*

Faith

Faith shows the reality of what we hope for;
it is the evidence of things we cannot see.

HEBREWS 11:1

USUALLY, WHEN AN ADDICTED PERSON enters Christian recovery, sobriety is hoped for but not yet seen. If the seed of faith, though small, is implanted in the sobriety seeker, and watered by the Word and encouraged by fellow believers, that faith will grow, and the things not seen, including sobriety, will likewise grow. Without the kind of faith that brings about sobriety, our hope is sparse. Our basis for faith is the character of God, the one who is always for us, who sees us as sober men and women, not as the slaves of addiction we once were.

Let your faith that God will nourish your sobriety enable you to see the invisible, believe the unbelievable, and receive the impossible in your recovery.

† *God, my faith may have started small and may even yet be smaller than I'd like, but it is growing, as is my sobriety. Help me see the sobriety that you see. Assist me in believing what is yet unseen. Aid me in receiving the impossible.*

Faith sees the invisible, believes the unbelievable, and receives the impossible.

CORRIE TEN BOOM (1892–1983)

You can find today's Scripture passage on page 1590 of *The Life Recovery Bible*.

Daily Strength

As your days, so shall your strength be.

DEUTERONOMY 33:25, ESV

FAILURE OR RELAPSE MAY COME WHEN WE START to feel as if we don't have the strength to go on with sobriety. It may appear much easier to relax our efforts and not take recovery so seriously. The problem is that often we really *don't* have the strength to go on because we've slipped back into the habit of relying on our own power—willpower—to make it through our days. God gives strength, but it's strength for today only, not for tomorrow.

God never requires more from us in a day than we're able to give. Through him, we can do more than we think we can.

✝ ***Dear Lord, I've learned through failure that I can't rely on sheer willpower to bring about my recovery. I need a recovery empowered by your strength. Father, watch over me, your child, and protect me. Shield me from the enemy's advances, and save me from my own futile efforts to be whole.***

Daily living by faith on Christ is what makes the difference between the sickly and the healthy Christian, between the defeated and the victorious saint.

A. W. PINK (1886–1952)

You can find today's Scripture passage on page 261 of *The Life Recovery Bible*.

In Light of Eternity

What we suffer now is nothing compared
to the glory he will reveal to us later.

ROMANS 8:18

IT'S NATURAL THAT, in recovering from addiction, our present sufferings press on us daily. And yet God would have us turn our thoughts about our present situation into seeing by faith what lies ahead. There is glory to be revealed to all who belong to Christ. Bearing up is so much easier when we determine to see our earthly lives in light of eternity. When your load gets heavy, bear it soberly, looking ahead to a greater eternity that will far outweigh today's woes.

† *Lord, living for my addiction was central to all I did. My addiction was always focused on the present moment and what brief "pleasure" it offered me. As far as the future was concerned, it really didn't exist. Now, though, my life is all about the present* and *the future. My past falls away when I think about a positive future here in this life and the glory to be revealed when I'm in eternity. I wouldn't go back to yesterday for any price. Thank you, Lord, for the glory to be revealed in me.*

How light is death, compared with the weight of glory? . . . How short, in respect of eternity? The present suffering is not worthy of the glory which shall be revealed in the children of God.

THOMAS WATSON (1620–1686)

You can find today's Scripture passage on page 1442 of *The Life Recovery Bible*.

God Is Faithful

If we are unfaithful,
he remains faithful,
for he cannot deny who he is.

2 TIMOTHY 2:13

ANY CHRISTIAN WHO HAS SUFFERED FROM AN addiction can recall times of personal unfaithfulness to God. It simply goes with addiction. We may have, at times, chosen our addiction over a calling from God. We may have hurt others with our unfaithfulness. But even in all our unfaithfulness, *God has remained faithful to us.* And so he will continue as the one who has our back at all times. That's simply the nature of the God we serve.

✝ *Wow, God! I am in awe when I consider how you have remained faithful to me even as I've often been unfaithful to you. For me, and the others I know, unfaithfulness seems to be part of the human condition. But, on the other hand, faithfulness is clearly part of your nature. You cannot be unfaithful. Lord, in your secure faithfulness to me, I find the power to go on in recovery. Your faithfulness is my support.*

> Have you been holding back from a risky, costly course to which you know in your heart God has called you? Hold back no longer. Your God is faithful to you, and he is adequate for you. You will never need more than he can supply, and what he supplies, both materially and spiritually, will always be enough for the present.
>
> J. I. PACKER (1926–2020)

You can find today's Scripture passage on page 1562 of *The Life Recovery Bible.*

Victory through Faith

Every child of God defeats this evil world, and
we achieve this victory through our faith.

1 JOHN 5:4

AN ADDICT READING THE NEW TESTAMENT can't help but notice the emphasis on faith. And rightly so. Ultimately, even with the aid of recovery programs and support groups, it must be faith—personal faith—that wins the day and hastens us across the finish line. If we have been born of God, then we *have*, by faith in Christ, defeated this evil world.

When we feel weak or discouraged or tempted, what we need is a fresh encounter with overcoming faith. This faith will prevail over our strongest emotions and temptations.

✝ *Father, there's so much you want to give me and to invest in me that I must receive by faith. Lord, my victory over this world and its abundant evils actually enables me to see that there is good in this world that can be received by faith. Restored relationships, a destiny designed by you, the enjoyment of nature, all of which I can access by faith alone. Yes, there is an enemy that rails against my faith, but even that enemy is defeated by the very faith he tries to destroy in me. Thank you, Father, for a sure victory that always prevails.*

> [Jesus] says to us: "Do not be afraid of the world. It is not an invincible enemy. It has been conquered. I have overcome it; so may you. I did it for you, and have weakened its power. You fight with a wounded, beaten foe. Believe me. My victory shall insure yours."
>
> JOHN ANGELL JAMES (1785–1859)

You can find today's Scripture passage on page 1633 of *The Life Recovery Bible.*

Let the Holy Spirit Guide

Let the Holy Spirit guide your lives.
Then you won't be doing what your sinful nature craves.

GALATIANS 5:16

ADDICTION IS A WORK OF THE SINFUL NATURE. God's remedy to a life led by the sinful nature is to be guided by the Holy Spirit. We cannot walk in the Spirit and at the same time gratify our sinful nature. When our carnal nature cries out, we must not consent to give in to it. We have a choice as to whether we will walk in the Spirit or give in to our cravings. One choice brings happiness and the fruit of the Spirit; the other brings death and the fruits of the sinful nature, addiction among them.

✝ *Lord, temptation is always to be overcome, never to be yielded to. So as part of me cries out for its illicit desires, I must have your Holy Spirit to help me resist. I must have the fruit of the Spirit to triumph over my sinful desires. May your will—the overcoming of wrong and hurtful desires—be done in my life.*

If thou wouldst conquer thy weakness, thou must never gratify it. No man is compelled to evil: his consent only makes it his. It is no sin to be tempted, but to be overcome.

WILLIAM PENN (1644–1718)

You can find today's Scripture passage on page 1505 of *The Life Recovery Bible.*

The Accuser

The accuser of our brothers and sisters
has been thrown down to earth—
the one who accuses them
before our God day and night.
And they have defeated him by the blood of the Lamb
and by their testimony.

REVELATION 12:10-11

MANY CHRISTIANS WHO HAVE BECOME addicted know that a good portion of Satan's victory in addiction isn't our acting out—it's the pile of condemnation that follows our acting out. We can almost hear Satan's accusations of us—not just before the throne of God but in our own hearts. It seems that condemnation is *the* primary motive of Satan in luring us back.

But here's the remedy: Don't listen to Satan's accusations. Refuse them in the name of Jesus. If you have confessed your sin, then receive the forgiveness provided for you in Christ, and move on. We conquer Satan's accusations only by the blood of the Lamb and by our testimony.

✝ ***Lord, the enemy is relentless in his accusations against me. If I fail in some way, he's there to pronounce judgment, even when he was the tempter. His bold deception would be devastating if it weren't for the fact that you have saved me from all the garbage Satan accuses me of. I have joy in knowing that, though I have an accuser, I have a great Silencer in Christ. He stops the mouth of the accuser. Thank you, God, that I'm no longer susceptible to Satan's lies and accusations.***

> [Satan] commenced his attack on our first parents by accusing God before them, and representing Him as one harsh and unnecessarily severe in His threatenings of wrath against their disobedience. Having led man into sin, he then turns round and becomes his accuser before God! He is a double-dyed accuser; equally accusing God to man and man to God.
>
> **ARCHIBALD G. BROWN (1844–1922)**

You can find today's Scripture passage on page 1660 of *The Life Recovery Bible*.

All the Days of My Life

You prepare a table before me
in the presence of my enemies;
you anoint my head with oil;
my cup overflows.
Surely goodness and mercy shall follow me
all the days of my life,
and I shall dwell in the house of the LORD forever.

PSALM 23:5-6, ESV

HOW LONG WILL GOODNESS AND MERCY follow us? Only all the days of our lives. God never stops pursuing us, even at our worst. Perhaps *especially* at our worst. God's door of mercy is open today and always. Our worst act need never be our final act.

✝ *Lord, only you know my life span and how many years I have left. But I know that no matter the number of my days I have here on the earth, your goodness and unfailing love will pursue me every single one of them. The door of your mercy never closes on me. Your salvation is as good as your Word. My future is this: I will live in your house forever!*

Every ransomed man owes his salvation to the fact that during the days of his sinning God kept the door of mercy open by refusing to accept any of his evil acts as final.

A. W. TOZER (1897–1963)

You can find today's Scripture passage on page 694 of *The Life Recovery Bible.*

The Mystery of God

Just as you cannot understand the path of the wind or the mystery of a tiny baby growing in its mother's womb, so you cannot understand the activity of God, who does all things.

ECCLESIASTES 11:5

TRYING TO EXPLAIN GOD TO UNBELIEVERS CAN seem complicated because he is . . . well . . . a mystery. We don't understand all of God's reasons or motives. We must often admit we don't know the answers to questions any reasonable person might ask. At such times, we should just enjoy pondering the mystery of God's love. Unanswered questions should never deter or detour us from our promised sobriety. We will have answers someday, but for now, we know all we need to know to have a recovered life.

† *Lord, there are many mysteries about life, about the Good News of the gospel, and about eternity. There are questions for which I don't have answers, but then I've had questions in the past that you did eventually answer. Some of your servants, like Robert Murray M'Cheyne, died at the young age of thirty. Why should that be so? And yet M'Cheyne didn't need to hear an answer to why he was called home to you so soon. He was content to be still and trust in you, the one who sees the end from the beginning. I, too, can trust you for all my unanswered questions.*

When Christ delays to help his saints now, you think this is a great mystery—you cannot explain it; but Jesus sees the end from the beginning. Be still, and know that Christ is God.

ROBERT MURRAY M'CHEYNE (1813–1843)

You can find today's Scripture passage on page 833 of *The Life Recovery Bible.*

Testimony Time

You will receive power when the Holy Spirit comes upon you. And you will be my witnesses, telling people about me everywhere—in Jerusalem, throughout Judea, in Samaria, and to the ends of the earth.

ACTS 1:8

IN OUR POST-ADDICTION LIVES, WE CAN'T KEEP our way of recovery to ourselves. Just as a court will have witnesses testify as to what happened in the matter at hand, we are compelled by concern for those coming behind us to tell them of our own recovery experience.

Though it's unwise to do so early in recovery, it would be beneficial at some point to write out your "testimony" for the sake of others. Be willing to share your experience—even your lapses and what may have caused them. God will give you the right words, just as he's given you the very experience you will testify about.

† *Lord, help me know when to speak of my recovery and when to let my actions speak for me. I want all I say about my journey to be true. When you give me opportunities, may I speak boldly and truthfully about my entrance into sobriety and how what I've been through can help others.*

If lips and life do not agree, the testimony will not amount to much.

HARRY IRONSIDE (1876–1951)

You can find today's Scripture passage on page 1381 of *The Life Recovery Bible*.

The Perfecting Nature of God's Work in Us

You are to be perfect,
even as your Father in heaven is perfect.
MATTHEW 5:48

GOD DOESN'T DO THINGS HALFWAY. His goal is complete recovery. However, he's in no hurry to complete his work. Every believer, even one without a history of addiction, is in some sort of recovery. We all learn, observe, make mistakes, and grow. All through the process, God is at work. Even today, though you may or may not see it openly, God has his hand on you, guiding you along your recovery journey.

† *Lord, being perfect is impossible! And yet that's what you want from me. But then I read that my perfection is to be as you, in heaven, are perfect. My perfection, then, comes from you. In my own strength, there is no perfection to be found. But if my perfection comes from you, I cannot fail. Oh, God, what a treasure, then, is being perfect!*

It is only imperfection that complains of what is imperfect. The more perfect we are, the more gentle and quiet we become toward the defects of others.
FRANÇOIS FÉNELON (1651–1715)

You can find today's Scripture passage on page 1204 of *The Life Recovery Bible*.

OCTOBER 13

The Hidden Life

You died to this life, and your real life
is hidden with Christ in God.

COLOSSIANS 3:3

WE KNOW THAT, AS BELIEVERS, we are "in Christ." That's our source of victory. But do we understand that we are "hidden" in Christ? Hidden from the world's temptations, from our corrupt old nature, from the enemy's tactics against us. We are hidden precisely because we're also "dead," having died to all that would corrupt us. What joy to know we are dead, yet we live. What happiness to know we're hidden in Christ yet in full view of others as a trophy of God's recovering work.

✝ *God, thank you that I'm now "hidden" with Christ! I'm hidden from all that would seek to devour me through addiction. In this hiding place, I'm always safe, always secure, and I have a well of happiness always accessible to me. Thank you that in dying to my old, open life, I'm now alive in Christ, hidden and happy.*

> There is nothing so deep, nothing so hidden, as the life of God in the soul. It seems to be enshrined in the lowest depths of a man's heart. It does not float upon the surface, like a cork upon the water, but sinks deep, very deep, into the very bottom of the soul. Therefore hidden from the eyes of a profane world; hidden from the professing world; and what is more, sometimes hidden from the subject of it himself. A child of God often cannot see his own faith, nor can he discern the life that is bubbling and streaming up in his own bosom. It is not a lake, spread abroad in the meridian sunshine to attract every eye; nor is it a brook that flows babbling on over the clear pebbles; but it is a well. . . . Therefore hidden from view.
>
> J. C. PHILPOT (1802–1869)

You can find today's Scripture passage on page 1534 of *The Life Recovery Bible.*

The Hand of God

[Jesus said,] "My Father, who has given them to me, is greater than all, and no one is able to snatch them out of the Father's hand."

JOHN 10:29, ESV

HAVE YOU EVER THOUGHT OF YOURSELF as a gift to Christ from God the Father? John tells us that we have been given to Christ by our heavenly Father, who is greater than all our adversaries and addictions. Even more, we are so secure in Christ, no one—not even the enemy of our souls and the source of our addiction—can snatch us from God's firm hand.

† *Thank you, Lord, that you have included me as a gift to your Son, Jesus. I praise you that, in your hand, I'm inaccessible to my mortal enemy. Neither can I be snatched away from your hand. This gift to your Son is irrevocable. Though many attempts have been made and will be made to lure me away, those attempts will be met with certain failure. The enemy cannot prevail against you!*

> There is always something plucking at Christ's sheep: the lust of the flesh, the lust of the eyes, the pride of life, the devil, and the world are ever striving hard to destroy them; but they shall not succeed. Think you the devil will give up his kingdom without a mighty struggle? Oh no, he goes about as a roaring lion seeking whom he may devour; he wars a constant warfare with all who keep the commandments of God and have the testimony of Jesus Christ—but the word of God is pledged that he shall never prevail. Not all the powers of darkness shall avail to quench one single spark of real gospel faith.
>
> J. C. RYLE (1816–1900)

You can find today's Scripture passage on page 1358 of *The Life Recovery Bible*.

OCTOBER 15

Nothing Is Wasted

After everyone was full, Jesus told his disciples,
"Now gather the leftovers, so that nothing is wasted."
JOHN 6:12

OF ALL GOD'S GREAT ATTRIBUTES, surely one of them is his unwillingness to waste anything. We are often reminded of our wasted time in the throes of addiction, but God, in his great economy, will not see those years go to waste. If we will listen and watch, God will teach us to look beyond our past and trust him to make a future out of it. This is our God—the God who wastes nothing.

† *Lord, you know how wasteful I've been in my past. But you, God, are never wasteful. Where I see ruins, you see the building blocks for success. Where I see ashes, you see fire. Where I see hopelessness, you see hope. Where I have wasted, you see a chance for restoration. Help me, Father, to see the good things you will do with what I have thought of as only "waste."*

> You must learn, you must let God teach you, that the only way to get rid of your past is to get a future out of it. God will waste nothing.
> PHILLIPS BROOKS (1835–1893)

You can find today's Scripture passage on page 1349 of *The Life Recovery Bible.*

The Evil behind the Mask of Light

Even Satan disguises himself as an angel of light.

2 CORINTHIANS 11:14

NEVER ALLOW YOUR MIND TO SUBMIT to the overtures of the enemy. Taking his bait will result in a return to the slavery from which you have been set free. And we know by now the bait he uses. We've seen it before—and so often, it's dressed up in glitz, so as to appear as light, not the darkness it is. The temptation is to remember the high, to crave it afresh, to think of it as light and desirable. A sign of growth in recovery is the ability to see the evil behind the mask of light and to instantly reject the invitation to indulge.

† *Lord, what you give hungry men and women is real and true, not a religion where one must work for approval. The enemy has his many temptations and often uses them to the best effect in order to recapture me in addiction. But I've seen the glitz. I've experienced the temporary thrills—and they are nothing to me as I rely on you. Though Satan disguises himself well, I easily rip off his mask of light and see his darkness for what it really is. And I overcome.*

Satan tempts to sin under a pretense of religion. He is most to be feared when he transforms himself into an angel of light. He came to Christ with Scripture in his mouth: "It is written." The devil baits his hook with religion.

THOMAS WATSON (1620–1686)

You can find today's Scripture passage on page 1492 of *The Life Recovery Bible*.

Come Closer

So humble yourselves before God. Resist the devil, and he will flee from you. Come close to God, and God will come close to you.

JAMES 4:7-8

FACE IT—RECOVERY FOR THE CHRISTIAN is a miracle. We simply could not recover on our own. God's love for us is shown in his presence during our recovery. He's the author of the miracle happening now in our lives. We must remember when we pray for a miracle, God shows up. And that's the miracle we really want. All else, including our recovery, springs from God's presence.

As you walk the path of recovery, know that you don't have to walk it alone. Draw near, then, to God, and he will draw near to you.

✝ *God, when you seem distant, that's the signal for me to move closer to you. When I do, I'll find that you have come closer to me. And in your closeness, your presence sustains me in both my trials and my triumphs.*

Hear this command, and practice it; get near to God in Christ Jesus, and you shall soon find him come to your help in every hour of need.

CHARLES SPURGEON (1834–1892)

You can find today's Scripture passage on page 1605 of *The Life Recovery Bible.*

Choose Wisely

God chose to save us through our Lord Jesus Christ,
not to pour out his anger on us.

1 THESSALONIANS 5:9

POSE THIS QUESTION TO YOURSELF: What does God want for me? Be specific. Don't just say, "Sobriety." Think about it before you answer. Then make a mental or written list of God's desired provision for you. When you're done, ask yourself: What does Satan want for me? Again, make a mental or written list of what you know to be Satan's desired end for you. What has been his desired end in some of your addicted friends? Now compare the lists.

Reflect on the lists you've created. You get to choose which list you prefer. Base your every decision on the choice you make. Choose wisely.

† *God, it's not hard for me to contrast the pros and cons of addiction with the pros and cons of sobriety. Frankly, there is no comparison. As I consider the lists I've made, help me to reflect on what kind of future you desire for me versus the future Satan desires for me through addiction. Help me keep those two images in my mind as I go about my day. Help me lean into the one clear choice as I also reject the more destructive option.*

Of one thing I am perfectly sure: God's story never ends with ashes.

ELISABETH ELLIOT (1926–2015)

You can find today's Scripture passage on page 1541 of *The Life Recovery Bible*.

OCTOBER 19

Are We Neglecting Our Salvation?

What makes us think we can escape if we ignore this great salvation that was first announced by the Lord Jesus himself and then delivered to us by those who heard him speak?

HEBREWS 2:3

TO NEGLECT OUR SALVATION IS TO neglect recovery. How do we neglect salvation and recovery? By not making them our number one priority. Anything we put ahead of our relationship to Christ, anything we prefer over sobriety, short-circuits our recovery. According to Merriam-Webster, the opposite of *neglect* is *cherish*. If cherish isn't how we consider our salvation and our recovery, it's time to rehearse again the tragedy of addiction and the benefits of sobriety.

† *Father, neglecting my great salvation is never an option for me. I cherish my relationship with you. I place my worship of you above all else. Show me more ways to demonstrate my appreciation for being saved from addiction—and saved to happiness.*

Salvation is represented, as a sovereign remedy for all our moral maladies. It is that which will restore us to spiritual health—and will make us holy, happy, and honorable. . . . It presents all that we can need to revive, refresh, and delight us. It contains a free, full, and immediate pardon, for all our sins, a title to everlasting life and happiness, a complete deliverance from sin, Satan, death, and Hell. It is a great salvation!

JAMES SMITH (1802–1862)

You can find today's Scripture passage on page 1579 of *The Life Recovery Bible*.

Leaving It Up to God

If you sinful people know how to give good gifts to your children,
how much more will your heavenly Father give
good gifts to those who ask him.

MATTHEW 7:11

THE MISPERCEPTION THAT GOD IS RELUCTANT to give us what we desire is too costly an error for the person in recovery to consider. In seeking sobriety, we're desperate enough to know how much we need a miracle from God.

A good father always gives good gifts to his children. Jesus tells us *how much more* our heavenly Father will give us good things if we but ask him, trust him as we would a good father, and believe. For those of us who know addiction, surely a joyful life of sobriety is our number one request—and God will answer that prayer.

✝ *God, learning to see and appreciate you as my true Father makes recovery easier. No earthly father would deny a hurting child the remedy for pain. How much more, then, can I trust you to provide for me, your child. Lord, I cry out to you for a deeper parent-child love and relationship. Hear my plea, Father.*

If an earthly parent does not allow his little ones to starve, but instead freely ministers to their needs, then certainly God will respond to the cries of His own children. They were but the begetters of our bodies; He the maker of our souls. Their resources are very limited; His are infinite!

A. W. PINK (1886–1952)

You can find today's Scripture passage on page 1206 of *The Life Recovery Bible*.

OCTOBER 21

The Most Beautiful Thing

He renews my strength.
He guides me along right paths,
bringing honor to his name.

PSALM 23:3

THE RESTORATION WORK OF GOD IN THE LIFE of a human soul is the most magnificent and beautiful thing in the world. And that work is present within all of us who are recovering from whatever addictions were part of our past. A healing moment can be had at any time during the day when we pause to consider the beauty of God's restoring work within us. Learn to look for those times when you can pause and whisper thanks for how God is restoring you.

† *God, I love the word* restoration *for, in restoration, I'm able to experience your healing power at work. Surely it began with forgiveness of all I've done that brought me so low in life. But beyond that initial forgiveness, you have provided a wonderful demonstration of your love for me in practical ways. You bring the right people into my life, you provide the right teaching that builds me up, and you meet me in prayer every time I call on you. Thank you, Lord, for this most beautiful thing called* restoration.

When God forgives, He at once restores.

THEODORE EPP (1907–1985)

You can find today's Scripture passage on page 694 of *The Life Recovery Bible.*

Relentless

The Son of Man came to seek and
save those who are lost.

LUKE 19:10

THE LORD CAME TO EARTH IN THE PERSON of Jesus Christ with a mission in mind. He wasn't here just for a visit; he was here to save those who were lost. He was here to save *us*. How committed was he in this mission? He was relentless. He suffered death on the cruel cross in order to fulfill his mission. That is commitment.

We, too, must be relentless in our mission of recovery. We must be steadfast and unmovable despite frequent temptations to chuck it all and default to our addiction. Consider the depth of your commitment to total recovery, acknowledging that your foe is also relentless in his attacks against you. Nevertheless, you will succeed because you *must* succeed.

† *Father, when I consider the relentless nature of Christ's commitment to his mission, I'm reminded of my own mission of recovery. I will be steadfast and relentless in maintaining sobriety and overcoming the magnetic pull of my old life. Thank you, Lord, for the example I have in Christ. May his relentlessness be my guide in recovery and in my battle against a persistent foe.*

> Looked at from an earthly viewpoint, could any life have been more narrow in its condition than Christ's? Think who he was—the Son of God, sinless, holy, loving, infinitely gentle of heart. Then think of the life into which he came—the relentless hate that was about him, the bitter enmity that pursued him, the rejection of love that met him at every step. Think of the failure of his mission, as it seemed, and his betrayal and death. Yet he was never discouraged. He never grew bitter.
>
> J. R. MILLER (1840–1912)

You can find today's Scripture passage on page 1324 of *The Life Recovery Bible*.

OCTOBER 23

Thankful Hearts

Sing psalms and hymns and spiritual songs to God with thankful hearts. And whatever you do or say, do it as a representative of the Lord Jesus, giving thanks through him to God the Father.

COLOSSIANS 3:16-17

THANKFULNESS IS THE FOREVER MINDSET of the addict who is on the recovery journey. From the beginning, where we can be grateful for God's rescuing us, each mile of the way—even across rough terrain—brings a song into our hearts. God's Word feeds us on the journey—and we find no leftovers along the way. Like the Hebrews on their journey in Exodus, who were given fresh manna every day, we are given strength to overcome every morning. To neglect the "manna" is to starve. To partake is to be strengthened—and thankful.

✝ *Lord, I raise my voice to you in song, knowing you listen to the words in my heart. They are words of thankfulness, songs and hymns of praise and worship to you. I have so much to be thankful for—and I well know this. Hear my heart, O God.*

Careful for nothing, prayerful for everything, thankful for anything.

D. L. MOODY (1837–1899)

You can find today's Scripture passage on page 1534 of *The Life Recovery Bible*.

Our Unpredictable God

[Jesus] spit on the ground, made mud with the saliva, and spread the mud over the blind man's eyes. He told him, "Go wash yourself in the pool of Siloam" (Siloam means "sent"). So the man went and washed and came back seeing!

JOHN 9:6-7

WE MARVEL AT THE UNIQUE WAYS GOD BROUGHT about healing in the Bible. Who would ever consider mixing dirt and saliva to make mud to smear on a blind man's eyes? This and other stories of healing in the Bible tell us that when God heals, he does it according to his plan for that healing and that individual. In the same way, not all recoveries from addiction look alike. There are surely similarities in recoveries but not exact duplicates. As you walk through recovery, you may be surprised at how God works with you. He may not bring recovery in the way you expect.

Let God lead you through your restoration. He can work the miracle you need, though not necessarily in the way you imagine.

† ***Lord, so often it seems you are the God of surprises. In my recovery journey, do what you will in the way you will. I accept your route to wholeness. Help me see your designed pathway to wholeness. Keep me from looking in the wrong places or assuming that the way you brought my friend to sobriety is the same path I need to walk. Surprise me, if that's what it takes.***

Have you been asking God what He is going to do? He will never tell you. God does not tell you what He is going to do—He reveals to you who He is. Do you believe in a miracle-working God, and will you "go out" in complete surrender to Him until you are not surprised one iota by anything He does?

OSWALD CHAMBERS (1874–1917)

You can find today's Scripture passage on page 1356 of *The Life Recovery Bible.*

Filled with Joy

We also pray that you will be strengthened with all his glorious power so you will have all the endurance and patience you need. May you be filled with joy.

COLOSSIANS 1:11

POWER FOR LIVING COMES FROM BEING IN the presence of the Lord. Absolute power comes from continuously *living* in the presence of the Lord. There are no shortcuts. Paul's wish for the Colossians was for them to be made strong *with all of God's glorious power* so that they might have the necessary endurance and patience and, with that, joy. And abundantly so. Every one of us needs that power, that strength that comes from God, so that we, too, can have the endurance, patience, and joy God desires for us.

† *Father, what a journey I'm on! It's a trek that requires supernatural power for living. It calls for your daily, moment by moment presence. It requires Holy Spirit–induced joy. It takes a ton of endurance and patience . . . all of which you supply abundantly. Yes, Lord, I am filled with joy. I have everything I need!*

If you look up into His face and say, "Yes, Lord, whatever it costs," at that moment He'll flood your life with His presence and power.

ALAN REDPATH (1907–1989)

You can find today's Scripture passage on page 1531 of *The Life Recovery Bible.*

God's Favor

His anger lasts only a moment,
but his favor lasts a lifetime!
Weeping may last through the night,
but joy comes with the morning.

PSALM 30:5

WE WHO ARE GOD'S CHOSEN CHILDREN ENJOY his favor. We may think that much of our future depends on others and how they may react to our past addiction. But God knows about such people, and in spite of others' skepticism toward us, he moves in the hearts of those we deal with by giving us favor in their eyes.

In every circumstance, be your redeemed self. Be transparent. Trust God to bring you favor in the eyes of those you encounter. God is far bigger than their prejudices. He withholds no good thing from those who walk uprightly.

✝ *Father, thank you that I've found favor in your eyes—and that you grant me favor in the eyes of those with whom you will have me connect. I'm not concerned about pleasing others at any expense, knowing that by pleasing you first, I will do right by others, as well. Praise you, Lord, for favor that lasts a lifetime!*

Free and warm reception into the divine favor is the strongest of all motives in leading a man to seek conformity to Him who has thus freely forgiven him all trespasses.

HORATIUS BONAR (1808–1889)

You can find today's Scripture passage on page 698 of *The Life Recovery Bible*.

The Promise of Safety

In peace I will lie down and sleep,
for you alone, O LORD, will keep me safe.

PSALM 4:8

DURING OUR SOJOURN IN THE FAR LAND OF addiction, there were many times we were in an unsafe situation. Perhaps our very lives were in danger because of decisions we made that were influenced by our addiction. How much different our post-addiction lives are! Now we are made to dwell in safety by our delivering God. We can live in peace, and we can sleep in peace because he has promised to keep us safe. God's peace is ours today. It's ours right now, but we must make sure that we no longer court danger through carelessness or relapse.

✝ *Lord, like the hymn "Amazing Grace" says, I can sing with certainty that your grace has brought me through many dangers, toils, and snares. There may be more challenges ahead, but you will bring me through each one. You will lead me home!*

Through many dangers, toils and snares,
I have already come;
'Tis grace has brought me safe thus far,
And grace will lead me home.

JOHN NEWTON (1725–1807)

You can find today's Scripture passage on page 682 of *The Life Recovery Bible.*

Teach Us to Number Our Days

Teach us to number our days
that we may get a heart of wisdom.

PSALM 90:12, ESV

WHEN WE WERE DEEP IN OUR ADDICTION, most likely we didn't "number our days" or pay much attention to the passing of time. In fact, during the worst days, time may have seemed to stand still—or not matter at all. When one is in the throes of addiction, time becomes irrelevant. Now that we are in recovery, we're more aware of life's brevity and the preciousness of the time we have here on earth. As a result, we can pray for God to teach us to number our days, counting each day of sobriety as evidence of God's miracle in our lives. Time that once stood still has now become a treasured gift from God. And what is the result of numbering our days? A heart of wisdom.

✝ *God, time is so important here on earth, and what is earthly time compared to eternity? You well know how I've squandered some of my time so far, but now I pray, like the psalmist, for you to teach me to number my days so I may gain a heart of wisdom. Help me to seize each day for you.*

Let me remember how brittle my years are; and let me seize hold in them upon the things which cannot be shaken.

ALEXANDER SMELLIE (1857–1923)

You can find today's Scripture passage on page 744 of *The Life Recovery Bible.*

Patterning

Those who say they live in God should
live their lives as Jesus did.

1 JOHN 2:6

FOR CERTAIN MEDICAL CONDITIONS, a patient must learn to do routine things all over again. Someone who has had a stroke and "forgotten" how to walk may have to have their legs "patterned" to walk again. This is the forced repetition of the desired movement over and over until the body "gets it" and begins, slowly at first, to resume the desired movements on its own.

There are aspects of recovery that are similar to patterning. We are shown the way to live in sobriety, and as we do what we know we must do, it eventually becomes natural to us . . . unless we give up too soon. Jesus was the one who set the pattern for us. If we do what he taught, we will live securely and soberly.

✝ ***God, help me as I pattern my life after Christ, being his follower. As I pattern my life in accordance with the way it should be lived, may I become more and more Christlike and less and less prone to missteps and even sin. May part of my recovery be a successful patterning of the right way to live.***

Christians are to set all Christ's moral actions before them as a pattern for their imitation. In His life a Christian may behold the lively picture or lineaments of all virtues, and accordingly he ought to order his conversation in this world.

THOMAS BROOKS (1608–1680)

You can find today's Scripture passage on page 1629 of *The Life Recovery Bible.*

Our God Never Grows Weak or Weary

Have you never heard?
Have you never understood?
The LORD is the everlasting God,
the Creator of all the earth.
He never grows weak or weary.
No one can measure the depths of his understanding.
He gives power to the weak
and strength to the powerless.

ISAIAH 40:28-29

THERE ARE TIMES IN RECOVERY WHEN WE have no might. That's God's cue to increase our strength. When we would faint, he enlivens us. He who is mighty, he who is the everlasting God, the Creator, *our* Creator, never grows weak or weary. Like an inexhaustible sun, he supplies light and power for those in darkness. All our estimations of God's attributes and powers are grossly underestimated. The Lord of all cares for the likes of us beyond all reason. Beyond all measure. Day by day, it's our privilege and joy to love him and to enjoy him.

✝ *Ah, Lord, I see that being strong isn't a matter of striving; it's relying on you for strength. While that sounds so passive, it's not really. Resting in you, depending on you for power, is an active step of faith. Lord, you see my weariness at times. Bolster me with your own strength as I lay down my own puny powers. Thank you for giving power to the weak and strength to the powerless. Thank you for loving and strengthening me.*

This, this is the God we adore,
Our faithful, unchangeable Friend,
Whose love is as great as His power,
And neither knows measure or end.

JOSEPH HART (1712-1768)

You can find today's Scripture passage on page 892 of *The Life Recovery Bible*.

No Longer Enslaved

We know that our old self was crucified with him in order that the body of sin might be brought to nothing, so that we would no longer be enslaved to sin.

ROMANS 6:6, ESV

THE SOURCE OF OUR SLAVERY WAS OUR OLD self acting as a playground for Satan's fatal games. Our only solution is not reformation of the old self—indeed, the old self cannot be reformed—but the utter and final death of the old self.

No, we cannot affect this vital homicide, but neither do we need to. In the crucifixion of Christ, we see that our old self was with him on the cross. The goal of our body of sin being brought to nothing was accomplished, thus freeing us from enslavement.

Paul starts today's verse with "We know." But *do* we know? If we know, we will reckon ourselves dead to sin and alive to Christ by faith. This, then, is the biblical solution to addiction: removing from our lives the old person prone to addiction and reckoning ourselves alive in Christ. All this is accomplished in us as we live out the faith of God's Word.

† *God, truth be told, it's not really addiction itself that's my problem—it's me. I would have no pull toward addiction unless something in me responded to the siren call. Father, the very best gift you can give me in overcoming addiction is the very one you have given me: You have done away with the "me" that is attracted to my addiction. It all was accomplished on the Cross. Christ's death was the death of my old self. Thanks be to God!*

Above all the grace and the gifts that Christ gives to his beloved is that of overcoming self.

FRANCIS OF ASSISI (1181–1226)

You can find today's Scripture passage on page 1438 of *The Life Recovery Bible.*

He Will Fulfill His Purpose for Me

I cry out to God Most High,
to God who will fulfill his purpose for me.

PSALM 57:2

GOD HAS A PURPOSE FOR EVERY LIFE—a perfect and divine purpose—that is unique to each individual. But the only way to access and live out this purpose is through faith. Not passive, hit-or-miss faith but constant faith throughout a lifetime. Yes, there are highs and lows, but the line of faith accommodates those. During the darker, colder season, faith looks toward spring. It does not surrender to the chilly winds of winter. Find *your* purpose. Live it out. Live it out boldly. No one can but you. Rejoice in your calling. You will find great happiness there—and nowhere else.

† *God, recovery from addiction would be enough of a gift for me. But you go even further by giving me a purpose to fulfill, one that no one else can do. I rejoice as I anticipate being effective in ways that I could never have done while in my addiction. When I go through waiting times, I will be patient, knowing that spring follows winter and so will my life bear its fruit in due time. Thank you now, Father, for what you plan to accomplish through me.*

When we begin to grasp what the Lord has done for us, and what He has promised He will yet do, we are able to press forward into our callings and purposes. When we apprehend the full surety of Gospel hope, we are quickened unto our good work in the world.

THOMAS CHALMERS (1780–1847)

You can find today's Scripture passage on page 718 of *The Life Recovery Bible*.

NOVEMBER 2

He Set Me Free

In my distress I prayed to the Lord,
and the Lord answered me and set me free.

PSALM 118:5

GOD IS THE GOD OF THE DISTRESSED. When we call on him, he answers and sets us free. Sometimes we put so much emphasis on addiction that we forget our other distresses. We are complex humans, and opportunities for distress come from many directions. As you rely on Christ for your addiction, take your other distresses to him as well. He can handle them all.

† *God, sometimes there were other factors in my life that led to my addiction. Distress, stress, anxiety, adversity . . . some of those were like a foot in the door that brought about my dependency. Part of my recovery must be to cast all of these on you, knowing you will answer and set me free. With you guarding me, I cannot fail.*

> He has known us in all *past* adversities, He will know us in the *present*, and in all that are *future*. Believer, one friend will be sure to know you in *trouble*, will be sure to visit you in sickness, and to help you in your distress—and that is your God. And if God is for you, who can to any purpose be against you?
>
> JAMES SMITH (1802–1862)

You can find today's Scripture passage on page 762 of *The Life Recovery Bible.*

Dealing with Our Sin

Remember, it is sin to know what you
ought to do and then not do it.

JAMES 4:17

ADDICTION OBSCURES THE VOICE OF GOD. It impairs our spiritual senses to the extent that we may even have thought God was okay with our addiction. But God doesn't approve of the things that work for our destruction, including addiction. Whatever substance or activity impairs our delight in the Lord must be dealt with as sin. When we are diligent about this, we find our sense of God returning. The dark veil is torn away. The vision is made clearer.

† *God, please continue to remove the veil that sometimes obscures my view of you. Let there be transparency in our relationship. Convict me when I sin, and then forgive me as I confess it to you. Make me aware of both my sins and your amazing grace exercised on my behalf. Clear my brain of the fog that weakens my reason and impairs my conscience. I want to see you more clearly, Father, day by day.*

> Whatever weakens your reason, impairs the tenderness of your conscience, obscures your sense of God, or takes off your relish of spiritual things; in short, whatever increases the strength and authority of your body over your mind, that thing is sin.
>
> **SUSANNA WESLEY (1669–1742)**

You can find today's Scripture passage on page 1606 of *The Life Recovery Bible.*

Our Perfect Father

For us,
There is one God, the Father,
by whom all things were created,
and for whom we live.

1 CORINTHIANS 8:6

NONE OF US HAVE HAD PERFECT FATHERS. Perhaps some of us have had fathers who failed us miserably. We are blessed, though, in that our heavenly Father is the perfect Father we may never have had. Only God can know the exact kind of father each individual needs and then actually *be* that Father. Breaking free from addiction is greatly enhanced by knowing and loving a perfect Father who both broods over us in love and builds us up to be mature men and women ourselves, able to stand against any adversity, including the adversity of addiction. That's the most important father-child relationship for us to pursue.

† *Lord, you know how certain family dynamics may have played into my addiction. No parents are perfect, even mine. They made mistakes, and they also did many things right. For whatever their participation in my addiction, I forgive them. I know now that you are the only perfect parent. You are the Father who will love me always and discipline me in the most effective way when necessary. Continue to show me from your Word how your paternal love for me is aiding in my recovery. Yes, you are the one Father I will also be accountable to and loved by.*

> He remembers our frame and knows that we are dust. He may sometimes chasten us, it is true, but even this He does with a smile, the proud, tender smile of a Father who is bursting with pleasure over an imperfect but promising son [or daughter] who is coming every day to look more and more like the One whose child he is.
>
> A. W. TOZER (1897–1963)

You can find today's Scripture passage on page 1465 of *The Life Recovery Bible.*

Counting My Blessings

Let your good deeds shine out for all to see, so that everyone will praise your heavenly Father.

MATTHEW 5:16

MORE THAN ONCE, I've caught myself rehearsing all the major mistakes I've made. Why do I do that? Talk about an open door to depression! Talk about a trigger! Instead, why don't I recount all the blessings I've received and all the right moves I've made?

Somehow, in our addiction, our perception of life changes. We may become negative toward others, our station in life, ourselves, and even God, who has called us to be shining lights so that others will see and give glory to God. We can't be shining lights if we are negative about ourselves or our condition.

We must learn to turn our thoughts of past mistakes and present circumstances from negative thoughts into positive ideas that propel us forward.

Don't stay stuck. Turn off the loop that keeps repeating your failures, bad choices, and broken relationships. Turn on the loop that edifies.

✝ *God, surely you hear the mental recording of past mistakes that loops and loops through my memory, causing me to relive painful moments from my past. As part of my recovery, that recording must be forever destroyed. You will need to help me with this, Father. Every time the recording starts, help me catch it immediately and turn it off. Every single time! Help me, instead, to remember the good things about my past. Let there be a new recording that loops in my memory. One that glorifies you and hastens my recovery.*

We must have the glory sink into us before it can be reflected from us. In deep inward beholding we must have Christ in our hearts, that He may shine forth from our lives.

ALEXANDER MACLAREN (1826–1910)

You can find today's Scripture passage on page 1202 of *The Life Recovery Bible.*

The Divine Purchase

God paid a high price for you,
so don't be enslaved by the world.
1 CORINTHIANS 7:23

WHAT IS THE WORTH OF A MAN OR WOMAN in God's eyes? What is the worth of an addict? The Bible is clear that every person's worth is equal to the life of God's Son. We are each purchased by the blood of Christ. That is our worth. That is *your* worth. Addiction attempts to destroy our sense of worth. We must return to acknowledging God's value for each of us. A cornerstone of recovery is accepting ourselves as beloved children of God, bought by the blood of an innocent Lamb.

† *Lord, when I think of myself as being of little worth, remind me that you place the value of my life as the value of your Son. I am not worthless. I am extremely valuable in your eyes. That fact must be rooted in my mind. Help me plant it there for good, Lord.*

> Jesus Christ has set a high value and estimate upon the soul. He made it and He bought it; therefore He best knows the value of it. He sold Himself to buy the soul.
>
> THOMAS WATSON (1620–1686)

You can find today's Scripture passage on page 1464 of *The Life Recovery Bible*.

God Is Always There

"Can anyone hide from me in a secret place? Am I not everywhere in all the heavens and earth?" says the LORD.

JEREMIAH 23:24

WHERE WAS GOD DURING OUR DARKEST DAYS of addiction? His eye was upon us then, as it is now, of course. We are never without his presence and scrutiny. Even now, as we recover from addiction, God's welcoming presence is near. He sees all and fills all. How can we not trust such a tender caregiver as our God?

† *Father, nothing about my life is hidden from you. You are aware of my every movement, my every desire, my every thought. May your ever-presence bring me confidence and cause me to remember that I'm never alone. You are my constant companion. You watch over me with eagle eyes.*

A God whose presence and scrutiny I could evade would be a small and trivial deity. But the true God is great and terrible, just because he is always with me and his eye is always upon me. Living becomes an awesome business when you realize that you spend every moment of your life in the sight and company of an omniscient, omnipresent Creator.

J. I. PACKER (1926–2020)

You can find today's Scripture passage on page 964 of *The Life Recovery Bible*.

Day by Day

Don't worry about tomorrow, for tomorrow will bring its own worries. Today's trouble is enough for today.

MATTHEW 6:34

ONE OF THE STAPLES OF RECOVERY MINISTRIES is the "one day at a time" approach—and wisely so. Each day is fresh to us from God, bursting with opportunities for growth—and sobriety. But with each new day there also lurks the dark cloud of potential relapse. For this reason, every day we must reaffirm our commitment to Christ and our dependence on the Holy Spirit. If every day we say, "I will walk in sobriety today," we will win our lives back.

✝ *Father, the burden of today finds ample strength in your provision. Tomorrow will find strength for tomorrow. Each day is a gift from you. Help me make the most of it by greeting each day with thankfulness and assurance that all will be well. Day by day, I will trust you and walk in sobriety.*

> It is not the cares of today, but the cares of tomorrow, that weigh a man down. For the needs of today we have corresponding strength given. For the morrow we are told to trust. It is not ours yet. It is when tomorrow's burden is added to the burden of today that the weight is more than a man can bear.
>
> GEORGE MACDONALD (1824–1905)

You can find today's Scripture passage on page 1206 of *The Life Recovery Bible.*

Tear Down the High Places

They provoked him to anger with their high places;
they moved him to jealousy with their idols.

PSALM 78:58, ESV

THE "HIGH PLACES" OF THE OLD TESTAMENT were where the disobedient Hebrews worshiped their idols. God instructed them to repent of this false worship and to tear down the high places.

This begs the question: Are there high places today where we worship idols? If we consider an idol as something we place ahead of our devotion to God, then most of us who come out of addiction will say yes. Tearing down our high places will mean removing from our presence the tools of our addiction, abandoning places where our addiction occurred, and not partaking of "idol worship" with acquaintances who are still using.

† ***Father, my addiction has the earmarks of idolatry. At its worst, the thoughts of it were with me daily. In a sense, I drew what little life I had from my addiction. It was literally one of my "high" places. But now, in recovery, I dismantle every altar, every idol, every bit of devotion in favor of worshiping only you. Any future attempts at idolatry will not be tolerated but cast down immediately.***

Nor need we go far, if we would but be honest with ourselves, to find out each our own idol—what it is, and how deep it lies, what worship it obtains, what honor it receives, and what affection it engrosses. Let me ask myself, "What do I most love?" If I hardly know how to answer that question, let me put to myself another, "What do I most think upon? In what channel do I usually find my thoughts flow when unrestrained?" for thoughts flow to the idol as water to the lowest spot in a field.

J. C. PHILPOT (1802–1869)

You can find today's Scripture passage on page 735 of *The Life Recovery Bible.*

NOVEMBER 10

Nailed to the Cross

Those who belong to Christ Jesus have nailed the passions and desires of their sinful nature to his cross and crucified them there.

GALATIANS 5:24

ADDICTION IS AMONG THE "passions and desires" that are counter to our spiritual lives. We who now belong to Christ have crucified the sinful nature and its attendant passions. Though this is true, we may object by saying we don't *feel* this is so, and as proof we offer our continuing desires for the substance of our addiction. But God does not deal in feelings. God deals in facts. If you are in Christ, you *have* crucified the flesh and its appetites. Now God calls you to believe this reality and walk it out.

† *Lord, long ago I realized that death was the only way out of addiction. And now I see that your Word teaches exactly that. You even show me that I already have died, because when Christ was on the cross, he took not only my sins but also that part of me drawn to addiction. By faith, I acknowledge that my passions and desires were nailed to the cross. I now live by the power of the resurrected Christ. The old me who thrived on addiction is indeed dead.*

> True believers are no hypocrites. They crucify the flesh with its evil desires and lusts. Inasmuch as they have not altogether put off the sinful flesh they are inclined to sin. . . . But they will not do the things to which the flesh incites them. They crucify the flesh with its evil desires and lusts by fasting and exercise and, above all, by a walk in the Spirit. To resist the flesh in this manner is to nail it to the Cross. Although the flesh is still alive it cannot very well act upon its desires because it is bound and nailed to the Cross.
>
> MARTIN LUTHER (1483–1546)

You can find today's Scripture passage on page 1505 of *The Life Recovery Bible*.

Walking Wisely

Look carefully then how you walk,
not as unwise but as wise.

EPHESIANS 5:15, ESV

WHEN WE ENTER RECOVERY, we can look back and see the foolishness of addiction. It may seem as though we were mesmerized to have become so dependent on something that was created, rather than on the Creator.

Wisdom is waking up to see reality and acting accordingly. We learn to walk in a newfound wisdom, having turned away from our prior foolishness.

Recovery is an ongoing gathering of wisdom and walking it out daily.

† *Father, I find many references in the Bible to "walking." One admonition is to walk carefully, not as unwise but as wise. This walk is far different from the walk of addiction. This walk has confidence and purpose, leading to a bright future. This walk is reserved for the wise man and woman. Lord, I choose to be that person. I choose to walk wisely.*

A walk is made up of steps, taken one at a time. One wrong step may prove fatal, and may lead into backsliding and sin, or into terrible sorrow and suffering. . . . All about us are the devil's snares and pitfalls. We walk in danger constantly. Then watch your step and know where the next step will lead you.

RUTH PAXSON (1875–1949)

You can find today's Scripture passage on page 1515 of *The Life Recovery Bible.*

NOVEMBER 12

Our Diminishing Fears

"I hold you by your right hand—
I, the LORD your God.
And I say to you,
'Don't be afraid. I am here to help you.'"

ISAIAH 41:13

FEAR IS A REALITY DURING ADDICTION. In fact, many find that, during addiction, their fears have increased—some to the point of becoming fearful of life itself. Recovery includes watching our fears diminish as we seek the Lord and learn to fear him only. He is the refuge for the fearful addict. Seek him. He will answer, and he will deliver.

† *God, you know my fears. In seeking you, I have sought to be free from fear. I know that fear is not from you but from my enemy. His lies are attempts to have me so consumed with fear that I can't enjoy a successful life. Praise you, Father, that you answer my cries for freedom. The only fear I seek is the fear of you that you instruct me to have.*

Fear is born of Satan, and if we would only take time to think a moment we would see that everything Satan says is founded upon a falsehood.

A. B. SIMPSON (1843–1919)

You can find today's Scripture passage on page 893 of *The Life Recovery Bible.*

Triumphal Procession

Thanks be to God, who in Christ always leads us
in triumphal procession, and through us spreads
the fragrance of the knowledge of him everywhere.

2 CORINTHIANS 2:14, ESV

WE ALL DESIRE TO LIVE WHAT'S COMMONLY called the "victorious Christian life." No one wants to live a life of defeat.

In Christ, we find the victory we so desperately need. In fact, all our victories can be traced back to one greater victory. If we never take our eyes off the victory over sin and death when Christ died for our sin and rose again, we win in life no matter our circumstances.

Christ's victory on our behalf trumps all that life might throw at us. His victory is *our* victory, and in it we are vessels through whom God will spread the fragrance of the knowledge of him everywhere we go.

✝ *Lord, you have made victory so easy, but we make it so hard. You want us simply to trust in you and walk in your ways. And yet we so easily want to walk in our own ways. May I always choose triumph instead of defeat. May a triumphal procession enable me to spread the fragrance of the knowledge of you everywhere.*

Prayer is life passionately wanting, wishing, desiring God's triumph. Prayer is life striving, toiling everywhere and everywhen for that ultimate victory.

G. CAMPBELL MORGAN (1863–1945)

You can find today's Scripture passage on page 1482 of *The Life Recovery Bible*.

Made Complete

May you experience the love of Christ, though it is too great to understand fully. Then you will be made complete with all the fullness of life and power that comes from God.

EPHESIANS 3:19

GOD'S GOAL IS THAT WE BE COMPLETE IN HIM and live as completed individuals.

We're all born incomplete. Growing up, we remain incomplete, though we sincerely desire to become complete. So, unless we're firmly rooted in Christ when we're young, we're susceptible to the false promises of completion our addiction offers.

Oddly, not only does addiction not make us complete, it further erodes the person we are. God's remedy for man's incompleteness is that we find our completion in Christ and learn to live as completed individuals. The more complete we see ourselves in Christ, the less likely we are to seek completion through false means.

✝ ***God, truth be told, I never felt complete in my addiction. In fact, I felt far less than whole. Even in the so-called afterglow of addiction, what I thought was a promise of fullness failed me once again. I know by bitter experience that there is no completion of self in addiction. But you complete me entirely—spirit, soul, and even body.***

> O my brother [and sister]! come and consent more fully to God's way of holiness. Let Christ be your sanctification. Not a distant Christ to whom you look, but a Christ very near, all around you, in whom you are. Not a Christ after the flesh, a Christ of the past, but a present Christ in the power of the Holy Ghost. Not a Christ whom you can know by your wisdom, but the Christ of God, who is a Spirit, and whom the Spirit within you, as you die to the flesh and self, will reveal in power.
>
> **ANDREW MURRAY (1828–1917)**

You can find today's Scripture passage on page 1513 of *The Life Recovery Bible*.

Self-Control

A person without self-control
is like a city with broken-down walls.

PROVERBS 25:28

AT OUR ADDICTED WORST, we were like cities broken into, left without walls. Our inability to control ourselves left us prey to destruction. The blessing of recovery is a return to self-control. The walls that come down brick by brick are now rebuilt as not just walls but boundaries that keep destruction out of our reach.

Pay attention to the increasing opportunities to exercise self-control. It's evidence of your progressing recovery.

† *Father, I soon tired of being like a city with broken-down walls. The wall I want broken down now is the brick wall that has separated me from you. As I tear down that wall, I find an increasing ability to control my actions and to make sound decisions. Continue, Lord, to show me ways to make the right choices and to exercise self-control, especially when tempted.*

> Think what the want of self-control is costing men continually! One moment's dropping of the reins and a wrong decision is made, a temptation is accepted, a battle is lost, and a splendid life lies in ruin. Let us achieve the grace of self-control.
>
> J. R. MILLER (1840–1912)

You can find today's Scripture passage on page 814 of *The Life Recovery Bible.*

Ask. Seek. Knock.

Keep on asking, and you will receive what you ask for.
Keep on seeking, and you will find. Keep on knocking,
and the door will be opened to you.

MATTHEW 7:7

ONE BLESSING THAT COMES FROM our disillusionment with addiction is that we embark on a quest for a new and different life—one of peace, not chaos. God tells us what to do on this quest. Ask, seek, and knock, and we will receive, we will find, and the door will be opened for us. The tragedy is that so few really do ask, seek, or knock. Or if they do, they give up when the door is not instantly opened. Be patient. Keep on asking. Keep on seeking. Keep on knocking. The promise of an open door is for you.

✝ ***Lord, you have seen me ask. You have heard my knocking. I believe you will open not just one door but many doors for me to walk through as I'm exiting my addiction. Open doors are, in fact, a promise from you, and I hold you to that promise as I knock.***

The tree of the promise will not drop its fruit unless it is shaken by the hand of prayer.

THOMAS WATSON (1620–1686)

You can find today's Scripture passage on page 1206 of *The Life Recovery Bible.*

Come Alive from the Deadening Effects of Addiction

Unless the Lord had helped me,
I would soon have settled in the silence of the grave.
I cried out, "I am slipping!"
but your unfailing love, O Lord, supported me.

PSALM 94:17-18

TO BE IN RECOVERY MEANS THAT WE HAVE escaped death from our addiction. This is no small thing. We are *alive.* We have a life to live, a call to answer, a destiny to pursue. We thank God that we were not delivered to the "silence of the grave" but remain *here* in the land of the living. Yes, our feet slipped—more than once—but the steadfast love of God held us up then and holds us up now. His arms are yet strong to save.

† *Oh, God, just to be in the land of the living is a wonderful gift. Thank you for my life—and for saving it when I felt myself slipping away in addiction. Lord, I love life. Keep me in this place where I experience true life. Never let me return to the life that is really death. Keep me from the silence of the grave by your unfailing love.*

> God just doesn't throw a life preserver to a drowning person. He goes to the bottom of the sea, and pulls a corpse from the bottom of the sea, takes him up on the bank, breathes into him the breath of life and makes him alive.
>
> R. C. SPROUL (1939–2017)

You can find today's Scripture passage on page 746 of *The Life Recovery Bible.*

Negativity

You should know this, Timothy, that in the last days there will be very difficult times. For people will love only themselves and their money. They will be boastful and proud, scoffing at God, disobedient to their parents, and ungrateful. They will consider nothing sacred. They will be unloving and unforgiving; they will slander others and have no self-control. They will be cruel and hate what is good. They will betray their friends, be reckless, be puffed up with pride, and love pleasure rather than God. They will act religious, but they will reject the power that could make them godly. Stay away from people like that!

2 TIMOTHY 3:1-5

WE WHO HAVE BEEN LOVERS OF PLEASURE and without self-control know the pull of temptation. Though we wish to rescue others, in so doing we must avoid those who may attempt to pull us back into the life we've left behind. These people will always be there. Some will never change. We must pray and be available, but we must listen to them with a cautious ear. Our words and actions may be used to help them, but their words and actions must never be allowed to influence us negatively.

† *Lord, when I look back on my life, I see many examples of the kind of behavior Paul wrote about to Timothy. At times, I've exhibited most of those attitudes and behaviors. Thank you that you've forgiven me for the entirety of my sins and that you replace my shortcomings with your Holy Spirit. Help me resist quickly any desires that would cause me to love only myself.*

Beware of pleasures. Many of them are innocent and healthful, but many are destructive. It is said that where the most beautiful cacti grow, there the most venomous serpents lurk. It is so with sin. Your fairest pleasures will harbour your grossest sins.

CHARLES SPURGEON (1834–1892)

You can find today's Scripture passage on page 1563 of *The Life Recovery Bible.*

Christian Contentment

True godliness with contentment is itself great wealth.
After all, we brought nothing with us when we came into
the world, and we can't take anything with us when we leave it.
So if we have enough food and clothing, let us be content.

1 TIMOTHY 6:6-8

WHEN WE WERE SEEKING CONTENTMENT in addiction, we searched in the wrong place. Our addiction led quickly to discontentment. Perhaps that experience best prepared us for true contentment in Christ. In him is a contentment that surpasses the world's version of contentment. We find in him our own willingness to entrust all to God. We are content at last with all he proposes for us.

✝ *Lord, to be discontent is to find fault with your provision. I accept fully all you give me. I don't seek wealth; I seek only those things that will carry over into eternity. When I may give signs of discontentment, I will remember that I once knew what real discontentment is and that I don't ever want to go back there again.*

Christian contentment is that sweet, inward, quiet, gracious frame of spirit, which freely submits to and delights in God's wise and fatherly disposal in every condition.

JEREMIAH BURROUGHS (1600–1646)

You can find today's Scripture passage on page 1557 of *The Life Recovery Bible*.

It's a Supernatural Life

Jesus replied, "I tell you the truth, unless you are born again, you cannot see the Kingdom of God."

JOHN 3:3

THE ELEMENTS THAT RELATE TO CHRISTIAN recovery are not readily understandable to the unbelieving world. The new birth is, of course, a prerequisite for experiencing Christian recovery. This new birth is not something we can bring about ourselves any more than we brought about our own physical birth. No, the new birth is a miracle of God's doing. At its heart, it's a supernatural event. And from the new birth all else that comes to us in recovery is, at its root, supernatural. When we learn to live as Christians, we soon learn that it cannot be done in one's own strength—it, too, requires the supernatural indwelling of the Holy Spirit. We were born again by God's Spirit, and now we experience the miracle of recovery the same way.

✝ ***God, first of all, thank you for my first birth. I wouldn't exist if you hadn't brought me into being through conception. Then I thank you for my new birth—my second birth. Thank you for the conception in my heart that pulled me toward you. That took a miracle, and I'm grateful for my new existence—and now my growth into spiritual adulthood as your maturing child.***

> To be born again is, as it were, to enter upon a new existence, to have a new mind, a new heart, new views, new principles, new tastes, new affections, new likings, new dislikings, new fears, new joys, new sorrows, new love to things once hated, new hatred to things once loved, new thoughts of God, and ourselves, and the world, and the life to come, and salvation.
>
> J. C. RYLE (1816–1900)

You can find today's Scripture passage on page 1344 of *The Life Recovery Bible.*

The Humility of Christ

"No," Peter protested, "you will never ever wash my feet!"
Jesus replied, "Unless I wash you, you won't belong to me."

JOHN 13:8

THE HUMILITY OF CHRIST IS SEEN IN HIS servanthood. He served the disciples by washing their feet . . . and today he serves us by washing away our sins, cleansing us from our addictions, and giving us new life to move forward.

It takes a special attitude to allow Jesus to serve us as he desires. But if we will not accept his offer of washing, we will remain broken. Never turn Christ away from washing your feet—or cleansing you from your addictions. That is his role as our Servant-Redeemer.

† *Father, I know that Christ demonstrated great humility when he left heaven to secure a place in his Kingdom for me and all others who believe. Lord, there is a lesson for me in observing Christ's lowliness in the Bible. Teach me to humble myself. Teach me to rise by going lower. Teach me how to serve by washing the feet of others.*

Do you wish to rise? Begin by descending. You plan a tower that will pierce the clouds? Lay first the foundation of humility.

SAINT AUGUSTINE OF HIPPO (354–430)

You can find today's Scripture passage on page 1363 of *The Life Recovery Bible*.

Pain as a Warning

Our present troubles are small and won't last very long. Yet they produce for us a glory that vastly outweighs them and will last forever!

2 CORINTHIANS 4:17

PAIN IS GOD'S WAY OF ALERTING US TO TROUBLE. It's a message that something must change in order to stop the pain. All of life's pains, including addiction, are sending a message. If we heed the message, we are spared. If we ignore the message, we perish. Every present trouble, trial, and temptation is merely a way of saying that there is coming to us an eternal weight of glory beyond all comparison.

If we feel pain, let us heed its message. Let us take it to the great Healer.

✝ ***God, it seems pain is a two-way signal. For me, it tells me something must change. For you, it's a summons to come to my aid. You soothe my pain, you help me make things right again, and most of all, you bring your healing presence. Where you find one of your children in pain, you speedily come to the rescue.***

> I am not a theologian or a scholar, but I am very aware of the fact that pain is necessary to all of us. In my own life, I think I can honestly say that out of the deepest pain has come the strongest conviction of the presence of God and the love of God.
>
> ELISABETH ELLIOT (1926–2015)

You can find today's Scripture passage on page 1485 of *The Life Recovery Bible*.

God's Unseen Hand

See, I have written your name on the palms of my hands.

ISAIAH 49:16

HOW CLOSE ARE WE TO GOD? Our names are engraved on the palms of his hands. We are surrounded by his protective walls. Trusting a seen hand is easily done. Hard is trusting an unseen hand. But as we learn more and more about the character of God, we find that his once invisible hands are becoming more and more obvious as he deals with us in kindness.

† *Father, it's my security in you that keeps me safe and gives me strength. You empower me to defeat every temptation and overcome every trial. Though I can't physically see you, I can see you clearly through the way you're working in my life. Keep me protected, Lord. Stretch out your hand to protect and bless me. Shelter me during the storms, and I shall remain safe.*

> Struggling believer, God cares for you, even for you, and loves you with an everlasting love! Your name is engraved on the palms of His nail-scarred hands—and when those hands are stretched out to protect and to bless, you cannot be forgotten. When others scorn you—he smiles upon you. When the storm is high and your heart is overwhelmed—he is at hand to shelter and to support you. Even when your foot has slipped and sin has come in—he will not cast you away, but will gently rebuke you and then graciously forgive and heal.
>
> GEORGE EVERARD (1828–1901)

You can find today's Scripture passage on page 903 of *The Life Recovery Bible.*

God Is Always at Work

He who watches over Israel
never slumbers or sleeps.
The LORD himself watches over you!
The LORD stands beside you as your protective shade.
The sun will not harm you by day,
nor the moon at night.
The LORD keeps you from all harm
and watches over your life.
The LORD keeps watch over you as you come and go,
both now and forever.

PSALM 121:4-8

ON THE DAYS WHEN IT SEEMS GOD IS SILENT, we wonder if he's truly in our lives to stay. Was our hope in this silent God for real? Why does he seem so far away?

But God *is* there. He never leaves. He never sleeps. He never has his eyes off us. Though he may feel absent today, there will be days ahead when we're once again assured of his felt presence. He never changes; the changes are in us.

✝ ***God, forgive me when I accuse you of being far away. I know you're always near. You're here with me now and will be throughout this day and every day, regardless of how I may feel. Watch over me, Father. Never let me stumble to a bitter end, but remain faithful on the path to recovery.***

Believer, endeavor in like spirit to say, "Nevertheless, since I belong to Christ, I am continually with God!" By this is meant continually upon His mind; He is always thinking of me for my good. Continually before His eye—the eye of the Lord never sleeps but is perpetually watching over my welfare. Continually in His hand—so that none will be able to pluck me out from it.

CHARLES SPURGEON (1834–1892)

You can find today's Scripture passage on page 769 of *The Life Recovery Bible.*

Call to Battle

God has given each of you a gift from his great variety of spiritual gifts. Use them well to serve one another.

1 PETER 4:10

GOD IS NOT RELUCTANT TO USE US. Never! God created us to be used as his hands and feet as we engage in acts of love to others. We might say God delights to use us as exporters of his love to others. We must get over the devilish notion that God merely puts up with us or must be persuaded to use us. No! Dare to believe your very purpose is for his use and was designed by him. When you find how he wants to use you and you step out in faith, miracles happen!

✝ *God, I desire to be part of a miracle in someone's life. Lead me in discovering ways to be there for people in need. Give me the necessary gifts to dispense to others. Open doors of opportunity for me to minister to hurting people. And, Lord, as I need miracles, I pray you'd send the right ones to help me over the bumps in the road. You delight to see your children encouraging each other. May I both give and receive as I open my life to others. The need is so great!*

Never, never, my young friend, were there such opportunities, or such means of holy usefulness, as there are now, and never were there such incentives to it. The world is in movement, and so is the church. The age of inactivity is past, the era of general action is come. The armies of good and evil are marching to the scene of conflict, and mustering in the valley of decision. [The Lord is] calling the hosts of the Lord to the battle, which is to rescue the world from the slavery of sin and Satan, and restore it to God. Victory is certain, and the shout of it will one day be heard, ascending to heaven from this regenerated earth. Will you be idle? What! at such a time? Will you have no share in such a triumph?

JOHN ANGELL JAMES (1785–1859)

You can find today's Scripture passage on page 1616 of *The Life Recovery Bible*.

NOVEMBER 26

Thanksgiving

Give thanks for everything to God the Father
in the name of our Lord Jesus Christ.

EPHESIANS 5:20

THE RECOVERED LIFE OF AN ADDICT IS a thankful life. The very fact that we're among the living is a cause for great gratitude. That God has brought us to a place where we can work out our recovery is also a reason for thanks. Our next prayer is to offer thanks for the days of recovery ahead of us, asking God to prepare us for the bumpy spots, to increase our hunger for him, and to connect us to the people who can help us in our recovery. Recovery is not a solo endeavor. We each need others to walk with us.

† ***Lord, you have my continual thanks for my ongoing recovery. Not just for recovery but for everything you're doing in my life. As I look back, it pains me to see where I once was, but it makes me thankful to consider that you didn't leave me there. You've brought me home to you. Yes, I am so thankful!***

The greatest Saint in the world . . . is not he who *prays* most, or *fasts* most; it is not he who gives most *alms,* or is most eminent for temperance, chastity, or justice; but it is he who is *always thankful* to God.

WILLIAM LAW (1686–1761)

You can find today's Scripture passage on page 1516 of *The Life Recovery Bible.*

An Invitation to a Feast

You prepare a feast for me
in the presence of my enemies.
You honor me by anointing my head with oil.
My cup overflows with blessings.

PSALM 23:5

GOD WAS WITH US IN ADDICTION, even if we didn't realize it. He prepared a table for us, not when we left our enemies but in the presence of our enemy: addiction. He anoints our heads, restoring our ability to think clearly, and he brings an overflow of blessings into our lives.

This invitation to feast is open to all who are addicted, but it seems so few come to the banquet. Make sure you're there at the feast.

† *Father, thank you for the feast you laid before me, even in the presence of my enemies. My cup overflows with your blessings. You are, above all else, a Giver of good things. You fill me even to overflowing. Praise you, Lord!*

We want to suck in, He wants to give out. We are empty and would be filled; He is full and flows over.

C. S. LEWIS (1898–1963)

You can find today's Scripture passage on page 694 of *The Life Recovery Bible*.

Live for What Is Right

He personally carried our sins in his body on the cross so that we can be dead to sin and live for what is right. By his wounds you are healed.

1 PETER 2:24

IS GOD'S POWER GREAT ENOUGH TO HEAL OUR deepest pain? Yes! *Emphatically* yes. It's an insult to God to say otherwise—to underestimate his concern and assume his power is not enough for us. The entire gospel message is that he himself bore our sins in his body so that we might die to sin (and addiction) and live righteously. His wounds are a balm to our pain. His wounds heal us.

† *Lord Jesus, my wounds became your wounds on the cross. By those wounds I am thereby healed. Allow me, then, as a right response to live for what is right. Deviation to choosing wrongly again will not happen. I see by faith your victory and mine on the Cross.*

Come, and see the victories of the cross. . . . Christ's wounds are thy healings, his agonies thy repose, his conflicts thy conquests, his groans thy songs, his pains thy ease, his shame thy glory, his death thy life, his sufferings thy salvation.

MATTHEW HENRY (1662–1714)

You can find today's Scripture passage on page 1614 of *The Life Recovery Bible.*

"Just This Once"

A little leaven leavens the whole lump.

GALATIANS 5:9, ESV

HAVE WE NOT ALL EXPERIENCED THE TRICK of Satan to tempt us to relapse "just a little" or "just this once"? We all know how that works. One small compromise with our addiction never suffices. It leads to some measure of relapse. We must be done forever with our addiction and know this internally. Small temptations will come, but when acted upon, they become larger temptations the next time. They become the leaven that leavens the whole lump.

Be done with your addiction forever. Silence the voice that promises "just this once."

✝ *God, I know the Satanic whisper that tells me I can indulge "just this once," or some other lie designed to pull me back into addiction. Lord, when that whisper happens, I pray you'll whisper louder that this victory is mine and I am no longer a slave to the bidding of my enemy. I can say no and mean it.*

> If you yield to Satan in the least, he will carry you further and further, till he has left you under a stupefied or terrified conscience: stupefied, till thou hast lost all thy tenderness. A stone at the top of a hill, when it begins to roll down, ceases not till it comes to the bottom.
>
> THOMAS MANTON (1620–1677)

You can find today's Scripture passage on page 1504 of *The Life Recovery Bible.*

Ablaze with Rejoicing

Always be full of joy in the Lord.
I say it again—rejoice!
PHILIPPIANS 4:4

WHEN YOU'RE HAPPY, REJOICE. When you're sad, rejoice. When you're confused, frustrated, or angry, rejoice. *Find* a reason to rejoice. Ignore your contrary feelings and just begin with a few words of rejoicing. Keep going until you find that you really do have much to rejoice about. Let rejoicing be your go-to remedy for down times. Let rejoicing set you ablaze again for the Lord you serve.

✝ ***Lord, in obedience to your Word, I rejoice. I rejoice now, and I rejoice when I don't feel very joyful. Even when things don't go my way, still I can rejoice in you, instead of moaning about my circumstances or foul mood. Rejoicing is always your remedy for me during my down times. You set me ablaze with a joy that radiates!***

Spirit-filled souls are ablaze for God. They love with a love that glows. They believe with a faith that kindles. They serve with a devotion that consumes. They hate sin with fierceness that burns. They rejoice with a joy that radiates. Love is perfected in the Fire of God.

SAMUEL CHADWICK (1840–1932)

You can find today's Scripture passage on page 1525 of *The Life Recovery Bible*.

Be Strong and Courageous

Love the LORD, all you godly ones!
For the LORD protects those who are loyal to him,
but he harshly punishes the arrogant.
So be strong and courageous,
all you who put your hope in the LORD!

PSALM 31:23-24

WE SPEND SO MUCH ENERGY RESISTING certain sins (often sins of the flesh) and so little effort resisting the demoralizing sins of discouragement and fearfulness, and we are thus robbed of our spiritual strength. Consider discouragement as horrid an invader to your life as the worst fleshly sin or addiction—and have none of it. Turn away.

† *Lord, I put my hope in you. I hear your call for me to be strong and courageous. I will stand strong in every aspect of my life. I will not allow discouragement or fear to rob me of my happiness. When tempted, I will call out for you to help me and encourage me. You are my steady source of strength.*

The Christian life is not a constant high. I have my moments of deep discouragement. I have to go to God in prayer with tears in my eyes, and say, "O God, forgive me," or "Help me."

BILLY GRAHAM (1918–2018)

You can find today's Scripture passage on page 700 of *The Life Recovery Bible*.

Delight in God's Word

Oh, the joys of those who do not
follow the advice of the wicked,
or stand around with sinners,
or join in with mockers.
But they delight in the law of the LORD,
meditating on it day and night.

PSALM 1:1-2

WE MAY BE INSTRUCTED TO READ OUR BIBLE as part of our recovery—and so we should. But reading isn't enough to change us. Learning to delight in God's Word enables it to become the agent of change it's meant to be. The more we pore over the Word and soak in it—even meditate on it—the more cleansing it will be to our souls, our minds, and our spirits.

Approach the Bible with awe. Read it, absorb it, then live it.

✝ *Lord, reading your Word is good—but it's not enough. As I approach the Scriptures, let me do so with awe. Let me read your Word as if eating it. As I read it slowly, not speeding through like an assignment, remind me to contemplate the meaning your Word has for me. Teach me out of your Word. Guide my steps, Father.*

> You must meditate and dwell upon what you read. . . . The more any man is in the contemplation of truth, the more deep and firm impression is made upon his heart by truth. Heavenly meditation brings out the sweetness that is in divine truths. . . . Those who meditate most, are most edified and enriched.
>
> THOMAS BROOKS (1608–1680)

You can find today's Scripture passage on page 680 of *The Life Recovery Bible*.

God Is Willing

We can say with confidence, "The LORD is my helper, so I will have no fear. What can mere people do to me?"

HEBREWS 13:6

CONFIDENCE IN GOD'S WILLINGNESS TO empower us against addiction is important; far less important is our own confidence in ourselves to beat addiction.

If there's a lesson for us in failure, it's that God so designed us to find happiness by relying on him in every aspect of life. It's no wonder when we thwart God's design and take on life in our own strength that we find ourselves out at sea. In this regard, temptations are useful in that they cause us to cast away our self-confidence and rely solely on God.

† *God, when I think of self-confidence, it reminds me that my self is confident because you continue to be faithful to me in my recovery. Every brick that comes down from the wall of separation has your fingerprints on it. Every temptation resisted is because you know my limits and see that I'm able to make it through unscathed. So, yes, I am confident—but confident because you have my back.*

Temptations are a file which rub off much of the rust of our self-confidence.

FRANÇOIS FÉNELON (1651–1715)

You can find today's Scripture passage on page 1594 of *The Life Recovery Bible.*

We Are His by Purchase

The Spirit is God's guarantee that he will give us the inheritance he promised and that he has purchased us to be his own people. He did this so we would praise and glorify him.

EPHESIANS 1:14

GOD HAS PURCHASED US WITH THE INTENT of keeping us. He has given us the Holy Spirit as a guarantee of that purchase. If you have been born again, that new life within you prevails against all sin, doubt, and adversity that would try to take you down. We see this in many Old Testament believers: Jacob, for instance, the deceiver who became a prince. David, the adulterer and murderer who was a man after God's own heart. In the New Testament, we see doubting Thomas and Peter the denier of the Lord. All these people were bought by the blood of Christ . . . just as we were. We were purchased as "keepers," and we have the Holy Spirit as the guarantee of our salvation.

✝ *Lord, you saved me to keep me. You purchased me with a no-return policy. I will always remember that you have the title deed to my life now. I treasure the Holy Spirit, my guarantee of your ownership. You now orchestrate the symphony that brings out the music in me. My salvation and all that pertains to it are mine . . . forever mine.*

Will God part with the objects of His highest love? Never!
Will Jesus surrender the purchase of His own heart's blood? Never!

JAMES SMITH (1802–1862)

You can find today's Scripture passage on page 1511 of *The Life Recovery Bible.*

Out of the Ropes of Death

The ropes of death entangled me;
floods of destruction swept over me.
The grave wrapped its ropes around me;
death laid a trap in my path.
But in my distress I cried out to the LORD;
yes, I prayed to my God for help.
He heard me from his sanctuary;
my cry to him reached his ears.

PSALM 18:4-6

GOD HEARS THE CRIES OF THE ADDICT. In love, he reaches out a saving hand to bring us out of the ropes of death. Our part is to take the outstretched hand of God and bid farewell to the pull of the grave.

When we cry, we must know that God hears us. We must watch for his saving hand. We must be willing to let go of the ropes of death and take hold of the hand of God.

† *Lord, I see your outstretched hand, and I take hold of it. You listen for my cry, and you come to my side. You are always ready to hear my prayer and to attend to my needs. You even anticipate my needs and dispatch the answer before I ask. God, you are true to me in every aspect, and this is the promise of recovery for me.*

There is no coming to heaven with dry eyes.

THOMAS ADAMS (1583–1652)

You can find today's Scripture passage on page 689 of *The Life Recovery Bible*.

DECEMBER 6

Prayer and Fasting

Is not this the fast that I choose: to loose the bonds of wickedness, to undo the straps of the yoke, to let the oppressed go free, and to break every yoke?

ISAIAH 58:6, ESV

FASTING COMBINED WITH PRAYER IS a time-honored practice for increasing our spiritual senses and making a breakthrough in our intercessions. Prayer and fasting loosen the bonds of addiction and allow the oppressed to go free. If fasting is medically safe for you (check with your doctor), begin with a one-day fast, choosing only water or weak tea to drink. Later, you may try a longer fast—making sure it's combined with prayer. Fasts are best conducted from evening to evening.[3]

✝ *Lord, my appetites have been my downfall. I pray that, should you lead me to fast, you'll give me the patience and self-discipline for it to be effective. As I fast, I pray for wisdom and insight into my recovery process. Remind me to intercede for others as I pray. Show me what you would teach me through prayer and fasting.*

> If you have been brought low through personal defeat; if there is a call in your soul to a deeper purifying, to a renewed consecration; if there is the challenge of some new task for which you feel ill-equipped—then it is time to inquire of God whether He would not have you separate yourself unto Him in fasting.
>
> ARTHUR WALLIS (1922–1988)

---

3 For a further study of fasts, one good source is *God's Chosen Fast* by Arthur Wallis.

You can find today's Scripture passage on page 913 of *The Life Recovery Bible.*

The Amazing Grace of God

Be on guard; then you will not be carried away by the errors of these wicked people and lose your own secure footing. Rather, you must grow in the grace and knowledge of our Lord and Savior Jesus Christ. All glory to him, both now and forever!

2 PETER 3:17-18

THERE IS A DANGER IN BECOMING SO sin focused, so addiction focused, we see only that instead of turning our eyes away to look instead at the amazing grace of God that is active in our own lives. A sin-focused life will lead to more sin. A grace-focused life removes the sting (and power) of sin and enables us to break free.

Yes, consider the power of sin, but then think more fully on the amazing grace and power of God.

✝ *God, though my addiction has been powerful, your grace is even more powerful in effecting change. I turn my eyes off my addiction to gaze more fully on my recovery and the amazing grace that has brought me this far and will lead me home.*

The ultimate test of our spirituality is the measure of our amazement at the grace of God.

MARTYN LLOYD-JONES (1899–1981)

You can find today's Scripture passage on page 1625 of *The Life Recovery Bible*.

A Happy Life

There is a path before each person that seems right,
but it ends in death.

PROVERBS 16:25

FOR EVERY NO GOD GIVES US REGARDING our lives, he has a reason. Perhaps that reason will never be revealed in this lifetime, but it is a reason nonetheless. The same is true for every yes God gives us regarding our lives.

We find a happy life in knowing that the paths we might choose for ourselves are never as good as the ones God has for us. For the addict, the path we once chose leads to death. Now, having escaped death, we must always choose the way God reveals, not the way that may seem right to us.

✝ *Father, you have said no to continued addiction in my life. You have said a bold yes to sobriety, health, and happiness. At times, my choices have not been wise ones. The path I chose led me in the wrong direction. Now, I accept that your path is the right one—the only one that leads to real happiness. Though I don't understand all the reasons for how you work out my recovery, I still trust you. Your past faithfulness has been all the assurance I need to trust you for the future.*

> Far more earnestly than we know, does God want us to be happy. It grieves a true human father to see his children unhappy. Our heavenly Father is pained and disappointed when his children on the earth are discontented and anxious, or when they do not rejoice.
>
> J. R. MILLER (1840–1912)

You can find today's Scripture passage on page 804 of *The Life Recovery Bible*.

"Follow Me"

Anyone who wants to serve me must follow me, because my servants must be where I am. And the Father will honor anyone who serves me.

JOHN 12:26

SERVING SATAN IS SERVING DEATH. Serving ourselves is serving folly. If we would lay down our service to Satan and self and pick up our cross and follow Jesus, we would find true life. The closer we have been to death, the more we will prize our life in Christ. Turn away from the folly of yourself and the death Satan brings. Choose only Christ today, and live.

✝ *Father, today and every day, I choose to follow Christ, to serve him, and to honor you. Lead me in the path I should take. Bring me quickly to my next step in recovery. Show me the right decisions to make, the right relationships to foster, and the right friendships to leave behind. Guide me in all I do as I follow Christ.*

Follow Christ in the denial of all the wills of self, and then all is put away that separates you from God; the heaven-born new creature will come to life in you, which alone knows and enjoys the things of God, and has his daily food of gladness in that manifold blessed, and blessed, which Christ preached on the mount.

WILLIAM LAW (1686–1761)

You can find today's Scripture passage on page 1362 of *The Life Recovery Bible*.

Partaking of the Bread of Life

Jesus replied, "I am the bread of life.
Whoever comes to me will never be hungry again.
Whoever believes in me will never be thirsty."

JOHN 6:35

NOT ALL OF CHRIST'S FOLLOWERS ARE CALLED to be evangelists. But in the community of those addicted, we find a field ready for harvest. Whatever gifts God has given us can surely be used in some way to bring hope and life to others who are now where we once were.

Evangelism is simply finding people who are seeking Christ. As one old story has it, evangelism is telling hungry people about a man who gives away free bread. As God fills you with himself, allow there to be an overflow that goes from you to others in need of Christ. He will show you how to share his Good News.

✝ *Lord, in my hunger, you fed me. In my thirst, you gave me living water. Part of who I am now is because I've dined on the bread of life. I know others, Father, who are hungry for something that satisfies, though they don't realize their hunger or how to be filled with the bread of life. I'm no evangelist, but I do want to help others find their recovery. Lead me to speak the right words, healing words, that will draw people to you for the bread of life and the living waters.*

> Jesus announces Himself as the bread which will sustain the life of the soul. Not merely some doctrine—but Himself. He is the bread; not merely bread—but the bread—the one true bread; without whom the soul cannot grow, nor its life be sustained. For only by this life-sustaining bread, can such sickly souls be nourished. As such, Jesus is necessary to the soul as its food—its bread.
>
> **HORATIUS BONAR (1808–1889)**

You can find today's Scripture passage on page 1350 of *The Life Recovery Bible*.

God Will Provide

"But we have only five loaves of bread and two fish!" they answered. "Bring them here," he said. Then he told the people to sit down on the grass. Jesus took the five loaves and two fish, looked up toward heaven, and blessed them. Then, breaking the loaves into pieces, he gave the bread to the disciples, who distributed it to the people. They all ate as much as they wanted, and afterward, the disciples picked up twelve baskets of leftovers.

MATTHEW 14:17-20

FACED WITH A HUNGRY CROWD OF five thousand and only five loaves of bread and two fish, the disciples wondered what to do. Send the people away? But Christ told them that what little they had was enough to meet the need.

What you have been given is enough to feed yourself and others. God will always multiply the little you have so that it will feed many. Never look to what you *don't* have. Consider instead what you *do* have and how God can multiply it to meet the need.

✝ ***Father, you don't just supply what I need—you supply more than enough. I only have to receive, by faith, all you have for me. My addiction at its worst made my craving insatiable. Now I pray for an intense hunger for you that fills me to overflowing. Multiply what you've given me, Lord. If there be leftovers, may I spread the supply around to those in need.***

Those who have but a little, yet when the necessity is urgent, must relieve others out of that little, and that is the way to make it more. Can God furnish a table in the wilderness? Yes, he can, when he pleases, a plentiful table.

MATTHEW HENRY (1662–1714)

You can find today's Scripture passage on page 1220 of *The Life Recovery Bible*.

El Roi

Thereafter, Hagar used another name to refer to the LORD, who had spoken to her. She said, "You are the God who sees me." She also said, "Have I truly seen the One who sees me?" So that well was named Beer-lahai-roi (which means "well of the Living One who sees me").

GENESIS 16:13-14

HAGAR, HAVING BEEN TURNED OUT with her son, Ishmael, by Abraham and Sarah, was desperate. She called on the Lord, and he answered her because he *saw* her. Truly saw her. For that reason, she knew that God was a God of seeing, *El Roi*. Notice that it took Hagar's desperation to come to know the God who sees. So, too, with addiction; our desperation is the open door to our God who sees, has always seen, and will see us through our recovery. He never *doesn't* see. He is always our *El Roi*.

✝ ***Father, you're my*** El Roi, ***the God who is always present, the God who always sees me. Watch over me closely, Lord. See to my recovery, notice my need for healing, and hear my desperate cries for help. Thank you for your watchful eye upon me and all I do.***

To keep continually in mind that God is always present with us; to live always as in God's sight; to act and speak and think as always under His eye—all this is eminently calculated to have a good effect upon our souls. Wide, and deep, and searching, and piercing is the influence of that one thought, "You are the God who sees me!"

J. C. RYLE (1816–1900)

You can find today's Scripture passage on page 24 of *The Life Recovery Bible.*

He Knows the Best Pathway

The LORD says, "I will guide you along the best pathway for your life.
I will advise you and watch over you."

PSALM 32:8

SOMETIMES DURING RECOVERY, we're at a loss as to what's next. Addiction was such a huge part of our lives, so now that it's gone, what will replace it? We can know that God has definite plans for us in our post-addiction years. Decision making may seem hard at first, but count on God speaking through your counselors, pastor, the Word, circumstances, and common sense. Know that it's God who has his eye upon you. It's God who will direct you on the pathway you should go. He has many means to reach open hearts.

✝ ***Lord, you know that, in the past, I've made some hasty and wrong decisions. Help me to be a better decider in the future. Speak to me through your Word, my spiritual mentors, prayer, and circumstances. Put a check in my spirit when I'm about to make a poor decision. Teach me, Father, how to decide rightly.***

The only way to dispossess the heart of an old affection is by the expulsive power of a new one.

THOMAS CHALMERS (1780–1847)

You can find today's Scripture passage on page 700 of *The Life Recovery Bible*.

The Fear of the Lord Is Clean

The fear of the LORD is clean,
enduring forever.

PSALM 19:9, ESV

WE POSSESS GREAT POWER FOR CHANGE through understanding and living in the fear of God. This godly fear is clean, pure, and foundational to our sobriety. Never be reluctant to embrace the one fear that ends all other fears.

It's commonly said that the fear of the Lord is "awe" of the Lord. It *is* that, but it's more than that. Awe rarely changes lives, but godly fear of the Lord brings the kind of change that leads to healing. Godly fear involves a love of our heavenly Father to the extent that we fear his disapproval. We live to please him because we love him. Perhaps some of us had fathers we loved but also feared—not because we feared that they would hurt or abuse us but because we feared their power over us. We may have feared unloving fathers because they could use their power to abuse us. God, the perfect Father, is worthy of our loving fear.

✝ *Father, for so long, I haven't truly feared you in the biblical sense. Thank you for forgiving the times I have slighted my fear of you—that fear that is clean and endures forever. I praise you that, by fearing you—and only you—I'm delivered from the fears of everything else. Fearing you makes me fearless against all else.*

The remarkable thing about God is that when you fear God, you fear nothing else, whereas if you do not fear God, you fear everything else.

OSWALD CHAMBERS (1874–1917)

You can find today's Scripture passage on page 691 of *The Life Recovery Bible*.

Doing Good in Evil Days

Make the most of every opportunity in these evil days.

EPHESIANS 5:16

WHEN WE SEE THAT OUR DAYS HAVE potential for evil, we must turn that on its head and declare that the days, though evil, present an opportunity for us to experience good and to do good. Time is a precious gift of God. Having wasted so much of it in our addicted past, we now must invest our time, and our lives, wisely. Every day presents us with an opportunity to do so. Take advantage of the time God has given you today. Do good.

✝ *God, you are the Lord of time. You have granted me a span of time on this earth. I pray that you would give me eyes to see the opportunities I have to do good in these evil days. Enlist me as a warrior helping those captured by the evil of addiction. I understand their experience and can help them . . . if you show me how, when, and where. Help me to do good, Lord, for the rest of my days.*

> Consider what has been said of the preciousness of time, how much depends upon it, how short and uncertain it is, how irrecoverable it will be when gone. If you have a right conception of these things, you will be more treasuring of your time than of the most fine gold. Every hour and moment will seem precious to you.
>
> JONATHAN EDWARDS (1703–1758)

You can find today's Scripture passage on page 1515 of *The Life Recovery Bible*.

Perfect Peace

You will keep in perfect peace
all who trust in you,
all whose thoughts are fixed on you!

ISAIAH 26:3

PERFECT PEACE! Think of it! How we've longed for even *im*perfect peace, and yet now, by trusting in God and fixing our thoughts on him, we are granted *perfect* peace. This peace quickly becomes an essential tool in our recovery protocol. Today, let's fix our thoughts on our heavenly Father and all his benefits. Let's trust in God. Let's enjoy the perfect peace that only comes from him.

✝ *Father, you are the giver of perfect peace. As I trust in you and fix my thoughts on you, I'm granted this peace. As I go through my day, remind me from time to time to turn my thoughts back to you, no matter how busy I might be. May your peace fully replace the turmoil of addiction. May your peace be my guide.*

> Perfect trust is blessed with perfect peace. The word [translated] "trust in God" comes from the Hebrew word which signifies to nourish. Why so? Because our trusting in God nourishes, it nourishes peace in the soul.
>
> THOMAS WATSON (1620–1686)

You can find today's Scripture passage on page 874 of *The Life Recovery Bible*.

Looking Forward

Look straight ahead,
and fix your eyes on what lies before you.

PROVERBS 4:25

WHAT CONTRIBUTES TO FAILURE . . . to relapse? Very often, it's taking our eyes off the straight path ahead of us and looking to tempting trails off the main road. Even when we know from experience those trails are thick with thorns, somehow the magnetic pull is in that direction. Keeping our eyes looking directly forward keeps us on the safe road and leads us to our better destination.

† *Father, I can see the road ahead through a slight mist. I see a few bumps along the way, I see a curve here and there, but beyond that, I see my destination of a life well-lived after addiction. I also see that, by the side of the road, treacherous traps await in the guise of roses with thorns, and beyond the roses, poisonous weeds. I dare not look that way, Lord, having more than once explored the eye-appealing attractions designed to lure me off the road. No, I look straight ahead, fixing my eyes on my divinely appointed destination, thanking you for it every step of the way.*

> In every way it is better to look forward than to look back. The life follows the eye; we live as we look. But what is there ever behind us to live for? There is no work there to do; no tasks wait there for accomplishment; no opportunities for helpfulness or usefulness lie in the past. Opportunities, when once they have passed by, never linger that tardy laggards may yet come up and seize them; passed once, they are gone forever. . . . We cannot impress ourselves in any way upon the past.
>
> J. R. MILLER (1840–1912)

You can find today's Scripture passage on page 792 of *The Life Recovery Bible*.

The Tongue of the Recovering Addict

Wise words satisfy like a good meal;
the right words bring satisfaction.
The tongue can bring death or life;
those who love to talk will reap the consequences.

PROVERBS 18:20-21

WHEN WE BECAME SAVED, when we trusted in Christ and were born again, *all* our being was born again, including our tongue. Where once, under the influence of addiction, we spoke words of death, now we speak words of life. Whichever way we speak—death or life—there will be fruit to eat, either bad fruit or good fruit. We know enough by now to desire the good fruit—the fruit of life. Let's watch our tongue today as we speak to those around us and to ourselves. Let's speak life, not death.

† *Father, you are Lord of my tongue. From my lips can come death or life. I choose life. Keep a guard over my words, Lord. May they have life-giving power to all who hear me. May they be life-giving to me, as well.*

God has invested sanctified speech with a life-giving power.
There is a vitality in the hallowed tongue peculiarly its own.

OCTAVIUS WINSLOW (1808–1878)

You can find today's Scripture passage on page 806 of *The Life Recovery Bible*.

Fruitfulness

When you produce much fruit, you are my true disciples.
This brings great glory to my Father.

JOHN 15:8

HOW WILL PEOPLE KNOW WE'VE RECOVERED from our addiction? One way to prove we are Jesus' disciples is to glorify God by bearing much fruit. There are certain fruits that are common to us all in recovery: love, joy, and patience, for instance. But every addict in recovery may have certain fruits that are more prominent in their life than in others. The solution is to be the *you* God plans you to be and let others be who God plans them to be. Fruit bearers all.

† *Father, I have a measure of faith that continues to grow. I pray, too, for fruit in my life to continue to grow. I pray for the power of Christ in me to bring forth the good fruit whose origin is in heaven. Lord, I am a true disciple. May my fruit show my commitment and bring great glory to you.*

Faith bears Fruit. It cannot help it, because it links the soul with Christ, so that the energy of His life pours into it through the artery of faith, and, as it comes in, so it must make a way for itself out.

F. B. MEYER (1847–1929)

You can find today's Scripture passage on page 1366 of *The Life Recovery Bible.*

Called to Servanthood

You have been called to live in freedom, my brothers and sisters. But don't use your freedom to satisfy your sinful nature. Instead, use your freedom to serve one another in love.

GALATIANS 5:13

FREEDOM OBLIGATES US TO SERVE OTHERS. The freedom to which we were called is God's investment in us. When we serve others, God sees and reaps the fruit of our servanthood. We must not use our newfound freedom as an occasion for the flesh. We've been there and done that, so we know better.

Where can you serve? God has a place for you. He will help you find it.

✝ *God, you have called me to freedom! And you have a plan for me to use that freedom, and it's in serving others. At its heart, addiction is a selfish way of life. In recovery, you're teaching me how to set myself aside and use my freedom for others. Bring people across my path who can use even just a word of affirmation from me—or more if I sense I can help meet their deeper need. In short, make me like you—sensitive to the needs of others.*

Forget yourself and live for others, for "it is more blessed to give than to receive."

A. B. SIMPSON (1843–1919)

You can find today's Scripture passage on page 1505 of *The Life Recovery Bible.*

Fill My Mouth, Lord

For it was I, the LORD your God,
who rescued you from the land of Egypt.
Open your mouth wide, and I will fill it with good things.

PSALM 81:10

IT'S INTERESTING TO THINK OF the numerous addictions that are taken orally. It's as if both God and Satan are offering to fill our mouths if we will open them wide. But only God's portion will satisfy. God, the Lord who has brought us out of the land of our addiction.

Today, open your mouth wide. God will fill it.

✝ ***Lord, fill me today! I open my mouth wide for you to give me sustenance. I will dine on the good things you bring into my life, blessing upon blessing. You have brought me home, Lord, home to yourself out of the land of my bondage. Bring forth your favors for me, Lord. My mouth is open wide for you to fill it!***

> "Open your mouth wide—*and I will fill it*!" That is, "I have the very blessings which you need. They are *from Me*—they are *for you*! . . . Do not doubt My benevolence, for this grieves My heart. I give you My word, that I will bestow My favors upon you *freely, plentifully,* and *frequently*! My word is plain—read it; it is faithful—trust it; it is honest—plead it; it is sure—expect the fulfillment of it. I have wrought for you in times past, I am in the same mind now as then—My nature is still as gracious and merciful. I will hear and bless you. I will do for you all I that have promised. I will give you all that you ask of Me in faith, that is, giving Me credit for honesty, faithfulness, and love. I will do exceeding abundantly *above* all that you ask or think!"
>
> JAMES SMITH (1802–1862)

You can find today's Scripture passage on page 737 of *The Life Recovery Bible*.

Staying the Course

I have fought the good fight, I have finished the race, and I have remained faithful. And now the prize awaits me—the crown of righteousness, which the Lord, the righteous Judge, will give me on the day of his return. And the prize is not just for me but for all who eagerly look forward to his appearing.

2 TIMOTHY 4:7-8

PAUL COULD SAY AFTER HIS YEARS of both plenty and deprivation that he had finished his race. He had stayed the course God had laid out for him. What remained now was the reception of a crown of righteousness, which, Paul reminds us, isn't just laid up for him but for all who love the Lord's appearing on that day.

Stay the course. Keep on the recovery road. The reward is great. The loss of not staying the course is unimaginable. Don't think twice about going back.

✝ *Father, here I am, in the midst of the race that is my life. I run with the second wind you've given me in Christ. I run with the prize awaiting me. I run for the crown of righteousness. I run to win, not to lose. I stay the course, Lord. I will finish well!*

Keep close intimacies with Jesus. We must live upon Christ, and we must die upon Christ.

MARY WINSLOW (1774–1854)

You can find today's Scripture passage on page 1564 of *The Life Recovery Bible*.

A Love That Gives

God showed his great love for us by sending Christ
to die for us while we were still sinners.

ROMANS 5:8

IF WE HAVE EVER DOUBTED GOD'S LOVE during our days of addiction, Paul offers the evidence of God's love in that it was present while we were yet in our addiction. Christ died for those addicted. He died for *us*. This is a love that knows no bounds. It's a saving love, a redeeming love, an everlasting love. And though it was ours then in our addiction, it is still ours in our present recovery. His healing love is ours today and every day.

✝ ***God, it's natural for a person to die for a good person but astonishing when someone will die for a sinner. And yet that's what Christ has done. While I was yet deep in addiction, Christ took me in as his own, dying for me, atoning for my sins, rising to new life so that I might have that new resurrection life. Father, I'm thankful beyond measure that you loved me before I even had the chance to love you.***

> The love of our Lord Jesus Christ towards sinners is strikingly shown in His steady purpose of heart to die for them. All through His life He knew that He was going to be crucified. There was nothing in His sufferings and crucifixion which He did not foresee distinctly, even to the minutest particular, long before it came upon Him. He tasted all the well-known bitterness of anticipated suffering. Yet He never swerved from His path for a moment. . . . Such love surpasses knowledge. It is unspeakable love—unsearchable love! We may rest on that love without fear. If Christ so loved us before we thought of Him, then He will surely not cease to love us after we have believed.
>
> J. C. RYLE (1816–1900)

You can find today's Scripture passage on page 1437 of *The Life Recovery Bible*.

The Shelter of God's Promises

While they were there, the time came for her baby to be born. She gave birth to her firstborn son. She wrapped him snugly in strips of cloth and laid him in a manger, because there was no lodging available for them.

LUKE 2:6-7

ON THIS CHRISTMAS EVE, we think of the low birth of Jesus in the stable of an inn so full of travelers there was no room for the Savior of the world to be born. Joseph and Mary needed shelter for the big event, and God provided, though we might think he would provide the best of facilities for Christ's birth.

The lesson, though, is that God's provision isn't based on man's perception of what ought to be. In being born in a stable, the future King of kings identifies with the lowly, the marginalized, the outcast, the addict.

Christmas is a time to remember the entrance into our world of one who is the Lord of another Kingdom, not of this world. A Kingdom in which he has made us citizens.

✝ *Father, as I anticipate Christmas tomorrow, I do so with joy. Tonight, we celebrate the eve of the birth of Christ. Tomorrow, we will open presents and, likely, experience a good meal in a warm home, perhaps with loved ones. And yet the central part of tomorrow's festivities is one very special gift, the likes of which have never been seen: the gift of a Savior from our sins and our addictions. Truly it's a marked day in the history of humankind—and a marked day for me, one who was set free because of Christ.*

Who can add to Christmas? The perfect motive is that God so loved the world. The perfect gift is that He gave His only Son. The only requirement is to believe in Him. The reward of faith is that you shall have everlasting life.

CORRIE TEN BOOM (1892–1983)

You can find today's Scripture passage on page 1290 of *The Life Recovery Bible*.

Contrast the Holidays

A child is born to us,
a son is given to us.
The government will rest on his shoulders.
And he will be called:
Wonderful Counselor, Mighty God,
Everlasting Father, Prince of Peace.

ISAIAH 9:6

TODAY MARKS THE MOST CELEBRATED of days for Christians. Our Redeemer was born on this day. A child was given to us, for us, by God. He is our wonderful Counselor, our mighty God, our everlasting Father, our Prince of Peace. Allow some time to contrast how your life is today with what it would have been like if Christ had not come. Where would you be now without a Redeemer? Where are you now *with* a Redeemer?

† *Father, thank you for the blessing of Christmas, commemorating the grand event of all grand events—the birth of the one who would save me from myself. Christmas is a joyous time and rightly so, Lord. May this day be a reminder of the very first Christmas present—a Savior. For, as we celebrate the day, we also celebrate our recovery.*

> It is here, in the thing that happened at the first Christmas, that the profoundest and most unfathomable depths of the Christian revelation lie. . . . God became man. . . . Nothing in fiction is so fantastic as this truth of the Incarnation.
>
> J. I. PACKER (1926–2020)

You can find today's Scripture passage on page 858 of *The Life Recovery Bible*.

DECEMBER 26

Constant Communion

Be still, and know that I am God!

PSALM 46:10

GOD WOULD HAVE US LEARN TO EXPERIENCE his voice, whether in stillness or in exaltation. We hear God best when our own inner selves are silenced. Often, we find our wandering thoughts jumping from one thing to another and ending up at some unwanted temptation. At such times, we have lost control not just of our thoughts but also our ability to hear God.

Being still before God is a part of our recovery that we must learn. It won't come naturally. But as we practice stillness, perhaps while meditating on a portion of God's Word, we slowly increase our ability to hear. And the more we experience his presence in stillness, the more we desire it.

Today, find time to be still before God. Praise him for his presence. Offer up thanks for saving you from addiction. Pray for eyes to see your next step and vision to see where he wants to use you. Develop your constant communion with God.

✝ ***Father, your presence in stillness isn't something I'm used to. In my addictive years, stillness before you wasn't something I experienced. Now, I come to you desiring to sense your presence in utter stillness. Help me learn to quiet my busy soul as I wait before you. Increase my ability to simply be still. Quiet the inward rabble that rebels against simply sitting in your presence.***

> Not only must the tongue hold its peace; the soul must be silent. Many may sit silently, refraining from discontented expressions, . . . yet inwardly they are bursting with discontent. This shows a complicated disorder and great perversity in their hearts. And notwithstanding their outward silence, God hears the peevish, fretful language of their souls.
>
> JEREMIAH BURROUGHS (1600–1646)

You can find today's Scripture passage on page 712 of *The Life Recovery Bible.*

The Invested Life

[Jesus said,] "Don't store up treasures here on earth, where moths eat them and rust destroys them, and where thieves break in and steal. Store your treasures in heaven, where moths and rust cannot destroy, and thieves do not break in and steal. Wherever your treasure is, there the desires of your heart will also be."

MATTHEW 6:19-21

EVERY LIFE IS AN INVESTMENT. We either invest in earthly treasures—including addictions—or we lay up heavenly investments that will pay better dividends both here and in eternity. Whatever earthly treasures are calling to you, turn a deaf ear. Instead, listen to the voice of God pointing you to where your true treasure lies.

† *Father, I give up on earthly treasures. They can be more of a burden than a blessing. They can also keep me from investing in heavenly treasure. Lord, I pray for opportunities to increase my eternal deposit with you where moth and rust cannot destroy. I pray this knowing that having heavenly treasure also brings me greater happiness here on earth.*

The position of the heart is sure to be affected by the place where the treasure is laid up. Shall sons of God give their hearts away to passing joys, which decay if they remain ours, and are liable at any moment to be taken from us?

CHARLES SPURGEON (1834–1892)

You can find today's Scripture passage on page 1205 of *The Life Recovery Bible.*

Impossible?

The disciples were astounded. "Then who in the world can be saved?" they asked. Jesus looked at them intently and said, "Humanly speaking, it is impossible. But with God everything is possible."

MATTHEW 19:25-26

HOW MANY TIMES ON OUR WORST DAYS have we confessed our situation to be impossible? And yet, Jesus looks at each one of us and pronounces our recovery as possible, even as a certainty. We must never disbelieve this vital assurance from the Lord. When the enemy whispers, "Impossible," we must shout back our Lord's powerful assertion: "Possible!"

† *Father, with you, all things that seem impossible to me, including my continued sobriety, are promised as possible through you. I pray that, when my faith is ebbing, you'll remind me that, even then, your power is made real in my life accomplishing the impossible—continued sobriety in the face of great temptation. You, then, Lord, get the glory for the "impossible" victory I shall enjoy.*

Faith does not operate in the realm of the possible. There is no glory for God in that which is humanly possible. Faith begins where man's power ends.

GEORGE MÜLLER (1805–1898)

You can find today's Scripture passage on page 1228 of *The Life Recovery Bible.*

He Will Take Care of You

I hold you by your right hand—
I, the Lord your God.
And I say to you,
"Don't be afraid. I am here to help you."

ISAIAH 41:13

WHO, REALLY, IS THE INITIATOR, DIRECTOR, and sustainer of our recovery? Is it not God, our heavenly Father, who has sought us out and brought us out? Is it not God himself who holds our hand as we recover? Is it not our God who tells us not to fear about how our recovery will work out? Has not God given us the promise of help when we need it? Is he not *here* now?

Why then would we ever turn away from God to a lesser helper? Today, be encouraged that it is our mighty God who will take care of you.

✝ *Father, you know that fear is often involved in my addiction battle. Fear of pain, fear of the past, fear of the future, fear of facing life; reasonable fear and unreasonable fear. And yet fear accomplishes nothing. It simply paralyzes me from any forward progress. Deliver me, Lord, from all my fears. Remind me of your words: Don't be afraid. I am here to help you. Yes, Lord, I hear you. I say no to fear and trust that you will take care of me.*

How very little can be done under the spirit of fear.

FLORENCE NIGHTINGALE (1820–1910)

You can find today's Scripture passage on page 893 of *The Life Recovery Bible.*

DECEMBER 30

The Faith Walk Never Ends

We walk by faith, not by sight.

2 CORINTHIANS 5:7, ESV

AS WE NEAR THE END OF THE YEAR, surely we are farther along the recovery path than when we began. No, we may not have fully arrived, but this is a journey on a lengthy road. We must never forget that—just as spiritual growth is something all Christians will enjoy for the rest of their lives, never arriving at perfection in this life—our recovery journey will continue next year and the year after that. We will walk by faith every step of the way. Though the journey has a few hills and curves and bumps, it's really a joyous one. Always look forward to a God-ordained future with expectation and joy.

† *Father, this year has been eventful to say the least. There have been surprises, joys, some sorrows, victories, setbacks, and much else pertaining to life itself. Though I'm not "there" yet, I have made progress. I'm not the person I was a year ago, and a year from now I will not be the person I am now. Through it all is your presence to guide me, encourage me, and be my friend. Thank you, Father. What a life you have given me!*

> The child of God is, from necessity, a joyful man. His sins are forgiven, his soul is justified, his person is adopted, his trials are blessings, his conflicts are victories, his death is immortality, his future is a heaven of inconceivable, unthought-of, untold, and endless blessedness. With such a God, such a Savior, and such a hope, is he not, ought he not, to be a joyful man?
>
> OCTAVIUS WINSLOW (1808–1878)

You can find today's Scripture passage on page 1485 of *The Life Recovery Bible.*

Reflecting on Where You've Been, Where You Are, and Where You're Going

The LORD God is my strength, and he will make my feet like hinds' feet, and he will make me to walk upon mine high places.

HABAKKUK 3:19, KJV

THE CALENDAR YEAR ENDS TODAY. Tomorrow will find us in a new year. Take time to reflect on where you were a year ago. Mark in your mind the progress you've made. Was there relapse? Long-term victory over addiction? No matter what your status today, you can, by faith, affirm that one year from now you will be farther along—and you will have grown in the knowledge of God and of yourself. May your soul, today and always, be consumed with a longing for God that far exceeds your longing for any earthly addiction.

✝ ***Lord, I want to take a moment to thank you for this past year with all its ups and downs, even some sideways detours I hadn't expected. Be with me this coming year, Lord, as I continue on the recovery journey. Bring into my life the very things I need to mature in my faith and to be an example of your ability to save a person from self-destruction. Praise you, Lord, now, next year, and always!***

The Christian life is not only one of happiness, but also of progress. A climbing from one high place of grace to another. It is not a grasping at gaudy bubbles that vanish with the touch, but the laying hold of spiritual certainties. For this feet like the hind's feet are needed. I understand that the peculiarity of the hind's feet is that they not only rest on the rocks, but cling to them, so that they can easily stand on high places. Such represent the feet of faith that rests on and cling to the great and precious promises of God. The Christian's prospects are mountains high.

JAMES SMITH (1802–1862)

You can find today's Scripture passage on page 1161 of *The Life Recovery Bible*.

A Final Word from Steve and Nick

THOUGH THIS YEAR HAS ENDED, and the devotions are over, your journey goes on. We pray this past year has seen you make great progress on your recovery.

We want to take a moment to encourage you as you pursue the good life God has called you to. We hope you'll continue to stay in the Word of God, to be part of an accountability group and strong Christian fellowship.

Finally, if you have found these devotions useful, you may want to go through them for at least one more year as supplemental to your other resources.

May God bless you in your new life in Christ.

Acknowledgments

TO MISTY,

Thank you for teaching me the richness of recovery.

I love you.

Steve

I MUST FIRST ACKNOWLEDGE GOD FOR HIS faithfulness to me personally. To him belongs the credit for changed lives as a result of this book.

I'd like to thank the folks at Tyndale House Publishers, particularly Jon Farrar and Erin Gwynne. Erin's careful edit of the manuscript was a godsend. I've long been a Tyndale fan, and to be published by them is a blessing.

Thanks to Greg Johnson, my agent, for his expertise and help.

Special thanks to Dr. Stephen Hufman, author of *A Desperate Need: A Guide to Treating Addictions and Recapturing Life*. I highly recommend Dr. Hufman's book.

Continual thanks to my family for their unqualified support of my writing.

Nick Harrison

About the Authors

STEPHEN ARTERBURN, M.ED., published his first book, *Hooked on Life*, in 1984. He has become a *New York Times* bestselling and award-winning author with more than fourteen million books in print, receiving four ECPA Gold Medallion "Book of the Year" awards for quality and impact. The Every Man's Battle series won two of those awards and has sold more than four million copies. Steve's publications have also been awarded one bronze, two gold, and two platinum ECPA sales awards. His most recent Gold Medallion win was 2020 in the Youth Nonfiction category where his book *Kirby McCook and the Jesus Chronicles* was winner of the Young Adult Book of the Year award.

Stephen is the developer and editor of ten specialty and study Bibles, three of which were nominated for the Bible of the Year Gold Medallion award. *The Spiritual Renewal Bible*, published in 1998, won the Bible of the Year Gold Medallion in 1999. *The Life Recovery Bible* has sold more than three million copies and is given away by Prison Fellowship and is the pew Bible for the Salvation Army. It is the second all-time-bestselling study Bible for Tyndale House Publishers, only exceeded by the *Life Application Study Bible*. For more than a decade, it has remained on the Top Ten Bestselling Bibles list. Steve also produced *Every Man's Bible*, which was published in 2004.

In addition to his writing, Stephen is an international speaker who has spoken in Australia, Ireland, Korea, Brazil, and Canada. In 2000, he was inducted into the National Speaker's Association Hall of Fame in Washington, DC. A large portion of his speaking time is allocated to raising money for women's resource and pregnancy centers. In 2016, he was featured in the farewell tour of Women of Faith, which he founded in 1996 and was attended by more than five million women in packed-out arenas. He is also the teaching pastor at Northview Church in Carmel, Indiana.

Stephen is a respected innovator dedicated to helping transform lives with God's truth all over the world. In 1988, he founded New Life Treatment Centers, a venture-capital-funded organization providing Christian psychiatric and addiction treatment in secular psychiatric hospitals. Because of the impact, growth, and profitability of this organization, he was awarded the Socially Responsible Entrepreneur of the Year award by Ernst and Young, Merrill Lynch, and *Inc.* magazine. He quickly grew that profitable organization to one hundred million dollars in revenues before he sold it to Thomas Nelson Publishers. At that time, he spun off "New Life Ministries" into the current, not-for-profit ministry producing the number-one syndicated Christian counseling talk show, *New Life Live.* Many people in remote locations say it is the only wise counsel available to them.

New Life has maintained its focus on three principles since 1988: true truth, redemptive relationship, and total transformation. New Life has a network of one thousand Christian counselors and therapists around the country who help the thousands of people who call 1-800-NEW-LIFE. What used to be done in hospitals and treatment centers happens now in weekend intensives involving both therapists and speakers. Every Man's Battle, Restore for women who have been betrayed, and Emotional Freedom and Intimacy in Marriage are some of the intensive weekend events New Life conducts.

Stephen's marketing and media mindfulness has landed him and his work with appearances on *Oprah*, *Good Morning America*, and *ABC World News Tonight.* Not surprisingly, he has been featured in *GQ*, *Rolling*

Stone, *USA Today*, *New York Times*, and, most recently, on the cover of *Recovery Magazine*.

Steve has degrees from Baylor University and The University of North Texas as well as two honorary doctorate degrees, including one from The California Graduate School of Theology. Steve resides with his family in Carmel, Indiana.

NICK HARRISON is the author of more than a dozen books, including *Magnificent Prayer*, *Power in the Promises*, *His Victorious Indwelling*, and five books in the One-Minute® Prayer series. Nick is a graduate of San Jose State University and a former senior editor at Harvest House Publishers. He is also a popular teacher and speaker at Christian writers' conferences. Nick lives in Oregon with his wife, Beverly. Nick and Bev are the parents of three adult daughters and grandparents to two boys and two girls. Nick's website, featuring his blog, can be found at nickharrisonbooks.com.

Other Books by Stephen Arterburn

Toxic Faith: Experiencing Healing from Painful Spiritual Abuse
The Spiritual Renewal Bible
The Life Recovery Bible
Every Man's Battle: Winning the War on Sexual Temptation One Victory at a Time
Every Man's Bible
Transformation: Turn Your Life Around Starting Today!
Healing Is a Choice: Ten Decisions That Will Transform Your Life and Ten Lies That Can Prevent You from Making Them
Lose It for Life: The Total Solution—Spiritual, Emotional, Physical—for Permanent Weight Loss
Healing Stones: A Sullivan Crisp Novel
Walking into Walls: Five Blind Spots That Block God's Work in You
The Seven Minute Marriage Solution: Seven Things to Start! Seven Things to Stop! Seven Things That Matter Most!
Worthy of Her Trust: What You Need to Do to Rebuild Sexual Integrity and Win Her Back
Take Your Life Back: How to Stop Letting the Past and Other People Control You
Kirby McCook and the Jesus Chronicles: A Twelve-Year-Old's Take on the Totally Unboring, Slightly Weird Stuff in the Bible, Including Fish Guts, Wrestling Moves, and Stinky Feet
The Soul of a Hero: Becoming the Man of Strength and Purpose You Were Created to Be

Other Books by Nick Harrison

Magnificent Prayer: 366 Devotions to Deepen Your Prayer Experience
Power in the Promises: Praying God's Word to Change Your Life
His Victorious Indwelling: Daily Devotions for a Deeper Christian Life
Promises to Keep: Daily Devotions for Men of Integrity
365 WWJD: Daily Answers to What Would Jesus Do?
Walking with Wesley: A Ninety-Day Devotional
One-Minute Prayers® for Those with Cancer
One-Minute Prayers® When You Need a Miracle
One-Minute Prayers® for Dads
One-Minute Prayers® for Husbands